American Heart Association

Learn and Live

Low-Calorie
cookbook

Also by the American Heart Association

The New American Heart Association Cookbook, Sixth Edition

American Heart Association Low-Fat, Low-Cholesterol Cookbook, Third Edition

American Heart Association Low-Salt Cookbook, Second Edition

American Heart Association Quick & Easy Cookbook

American Heart Association Meals in Minutes

American Heart Association Low-Fat & Luscious Desserts

American Heart Association To Your Health! A Guide to Heart-Smart Living

American Heart Association 6 Weeks to Get Out the Fat

American Heart Association Fitting in Fitness

American Heart Association 365 Ways to Get Out the Fat

American Heart
Association®

Learn and Live SM

Low-Calorie

c o o k b o o k

more than 200 delicious
recipes for healthy eating

Clarkson Potter/Publishers
New York

Published by Clarkson Potter/Publishers, New York, New York.
Member of the Crown Publishing Group, a division of Random House, Inc.
www.crownpublishing.com

CLARKSON N. POTTER is a trademark and POTTER and colophon are registered
trademarks of Random House, Inc.

Originally published in hardcover by Clarkson Potter/Publishers,
a division of Random House, Inc., New York, in 2003.

Your contribution to the American Heart Association supports research that helps make
publications like this possible. For more information, call 1-800-AHA-USA1 (1-800-242-8721)
or contact us online at http://www.americanheart.org.

Printed in the United States of America

Design by Jan Derevjanik
Illustrations by Nicole Kaufman

Library of Congress Cataloging-in-Publication Data
American Heart Association low-calorie cookbook: more than 200 delicious recipes for
healthy eating.—1st ed.
    Includes index.
1. Low-calorie diet—Recipes.   2. Low-fat diet—Recipes.   3. Reducing diets—Recipes.
I. Title: Low-calorie cookbook.   II. American Heart Association.
    RM222.2 .A47   2003
    641.5'635—dc21   2002011004

ISBN 0-8129-2855-5

10 9 8 7 6 5 4 3 2 1

First Paperback Edition

Front cover: Sichuan Fillet with Colorful Vegetables (pages 164–65)
Photograph by Susan Goldman

Contents

Acknowledgments

American Heart Association Consumer Publications
    Director: Jane Anneken Ruehl
    Senior Editor: Janice Roth Moss
    Science Editor: Ann Melugin Williams
    Editor: Jacqueline Fornerod Haigney
    Assistant Editor: Roberta Westcott Sullivan
Recipe Developers
    Andy Broder
    Linda Drachman
    Barbara Gollman
    Nancy S. Hughes
    Ruth Mossok Johnston
    Carol Ritchie
    Marcia K. Stanley
    DeeDee Stovel
    Robin Vitetta-Miller
Nutrient Analyst
    Tammi Hancock, R.D.

Introduction

eat wisely and eat well

Why a low-calorie cookbook from the American Heart Association? **Scientific** research continues to confirm the link between obesity and the risks for heart disease and other health problems. With the decline in physical activity and the increase in food consumption in the United States, the incidence of obesity is soaring. In two decades, the number of overweight Americans has doubled. Today, about half the adult population is overweight; 30 percent of us are obese. You don't have to look very far to see that weight management has become a primary concern for most of us—for someone we love, if not ourselves. The American Heart Association is committed to addressing that concern.

Since you've picked up this book, you probably already know that calories do count when it comes to body weight. That's why we made sure that every recipe in this book is truly low calorie—no more than 500 calories per serving (including entrées and desserts). But with fewer calories on your plate, you want every one of them to be delicious, nutritious, and satisfying. That's where we can help. This latest edition in the Association's library of cookbooks brings you easy-to-follow recipes for more than 200 delectable dishes that won't leave you feeling deprived in the slightest. Each recipe has been carefully analyzed for calorie count and several important nutrients so you can easily keep on track without worrying about the numbers.

Consider this cookbook a tool for success, not a diet book. Use it to maintain your already-healthful weight, to follow a weight-loss program, or to lose weight on your own, if your doctor approves. If you have a medical condition, you really need to check with your doctor before losing weight.

One of life's great pleasures is eating well. With these recipes in your kitchen and a commitment to a low-calorie lifestyle, you can enjoy both good health and good food.

How to Use This Book

The *American Heart Association Low-Calorie Cookbook* contains all the tools you need—recipes, health information, and cooking and shopping tips—to manage calorie consumption and eat well at the same time. It also provides nutrient analyses to help you determine how each recipe can fit into your eating plan.

nutrient analyses

Each nutrient analysis provides the calorie count and lists the amount of total fat, saturated fat, polyunsaturated fat, monounsaturated fat, cholesterol, sodium, carbohydrate, fiber, and protein in one serving.

All values except those for fats are rounded to whole numbers; fats are rounded to the nearest half gram. (Because of rounding and because total fat includes the fatty acids we list plus other fatty substances and glycerol, the values for saturated, monounsaturated, and polyunsaturated fat don't always add up exactly to the total fat value.) If the accurate nutrient value was not available for at least one ingredient listed in a recipe, you will see a dash instead of a number for that value.

Here are some other important things you should know about the analyses.

❖ Unless noted, the analyses do not include optional ingredients or suggested accompaniments. If you eat any of these, you need to count the additional calories, saturated fat, and other nutrients.

❖ The same is true for garnishes. We highly recommend them to enhance the appeal of foods. They are not included in the analysis, though. If you eat a garnish, remember to add it to your counts.

❖ The serving sizes listed in ounces, cups, or tablespoons are approximations. If you change the number of servings, the nutrient analysis will not be accurate unless you change it proportionately.

❖ When a recipe calls for an ingredient that may vary in amount (for example, a 2½- to 3-pound chicken), we analyzed the average of the range.

- When a choice of ingredients is listed (for example, 1 cup nonfat or low-fat yogurt, or 1 medium apple or pear), we used the first ingredient for the analysis.

- Most of the calories in alcohol evaporate when heated, and this reduction is estimated in the calculations.

- When analyzing marinated meat, poultry, or seafood, we used data that allowed us to calculate only the amount of marinade absorbed by the food. No similar data exist for how much marinade is absorbed by vegetables, so we included the total amount of the marinade in the analysis for vegetable dishes.

- For "acceptable vegetable oil," we use canola oil in the analysis. Acceptable vegetable oils include monounsaturated oils, such as canola and olive, and polyunsaturated oils, such as corn and safflower. (For more information on fats and oils, see pages 305–306 and 319.)

- The nutritional analysis for olive oil is the same whether for extra virgin, superfine, fine, virgin, or pure. Our recipes simply call for olive oil; the type you use is your choice. You may find that you prefer the smoother, fruitier taste of the pricier extra-virgin olive oil for uncooked dishes but want to use a more robust, less expensive olive oil for cooked dishes.

- Meat statistics were based on cooked lean meat with all the visible fat removed. For lean ground beef, we used 90 percent fat free.

- Although data aren't available to show how much sodium can be removed when rinsing salty foods such as olives, capers, feta cheese, and bottled roasted red bell peppers, we usually suggest rinsing those foods. If you do so, you can assume that the sodium level in dishes containing those ingredients is actually a little lower than the nutrient analyses indicate.

- When you buy commercial varieties of canned broth, salsa, low-fat flour tortillas, barbecue sauce, ketchup, Worcestershire sauce, soy sauce, and steak sauce, be sure to read the nutrition labels carefully. If you choose the products with the lowest amounts of sodium, you will closely replicate what we analyzed.

ingredients

All recipes are prepared with the lowest-fat, lowest-sodium ingredients appropriate for the dish. Feel free to experiment or substitute when necessary—as long as your ingredient substitutions do not add calories, fat, or sodium. For example, interchanging herbs, spices, and vinegars can give you variety and customize the recipe to your taste without substantially changing the nutritional value of the dish.

Similarly, whether you use fresh or dried herbs and fresh, bottled, or frozen lemon, lime, or orange juice won't affect the nutritional analysis of the food you prepare. Fresh is almost always tastier, however, especially in uncooked dishes.

If you are like many other cooks, you like to experiment with different peppercorns. We usually just call for pepper so you can follow your own preference. Freshly ground will give you more flavor, whichever color you choose.

Great taste adventures beckon with the almost-unbelievable variety of foods in the marketplace today. We've tried to incorporate a number of new ingredients in the following recipes. If you come across one you know little or nothing about, check the index under "Cook's Tips." You are likely to find a tip that will tell you how to select, prepare, and store the product.

When a recipe calls for an ingredient such as 1 cup chopped bell peppers, you may wonder how much of the product to buy. To make your shopping trip easier and more accurate, we gave equivalents in some of our recipes and included a list of commonly used ingredients and their equivalents in Appendix D.

We hope you will use the tools this cookbook provides, plus your own creativity, to make the very most of your low-calorie lifestyle. Be adventurous in cooking and eating, and enjoy the results in good health!

recipes

appetizers, snacks, and beverages

Curried Chicken and Chutney Spread

Sun-Dried Tomato Dip

Edamame Hummus

Melon Kebabs with Minted Citrus Sauce
   ❖ Tropical Kebabs with Gingered Citrus Sauce

Rice-Filled Vegetable Bowls

Garlic Crostini

Bruschetta with Crisp and Cool Pico de Gallo

Zesty Vegetable Wrap

Taco Tartlets

Strawberry and Peach Smoothie

Chocolate Espresso Cooler

Cranberry-Orange Ale

Wassail

curried chicken and chutney spread

Mango chutney and curry powder turn cream cheese into a "company's coming" appetizer and a great snack. Serve small scoops of this creamy chicken spread on cucumber slices, bell pepper squares, or celery sticks, or use it to fill phyllo shells.

- **1 cup diced cooked chicken or turkey, white meat only, skin and all visible fat removed (6 to 8 ounces cooked boneless, skinless chicken breasts or 1 small turkey tenderloin, about 8 ounces)**
- **2 ounces fat-free or reduced-fat cream cheese, softened**
- **¼ cup fat-free or low-fat plain yogurt**
- **3 tablespoons mango chutney**
- **1 teaspoon curry powder**
- **2 tablespoons sliced almonds (optional)**
- **¼ teaspoon paprika (optional)**
- **¼ teaspoon curry powder (optional)**

In a food processor or blender, process the chicken, cream cheese, yogurt, chutney, and 1 teaspoon curry powder to the desired texture. (If you want the consistency like chicken salad, coarsely chop the chicken with a knife and combine the ingredients in a small bowl.)

To serve, put the spread in a small bowl. Sprinkle with almonds, paprika, and ¼ teaspoon curry powder.

COOK'S TIP ON MANGO CHUTNEY

Mango chutney is like a sweet, fruit-based jam with a zesty attitude (from a touch of vinegar). Find it near the condiments or Indian foods in your grocery. Serve mango chutney as a dipping sauce for grilled meats, or spread ½ cup of it over a block of fat-free cream cheese for an instant appetizer with low-fat crackers and mixed vegetables on the side.

with almonds

Calories 68	Cholesterol 16 mg
Total Fat 1.5 g	Sodium 55 mg
Saturated 0.5 g	Carbohydrate 6 g
Polyunsaturated 0.5 g	Fiber 0 g
Monounsaturated 1.0 g	Protein 7 g

without almonds

Calories 59	Cholesterol 16 mg
Total Fat 1.0 g	Sodium 55 mg
Saturated 0.0 g	Carbohydrate 5 g
Polyunsaturated 0.0 g	Fiber 0 g
Monounsaturated 0.5 g	Protein 7 g

sun-dried tomato dip

The lineup of sun-dried tomatoes, garlic, and Italian seasoning makes this dip a surefire crowd pleaser. It's especially good with raw celery, carrots, cucumbers, broccoli, and cauliflower.

½ cup boiling water

18 dry-packed sun-dried tomato halves

1 cup low-fat cottage cheese, undrained

½ cup fat-free or low-fat plain yogurt

2 tablespoons fat-free, cholesterol-free, or light, reduced-calorie mayonnaise dressing

1 to 2 medium garlic cloves or ½ to 1 teaspoon bottled minced garlic

2 medium green onions (green and white parts)

½ teaspoon salt-free Italian seasoning, crumbled

½ to 1 teaspoon dried basil, crumbled

⅛ teaspoon pepper

⅛ teaspoon salt

In a small bowl, combine the water and tomatoes. Let stand for 10 to 15 minutes, or until softened.

Meanwhile, in a food processor or blender, process the cottage cheese, yogurt, mayonnaise, and garlic until smooth. Transfer to a small bowl.

Slice the green onions. Add to the cottage cheese mixture.

Stir in the Italian seasoning, basil, pepper, and salt.

Drain and finely chop the tomatoes. Stir into the cottage cheese mixture.

Cover and refrigerate for 2 to 48 hours. Stir before serving.

COOK'S TIP

You can use fat-free cottage cheese instead of low fat, but the texture of the dip won't be quite as pleasing.

Calories 37	Cholesterol 1 mg
Total Fat 0.5 g	Sodium 130 mg
Saturated 0 g	Carbohydrate 5 g
Polyunsaturated 0 g	Fiber 1 g
Monounsaturated 0 g	Protein 4 g

edamame hummus

Hummus is traditionally made with chick-peas, but shelled green soybeans, called edamame *(ed-ah-MOM-ee)*, offer a refreshing alternative. Serve this zesty, mildly sweet hummus as a dip with fresh vegetables or pita bread, or use a larger portion as a side dish.

8 cups water

16 ounces frozen shelled green soybeans, or edamame

½ cup fat-free or low-fat lemon yogurt

⅓ cup firm reduced-fat tofu, drained if necessary

¼ cup diced red onion

3 strips cooked low-fat turkey bacon or soy bacon

1½ tablespoons fresh lemon juice

1 teaspoon hot chili sauce

1 medium garlic clove, minced, or ½ teaspoon bottled minced garlic

1 small red bell pepper, diced

Pour the water into a small stockpot; bring to a boil, covered, over high heat. Reduce the heat to medium-high; cook the edamame, uncovered, for 5 minutes.

Meanwhile, fill a large bowl with ice water. Remove the edamame with a large slotted spoon or skimmer; plunge the edamame into the ice water to stop the cooking process and preserve the color. Let stand until chilled, about 5 minutes. Drain well.

In a food processor or blender, process the yogurt, tofu, onion, bacon, lemon juice, chili sauce, and garlic for 30 seconds; scrape down the sides of the bowl and process for 30 seconds. Add the edamame; process until the mixture is almost smooth, scraping down the sides of the bowl as necessary. Add the red bell pepper; pulse 8 to 12 times, until the desired consistency.

COOK'S TIP ON EDAMAME (SOYBEANS)

Rich in fiber, vitamins A and C, and protein, edamame is easy to prepare. You can microwave, steam, or boil it; shell it if necessary; and sprinkle lightly with salt. Little kids often like them, too. If your supermarket doesn't carry the frozen variety, check Asian food markets or health food stores. And be sure to look for fresh soybeans in the late spring through early summer.

Calories 43	Cholesterol 2 mg
Total Fat 1.5 g	Sodium 35 mg
Saturated 0.5 g	Carbohydrate 4 g
Polyunsaturated 0.5 g	Fiber 1 g
Monounsaturated 0.5 g	Protein 3 g

melon kebabs with minted citrus sauce

serves 7; 3 fruit skewers and 1 tablespoon sauce per serving

Double the flavor of these appetizers with double mint—fresh mint leaves and peppermint extract. A dipping sauce of orange and lime juices provides a pleasing contrast to the sweet melons.

- **21 fresh mint leaves (optional)**
- **21 1-inch cubes watermelon, honeydew melon, or cantaloupe, or a combination**
- **3 tablespoons fresh orange juice**
- **3 tablespoons fresh lime juice**
- **1½ tablespoons sugar**
- **¼ teaspoon peppermint extract**

Place 1 mint leaf and 1 melon cube on each of 21 toothpicks.

In a small serving bowl, stir together the remaining ingredients until the sugar has dissolved.

Place the bowl of sauce in the center of a serving platter. Arrange the skewered fruit around the bowl. To eat, dip the melon into the sauce.

tropical kebabs with gingered citrus sauce

Substitute cubes of mango and whole strawberries for the melon; frozen orange juice concentrate for the fresh orange juice; honey for the sugar; and grated gingerroot for the peppermint extract.

melon kebabs

Calories 29	Cholesterol 0 mg
Total Fat 0 g	Sodium 3 mg
Saturated 0 g	Carbohydrate 7 g
Polyunsaturated 0 g	Fiber 0 g
Monounsaturated 0 g	Protein 0 g

tropical kebabs

Calories 47	Cholesterol 0 mg
Total Fat 0 g	Sodium 1 mg
Saturated 0 g	Carbohydrate 12 g
Polyunsaturated 0 g	Fiber 1 g
Monounsaturated 0 g	Protein 1 g

rice-filled vegetable bowls

serves 10; 3 pieces per serving

Start your next dinner party with pizzazz by serving brightly colored bite-size stuffed vegetables.

- ⅓ cup uncooked medium- or short-grain rice, such as arborio or sushi rice
- 3 tablespoons unsalted, dry-roasted cashew halves, finely chopped
- 3 tablespoons shredded carrot
- 1 tablespoon plus 1 teaspoon plain rice vinegar
- 1 tablespoon honey
- 2 teaspoons low-salt soy sauce
- ¼ teaspoon salt
- ⅛ teaspoon cayenne
- 8 cherry tomatoes
- 8 baby green or yellow pattypan squash, 1 to 1½ inches in diameter
- 2 medium golden zucchini, green zucchini, or yellow summer squash
- 3 tablespoons sliced green onions (green and white parts)

Prepare the rice using the package directions, omitting the salt and margarine.

Stir the cashews, carrot, rice vinegar, honey, soy sauce, salt, and cayenne into the rice. Cover and refrigerate for at least 2 hours, or until chilled.

Meanwhile, cut very thin slices from the bottoms of the tomatoes so they will stand upright. Cut thin slices from the tops. Using a small melon baller or small spoon, scoop out the centers of the tomatoes, forming small cups; be careful to keep from cutting through the bottoms.

Cut the top third off the pattypan squash. Cut the zucchini crosswise into slices about ¾ inch thick. Using a small melon baller or small spoon, scoop out the centers of the pattypan squash and the zucchini, forming small cups; be careful to keep from scooping through the bottoms.

Stir the green onions into the rice mixture. (The mixture will be slightly sticky.)

Spoon 1 to 2 teaspoons rice mixture into each vegetable cup, depending on the size of the vegetable. Serve immediately or cover and refrigerate for up to 6 hours.

Calories 60	Cholesterol 0 mg
Total Fat 1.5 g	Sodium 89 mg
Saturated 0.5 g	Carbohydrate 11 g
Polyunsaturated 0.5 g	Fiber 1 g
Monounsaturated 0.5 g	Protein 2 g

garlic crostini

These versatile, colorful crostini, or "little toasts," are simple to make for snacks or weekend entertaining.

3 ounces French bread (baguette style), cut crosswise into 8 slices

1 tablespoon light tub margarine

½ teaspoon mild red-pepper sauce or ¼ teaspoon red hot-pepper sauce

½ medium garlic clove, minced, ¼ teaspoon bottled minced garlic, or dash of garlic powder

Preheat the oven to 350° F.

Put the bread slices on a baking sheet.

Bake for 12 minutes, or until hard and barely golden around the edges. Let cool completely, if desired.

Meanwhile, in a small bowl, whisk together the remaining ingredients. Spread over each toast.

Calories 69	Cholesterol 0 mg
Total Fat 2.0 g	Sodium 156 mg
Saturated 0 g	Carbohydrate 11 g
Polyunsaturated 0.5 g	Fiber 1 g
Monounsaturated 1.0 g	Protein 2 g

bruschetta with crisp and cool pico de gallo

serves 16; ½ cup pico de gallo and 2 slices bruschetta per serving

Fresh corn kernels, tomatoes, and red onion add a rainbow of flavor and color to this pico de gallo *(PEA-ko de GUY-oh)*. It gets its crispy crunch from jícama, cucumber, and radishes. Served without the toast, the pico de gallo also tastes great as a stand-in for salsa.

pico de gallo

- **2 medium ears of corn**
- **1 large cucumber, peeled and diced**
- **1 small jícama (about 12 ounces), peeled and diced (see Cook's Tip on Jícama, page 40)**
- **6 large radishes, diced**
- **1 medium orange bell pepper, diced**
- **2 medium tomatoes, seeded and diced**
- **½ to ¾ cup diced red onion**
- **½ cup snipped fresh cilantro or parsley**
- **3 tablespoons mild or hot-pepper jelly (jalapeño flavor preferred)**
- **3 tablespoons fresh lime juice**
- **1 tablespoon olive oil**
- **1 teaspoon red hot-pepper sauce, or to taste**

❖ ❖ ❖

- **1 French bread (baguette style) (about 8 ounces)**
- **Olive oil spray**

Remove the kernels from the ears of corn and put in a very large bowl. Holding the corncobs over the bowl, scrape them with the unsharpened side of a knife to extract the tasty juice.

Gently stir in the cucumber, jícama, radishes, bell pepper, tomatoes, onion, and cilantro.

Melt the jelly in a small microwave-safe bowl on 100 percent power (high) for 1 minute or in a small saucepan over low heat, stirring occasionally. Stir in

Calories 85	Cholesterol 0 mg
Total Fat 1.5 g	Sodium 101 mg
Saturated 0 g	Carbohydrate 17 g
Polyunsaturated 0.5 g	Fiber 3 g
Monounsaturated 1.0 g	Protein 2 g

the lime juice, olive oil, and red hot-pepper sauce. Pour over the chopped vegetables; stir well.

Preheat the oven to 450°F.

With a serrated knife, slice the baguette diagonally into 32 pieces, each about ¼ inch thick. Put the bread on a baking sheet; lightly spray the top of each slice with olive oil spray.

Bake in the top third of the oven for 5 minutes, or until the edges of the bread begin to brown and some of the centers are slightly golden. Some parts of the bread may still be a little soft.

To assemble, put 2 slices of toasted bread on each plate. For each serving, mound ½ cup pico de gallo on the bread, or serve the pico de gallo on the side.

COOK'S TIP ON PEPPER (JALAPEÑO) JELLY

Mild- or hot-pepper jelly makes a nice glaze for broiled or grilled chicken and a pleasant addition to marinades and salad dressings. It can be found with the jams and jellies in most grocery stores.

COOK'S TIP ON REMOVING CORN KERNELS

Husk and desilk the corn. Hold the cob at a slight angle on a cutting board or over a bowl. Using a sharp knife, cut along the cob and remove a few rows of kernels. Turn the cob and remove a few more rows. Continue until you've removed all the kernels.

zesty vegetable wrap

This sweet and hot, vegetable-packed snack is a quick cure when you have an attack of after-work or after-school munchies.

    2 tablespoons light sour cream

    2 tablespoons hot mango chutney or 2 tablespoons mango chutney plus ⅛ teaspoon cayenne

    3 tablespoons sliced green onions (green and white parts)

    1¼ cups packaged broccoli slaw mix

    1 reduced-fat 8-inch flour tortilla

In a medium bowl, stir together the sour cream and chutney. Stir in the green onions. Add the broccoli slaw, tossing to coat with the dressing.

To serve, spoon the broccoli mixture down the center of a tortilla; tightly roll jelly-roll style to enclose the filling. Cut into thirds; secure each piece with a toothpick.

Calories 286	Cholesterol 10 mg
Total Fat 3.0 g	Sodium 394 mg
Saturated 2.0 g	Carbohydrate 56 g
Polyunsaturated 0 g	Fiber 6 g
Monounsaturated 0 g	Protein 8 g

taco tartlets

Lime-spiked sour cream is a refreshing topping on warm taco filling in light, crisp shells.

15 frozen mini phyllo shells (2.1-ounce package)

4 ounces lean ground beef

½ teaspoon chili powder

½ teaspoon garlic powder

⅓ cup canned no-salt-added low-fat refried beans or canned no-salt-added pinto beans, rinsed if desired, drained

3 tablespoons fat-free or reduced-fat shredded Cheddar or Monterey Jack cheese, or a combination

15 black olive slices

3 tablespoons nonfat or light sour cream

½ teaspoon fresh lime juice

¼ teaspoon chili powder (optional)

3 tablespoons salsa (optional)

Preheat the oven to 375°F. Put the phyllo shells on a nonstick baking sheet and let thaw at room temperature for 10 minutes.

Meanwhile, in a medium nonstick skillet, cook the beef over medium-high heat for 6 to 7 minutes, or until browned on the outside and no longer pink in the center, stirring occasionally to turn and break up the beef. Pour into a colander and rinse under hot water to remove excess fat. Drain well. Wipe the skillet with paper towels. Return the beef to the skillet, turn off the heat, and stir in the chili powder and garlic powder.

If using pinto beans, process in a food processor or blender until smooth.

To assemble, spoon 1 teaspoon beans, then 1 teaspoon meat mixture into each shell. Sprinkle each with ½ teaspoon cheese. Top each with 1 black olive slice.

Bake for 6 to 8 minutes, or until the filling is warmed through and the cheese has melted.

Meanwhile, in a small bowl, whisk together the sour cream and lime juice. Spoon ½ teaspoon over each heated tartlet. Sprinkle with chili powder and top with salsa.

Calories 35	Cholesterol 4 mg
Total Fat 0.5 g	Sodium 60 mg
Saturated 0 g	Carbohydrate 4 g
Polyunsaturated 0 g	Fiber 1 g
Monounsaturated 0.5 g	Protein 3 g

strawberry and peach smoothie

Enjoy the summer flavors of strawberries and peaches anytime with this refreshing smoothie.

- **8 ounces frozen unsweetened strawberries, partially thawed**
- **8 ounces frozen unsweetened peaches, partially thawed**
- **3½ cups fat-free milk**
- **⅓ cup frozen orange juice concentrate**
- **½ cup confectioners' sugar**
- **½ teaspoon ground cinnamon**
- **¼ teaspoon almond extract**

In a food processor or blender, process all the ingredients until smooth. Pour immediately for a regular smoothie; for a thicker smoothie, place in the freezer for 1 to 2 hours, or until the desired consistency.

Calories 124	Cholesterol 2 mg
Total Fat 0.5 g	Sodium 64 mg
Saturated 0 g	Carbohydrate 26 g
Polyunsaturated 0 g	Fiber 2 g
Monounsaturated 0 g	Protein 5 g

chocolate
espresso cooler

Whether you are a chocolate lover or a coffee sipper, this will hit the spot.

¼ cup hot water

2 tablespoons instant coffee granules

2½ cups fat-free milk

3 ounces fat-free chocolate syrup

1 teaspoon vanilla extract

In a pitcher, stir together the water and coffee granules until the granules have completely dissolved. Stir in the remaining ingredients.

Fill four tall glasses with ice cubes. Pour ¾ cup chocolate mixture into each glass.

Calories 146	Cholesterol 3 mg
Total Fat 0.5 g	Sodium 99 mg
Saturated 0 g	Carbohydrate 28 g
Polyunsaturated 0 g	Fiber 0 g
Monounsaturated 0 g	Protein 6 g

cranberry-orange ale

Here's a sparkling thirst quencher to help you fit more fruit into your eating plan.

2 cups fresh orange juice

1 cup cranberry juice (sweetened with apple juice or white grape juice)

4 mint leaves (optional)

1 cup diet ginger ale

1 orange, sliced or quartered (optional)

In a pitcher, stir together the orange juice and cranberry juice. Refrigerate until serving time.

To serve, fill four tall glasses with ice. Put a mint leaf in each glass. Pour the ginger ale into the juice mixture; stir gently. Pour into each glass; garnish with orange slices. Serve immediately.

Calories 86	Cholesterol 0 mg
Total Fat 0 g	Sodium 18 mg
Saturated 0 g	Carbohydrate 20 g
Polyunsaturated 0 g	Fiber 0 g
Monounsaturated 0 g	Protein 1 g

wassail

A special treat for your next cold-weather gathering, wassail is a flavorful spiced beverage. Traditional wassail has a wine or ale base, then is flavored with spices and sweetened. Our version starts with apple juice, making it a great nonalcoholic alternative.

- **1 gallon (64 ounces) unsweetened apple juice**
- **½ cup sugar**
- **1 cinnamon stick, about 3 inches long**
- **2 teaspoons whole cloves**
- **2 teaspoons whole allspice**
- **1 teaspoon grated orange zest**
- **⅛ teaspoon ground ginger**
- **1 orange**
- **1 lemon**
- **1 cup dried cranberries**

In a large nonreactive stockpot (not aluminum or cast iron), combine the apple juice, sugar, cinnamon stick, cloves, allspice, orange zest, and ginger. Cover and refrigerate for 6 to 8 hours.

Shortly before serving time, heat the apple juice mixture, covered, over medium heat until warm, 10 to 15 minutes, stirring occasionally. Do not let the mixture boil.

Meanwhile, thinly slice the orange and lemon; remove the seeds.

To serve, strain into a serving bowl or insulated beverage container. Add the orange slices, lemon slices, and cranberries.

COOK'S TIP

To make removal of the cloves and the allspice easy, put them in a mesh tea ball or tie them in some cheesecloth before putting them in the stockpot. You can also use mesh tea balls to put herbs and spices in soups and stocks. This eliminates most straining and makes removal of solids a breeze.

Calories 84	Cholesterol 0 mg
Total Fat 0 g	Sodium 4 mg
Saturated 0 g	Carbohydrate 21 g
Polyunsaturated 0 g	Fiber 1 g
Monounsaturated 0 g	Protein 0 g

soups

Hot-and-Sour Soup

Chunky Vegetable Soup
    ❖ Chunky Vegetable Soup with Tuna

Barley and Vegetable Soup

Grilled Carrot Soup

White Corn and Rosemary Soup

Roasted Tomato and Chipotle Soup

Effervescent Cantaloupe Soup

Sole and Tomato Soup with Crushed Cumin Seeds

Slow-Cooker Chicken Vegetable Soup

Lima Bean Chowder with Ham

Slow-Cooker Spicy Lentil and Bulgur Soup

Sun-Dried Tomato Soup with Wild Mushrooms and Wild Rice

hot-and-sour soup

An interesting combination of chicken broth and beef broth serves as the base for this soup.

2 cups fat-free, low-sodium chicken broth

2 cups fat-free, no-salt-added beef broth

4 ounces boneless, skinless chicken breast, all visible fat removed, thinly sliced

1 cup sliced fresh shiitake mushrooms, stems discarded

½ cup shredded carrots

3 tablespoons plain rice vinegar or white vinegar

1 tablespoon low-salt soy sauce

2 teaspoons sugar

1 teaspoon toasted sesame oil

½ teaspoon white pepper

3 tablespoons cornstarch

½ cup water

½ cup sliced water chestnuts, rinsed and drained

½ cup sliced bamboo shoots, rinsed and drained

4 ounces soft or silken reduced-fat tofu, drained and diced

Egg substitute equivalent to 1 egg, or 1 large egg

In a large saucepan, bring the chicken broth and beef broth to a simmer over medium-high heat. Stir in the chicken, mushrooms, carrots, rice vinegar, soy sauce, sugar, sesame oil, and pepper. Return to a simmer. Reduce the heat; simmer for 4 to 5 minutes, or until the chicken is no longer pink in the center.

Put the cornstarch in a small bowl. Add the water, stirring to dissolve. Stir into the soup. Increase the heat to medium-high; cook for 1 to 2 minutes, or until slightly thickened, stirring occasionally. Reduce the heat to medium. Stir in the remaining ingredients except the egg substitute. Cook for 1 to 2 minutes, or until the soup is warmed through, stirring occasionally. Increase the heat to medium-high. Bring the soup to a simmer. Slowly drizzle in the egg substitute. Simmer for 8 to 10 seconds, then stir gently. Cook for about 30 seconds, or until the egg shreds look slightly fluffy, are somewhat opaque, and are stringlike when lifted with a spoon. Serve immediately.

Calories 66	Cholesterol 8 mg
Total Fat 1 g	Sodium 125 mg
Saturated 0 g	Carbohydrate 7 g
Polyunsaturated 0.5 g	Fiber 1 g
Monounsaturated 0.5 g	Protein 7 g

chunky vegetable soup

It's so flavorful, you'll want to keep this soup on hand for snacks, a light lunch, or a first course at dinner. Serve with salt-free oyster crackers.

- **2 teaspoons olive oil**
- **2 medium yellow onions, chopped**
- **8 cups chopped green or savoy cabbage**
- **8 cups fat-free, low-sodium chicken broth**
- **4 medium carrots, shredded**
- **2 cups canned no-salt-added diced tomatoes (preferably with Italian seasonings), drained, or 2 cups diced tomatoes**
- **2 cups chopped broccoli florets**
- **2 medium ribs of celery with leaves, chopped**
- **2 tablespoons snipped fresh Italian, or flat-leaf, parsley**
- **1 teaspoon dried dillweed, crumbled**
- **½ teaspoon dried summer savory, crumbled**
- **1 teaspoon salt**
- **Pepper to taste**

Heat a large stockpot over medium-high heat. Pour the oil into the pot and swirl to coat the bottom. Cook the onions until golden brown, 8 to 10 minutes, stirring occasionally. Stir in the cabbage; cook for 4 minutes.

Stir in the broth, carrots, tomatoes, broccoli, and celery. Reduce the heat to medium; bring to a boil. Stir in the remaining ingredients. Reduce the heat to low; cook until all the vegetables are tender, 20 to 30 minutes. (Cook slightly less time for tender-crisp vegetables.)

chunky vegetable soup with tuna

For an entrée soup, add two 12-ounce cans white tuna in distilled or spring water, rinsed and drained, right before serving. Serves 12; 1¼ cups per serving.

chunky vegetable soup

Calories 58	Cholesterol 0 mg
Total Fat 1.0 g	Sodium 265 mg
Saturated 0 g	Carbohydrate 10 g
Polyunsaturated 0 g	Fiber 3 g
Monounsaturated 0.5 g	Protein 3 g

with tuna

Calories 130	Cholesterol 24 mg
Total Fat 2.5 g	Sodium 318 mg
Saturated 0.5 g	Carbohydrate 10 g
Polyunsaturated 1.0 g	Fiber 3 g
Monounsaturated 1.0 g	Protein 17 g

barley and vegetable soup

serves 8; ¾ cup per serving

A bowl of this soup and a sandwich for lunch will carry you through the busiest days. Sautéing the barley brings out its rich, nutty flavor and texture.

- 1 teaspoon acceptable vegetable oil
- ½ cup pearl (or pearled) barley, sorted for stones
- 3 medium fresh mushrooms, chopped
- 6 cups fat-free, no-salt-added beef broth
- 1 medium potato
- 2 medium carrots
- 2 medium leeks (white part only)
- 1 medium rib of celery
- 1 teaspoon dried thyme, crumbled
- ½ teaspoon dried marjoram, crumbled
- ½ teaspoon dried mustard (optional)
- ¼ teaspoon ground allspice (optional)
- ⅛ teaspoon pepper
- ⅓ cup nonfat or light sour cream
- ¼ cup snipped fresh parsley

Heat a stockpot over medium heat. Pour the oil into the pot and swirl to coat the bottom. Cook the barley and mushrooms for 1 to 2 minutes, or until the mushrooms have softened, stirring occasionally. Add the broth. Increase the heat to high; bring the mixture to a boil. Reduce the heat and simmer, covered, for 15 minutes, stirring occasionally.

Meanwhile, peel the potato and chop into bite-size pieces (about 1 cup), peel and slice the carrots, finely chop the leeks (about ¾ cup), and slice the celery. Add to the barley mixture. Stir in the thyme, marjoram, mustard, allspice, and pepper. Simmer, covered, for 30 minutes, or until the vegetables and barley are tender, stirring occasionally.

To serve, ladle the soup into eight bowls. Top each serving with about 2 teaspoons of sour cream and a sprinkling of parsley.

Calories 105	Cholesterol 0 mg
Total Fat 1.0 g	Sodium 79 mg
Saturated 0 g	Carbohydrate 19 g
Polyunsaturated 0.5 g	Fiber 3 g
Monounsaturated 0.5 g	Protein 7 g

grilled carrot soup

Grilled carrots, sweet onion, and apple combine with gingerroot and curry powder for an exotic soup.

   Vegetable oil spray

8 medium carrots, peeled

2 medium sweet onions (Vidalia preferred), halved

1 medium apple (Gala preferred), quartered and unpeeled, or 1 medium parsnip, peeled

8 cups fat-free, low-sodium chicken broth

1 tablespoon minced peeled gingerroot

½ teaspoon salt

2 to 3 teaspoons curry powder (optional)

Lightly spray the grill rack with vegetable oil spray. Preheat the grill to medium-high.

Place the carrots, onions, and apple on the rack. Grill, covered if possible, until brown on all sides, 25 to 30 minutes, turning occasionally.

Transfer to a heavy stockpot or Dutch oven. Stir in the broth and gingerroot. Bring to a boil over medium heat, about 12 minutes, stirring occasionally. Stir in the salt and curry powder. Reduce the heat; simmer for 10 to 15 minutes, or until the vegetables and fruit are tender.

In a food processor or blender, process the soup in batches until the desired consistency. Return the soup to the pot and reheat if necessary.

Calories 67	Cholesterol 0 mg
Total Fat 0 g	Sodium 232 mg
Saturated 0 g	Carbohydrate 14 g
Polyunsaturated 0 g	Fiber 3 g
Monounsaturated 0 g	Protein 3 g

white corn and rosemary soup

serves 6; ¾ cup per serving

This year-round soup tastes just like a bowl of herb-flavored corn on the cob, creamy style. You'll be glad the recipe is so easy to make and so good that you'll want to serve it again and again. Double the batch and keep a supply in the freezer.

1 teaspoon olive oil

1 medium yellow onion, thinly sliced

1-pound package no-salt-added frozen baby gold and white corn or all-white whole-kernel corn

3 cups fat-free, low-sodium chicken broth

1 tablespoon chopped fresh rosemary or 1 teaspoon dried, crushed

¼ teaspoon salt

⅛ teaspoon white pepper, or to taste

Fresh rosemary sprigs (optional)

In a large, heavy pot, heat the olive oil over medium heat. Cook the onion for 3 to 4 minutes, or until translucent, stirring occasionally. Stir in the corn; cook for 4 minutes, stirring occasionally. Stir in the broth and rosemary; bring to a boil over medium heat. Add the salt and white pepper. Reduce the heat; simmer for 40 minutes (no stirring needed).

Working in batches, process the soup in a blender or food processor until almost smooth. Reheat.

To serve, garnish with rosemary sprigs.

COOK'S TIP ON MORTAR AND PESTLE

A mortar and pestle is a handy tool for crushing various foods, such as dried seeds and berries, peppercorns, herbs, and peeled garlic cloves. The bowl-shaped mortar holds the ingredients, and the short, tapered blunt rod known as the pestle is used to crush them. Sturdy materials such as porcelain and marble are used for both pieces.

Calories 63	Cholesterol 0 mg
Total Fat 1.0 g	Sodium 118 mg
Saturated 0 g	Carbohydrate 11 g
Polyunsaturated 0 g	Fiber 3 g
Monounsaturated 0.5 g	Protein 3 g

roasted tomato and chipotle soup

serves 4; ¾ cup per serving

The unique, deep flavor of this medium-spicy soup comes from roasting the tomatoes and including a chipotle pepper in adobo sauce.

Vegetable oil spray (olive oil spray preferred)
1½ pounds tomatoes, cored and halved crosswise (about 5 medium)
1 canned chipotle pepper packed in adobo sauce
2 medium onions, finely chopped
1 medium garlic clove, minced, or ½ teaspoon bottled minced garlic
1¾ to 2 cups fat-free, low-sodium chicken broth
½ teaspoon sugar
¼ teaspoon ground cumin
¼ teaspoon salt
1½ teaspoons olive oil (extra virgin preferred)

Preheat the broiler. Line a baking sheet with aluminum foil; lightly spray the foil with vegetable oil spray. Put the tomatoes with the cut side down on the foil; lightly spray the tomatoes with vegetable oil spray.

Broil the tomatoes 3 to 4 inches from the heat for 5 minutes, or until blackened. Put the tomatoes in a medium bowl. Cover the bowl; let stand for 20 minutes. Peel, retaining liquid.

Meanwhile, put the chipotle pepper on a nonporous surface, such as a plate; mash the pepper with a fork to a paste consistency.

Heat a Dutch oven over medium heat. Remove the pot from the heat and lightly spray with vegetable oil spray (being careful not to spray near a gas flame). Cook the onions for 3 to 4 minutes, or until translucent, stirring frequently. Stir in the garlic; cook for 15 seconds. Remove from the heat.

Add tomatoes with liquid, broth, and mashed chipotle to the Dutch oven. Break up large pieces of tomato. Bring to a boil over high heat. Reduce the heat; simmer for 15 minutes, stirring occasionally. Remove from the heat.

In a food processor or blender, process 1 cup soup and the remaining ingredients except olive oil until smooth. Return the mixture to the Dutch oven; stir in the olive oil. Let stand, covered, for 10 minutes.

Calories 92	Cholesterol 0 mg
Total Fat 2.5 g	Sodium 223 mg
Saturated 0.5 g	Carbohydrate 16 g
Polyunsaturated 0.5 g	Fiber 3 g
Monounsaturated 1.5 g	Protein 4 g

effervescent cantaloupe soup

Peppery sweet with a bubbly fizz, this no-cook chilled soup is an elegant way to start dinner or brunch.

2 large cantaloupes, cubed (about 8 cups)

1 cup fat-free liquid nondairy creamer

Juice of 2 medium limes

1 teaspoon imitation coconut flavoring

⅛ teaspoon cayenne

½ medium honeydew melon (optional)

2 cups diet ginger ale

8 sprigs mint (optional)

In a large bowl, combine the cantaloupe, creamer, lime juice, coconut flavoring, and cayenne.

In a food processor or blender, process about half the mixture until smooth. Pour into a large bowl. Repeat with the remaining mixture. Cover and refrigerate.

Scoop 48 small melon balls from the honeydew. Put in a medium bowl. Cover and refrigerate.

To serve, stir the ginger ale into the cantaloupe mixture. Ladle into eight shallow soup bowls. Garnish each serving with 6 honeydew balls arranged like a cluster of grapes; place a sprig of mint at the top of each cluster.

Calories 120	Cholesterol 0 mg
Total Fat 0.5 g	Sodium 22 mg
Saturated 0 g	Carbohydrate 26 g
Polyunsaturated 0 g	Fiber 1 g
Monounsaturated 0 g	Protein 1 g

sole and tomato soup with crushed cumin seeds

serves 8; about 1½ cups per serving

You can make the base of this soup ahead and freeze it, then add chunks of mild-flavored sole a few minutes before serving. Pass the red hot-pepper sauce for those who like more heat.

2 teaspoons olive oil

1 to 2 large yellow onions (Spanish preferred), chopped into 1-inch pieces

1¼ cups finely chopped celery, leaves included

4 medium garlic cloves, minced, or 2 teaspoons bottled minced garlic

64 ounces canned no-salt-added seasoned diced tomatoes, undrained

1 cup snipped fresh parsley

1 cup dry white wine (regular or nonalcoholic)

1 teaspoon dried thyme, crumbled

½ teaspoon crushed cumin seeds or ground cumin

1½ pounds mild, firm fish, such as sole or tilapia

½ teaspoon salt

¼ teaspoon black pepper

⅛ teaspoon cayenne, or to taste

1 teaspoon sugar (optional)

1 large lime, cut into eighths (optional)

Heat a large, heavy pot over medium heat. Pour the oil into the pot and swirl to coat the bottom. Cook the onions for 3 to 4 minutes, or until translucent, stirring occasionally. Add the celery and garlic; cook until the celery is crisp-tender, about 4 minutes, stirring occasionally. Add the tomatoes, parsley, wine, thyme, and cumin. Simmer, covered, for 30 minutes (no stirring needed). The soup base can be cooled and frozen for up to six months at this point.

Shortly before serving, rinse the fish and pat dry with paper towels. Cut the fish into bite-size pieces. Add to the soup; simmer for 6 to 8 minutes, or until the fish is opaque and flakes easily when tested with a fork. Stir in the salt, black pepper, and cayenne. Adjust the seasonings with the sugar, if needed. Garnish each serving with a wedge of lime to squeeze into the soup.

Calories 175	Cholesterol 41 mg
Total Fat 2.5 g	Sodium 261 mg
Saturated 0.5 g	Carbohydrate 16 g
Polyunsaturated 0.5 g	Fiber 4 g
Monounsaturated 1.0 g	Protein 19 g

slow-cooker chicken vegetable soup

Whether the brand of soup vegetables you choose includes three varieties or ten, this soup will help you fit in your daily five or more servings from the veggie and fruit group.

16 ounces no-salt-added frozen vegetables for soup

1 cup sliced leek (white part only)

¾ cup diagonally sliced celery

½ cup sliced parsnip (optional)

4 boneless, skinless chicken breast halves (about 4 ounces each), all visible fat removed

4 cups fat-free, low-sodium chicken broth

1 teaspoon all-purpose salt-free seasoning

½ teaspoon salt

1 teaspoon dried dillweed, crumbled

¼ to ½ teaspoon pepper

¼ teaspoon crushed red pepper flakes (optional)

Using a knife, break up the soup vegetables. Put them in a slow cooker. Top, in order, with the leek, celery, parsnip, and chicken.

In a 4-cup glass measure or medium bowl, stir together the remaining ingredients. Pour over the chicken and vegetables.

Cook, covered, on low for 8 hours or on high for 5 to 7 hours, or until the chicken and vegetables are tender. Skim off any scum, if necessary.

Transfer the chicken to a cutting board. When it is cool enough to handle, cut or tear the chicken into chunks. Return the chicken to the slow cooker and serve.

COOK'S TIP

If you have dabs of different vegetables in your freezer, this recipe is a handy way to use them. Put together a pound of your favorite mixture, and substitute it for the packaged soup veggies.

Calories 143	Cholesterol 44 mg
Total Fat 1.5 g	Sodium 339 mg
Saturated 0.5 g	Carbohydrate 11 g
Polyunsaturated 0 g	Fiber 2 g
Monounsaturated 0 g	Protein 21 g

lima bean chowder
with ham

serves 5; about 1 cup per serving

A creamy base with chunks of tender-cooked vegetables and plump beans teams with a hint of ham for added flavor. The result is a hearty, heart-warming soup.

- 1 tablespoon light stick margarine
- 2 medium ribs of celery, cut crosswise into ½-inch pieces
- 2 medium carrots, cut crosswise into ¼-inch pieces
- 2 cups fat-free, low-sodium chicken broth
- 15.5-ounce can no-salt-added lima beans, butter beans, or navy beans, rinsed if desired, drained, or 1 cup frozen no-salt-added lima beans or butter beans, cooked
- ½ cup diced low-fat, lower-sodium ham
- ½ cup frozen no-salt-added or canned pearl onions (rinsed and drained if canned)
- ½ teaspoon dried thyme, crumbled
- ½ teaspoon garlic powder
- ⅛ teaspoon pepper
- 1 cup fat-free milk
- ⅓ cup all-purpose flour

Heat a medium saucepan over medium heat. Cook the margarine, celery, and carrots for 3 to 4 minutes, or until the vegetables are tender-crisp, stirring occasionally.

Stir in the broth, beans, ham, onions, thyme, garlic powder, and pepper. Bring to a simmer over medium-high heat. Reduce the heat to medium-low; cook, covered, for 10 minutes, or until the vegetables are tender, stirring occasionally.

In a small bowl, whisk together the milk and flour until most lumps are gone. Whisk into the soup. Increase the heat to medium-high; cook, uncovered, for 3 to 4 minutes, or until the mixture is thickened, stirring occasionally.

COOK'S TIP

If your grocery doesn't carry no-salt-added butter beans, try health food stores.

Calories 166	Cholesterol 6 mg
Total Fat 2.0 g	Sodium 188 mg
Saturated 0.5 g	Carbohydrate 28 g
Polyunsaturated 0.5 g	Fiber 5 g
Monounsaturated 0.5 g	Protein 10 g

slow-cooker spicy lentil and bulgur soup

When prepared in a slow cooker, lentils remain whole and keep a nice consistency. Hearty and almost fat free, this soup has a fresh, light taste. Serve the soup with a whole-wheat baguette.

- **1 cup chopped carrot**
- **1 large onion, thinly sliced or chopped**
- **⅓ cup peeled and chopped celeriac or ½ cup chopped celery**
- **½ cup water**
- **2 cups dried lentils**
- **6 cups water**
- **28-ounce can peeled Italian plum tomatoes, undrained, chopped**
- **2 tablespoons red wine vinegar**
- **1 tablespoon sugar**
- **1 teaspoon grated lemon zest**
- **¼ to ½ teaspoon cayenne**
- **½ cup uncooked bulgur**

Put the carrot, onion, celeriac, and ½ cup water in a slow cooker. Cook, covered, on high for 45 minutes, or until soft and fragrant.

Meanwhile, sort the lentils, removing any stones or shriveled pieces; rinse the lentils. Add the lentils and 6 cups water to the slow cooker. Cook, covered, on high for 3 hours, or until the lentils are soft but not mushy.

Add the remaining ingredients except the bulgur. Cook, covered, on high for 1 hour, or until the flavors are well blended. Turn off the slow cooker.

Add the bulgur and let stand, covered, for 1 hour, or until softened.

COOK'S TIP ON CELERIAC

Celeriac, or celery root, is a knobby brown root vegetable with a celerylike flavor. Discard any stalks or leaves, then scrub the root thoroughly and peel it. Celeriac is a great addition to soups, salads, and sauces. It also complements potatoes, can be used raw as a dipper, and is an interesting side dish. If you want to eat raw celeriac, soak it for 1 to 2 minutes in cold water to cover, adding 2 tablespoons of lemon juice per pound of celeriac. This will help keep it from turning brown.

Calories 156	Cholesterol 0 mg
Total Fat 0.5 g	Sodium 137 mg
Saturated 0 g	Carbohydrate 29 g
Polyunsaturated 0 g	Fiber 12 g
Monounsaturated 0 g	Protein 11 g

sun-dried tomato soup with wild mushrooms and wild rice

Earthy and robust, this soup has a stewlike consistency. With a crisp green salad and fresh, hot bread, you can feed a crowd.

2 teaspoons olive oil

3½ cups diced onion (yellow preferred)

3 medium garlic cloves, finely chopped, or ½ tablespoon bottled minced garlic

1½ pounds wild mushrooms, such as shiitake, oyster, chanterelle, or morel, chopped

4 ribs of celery with leaves, chopped

2 cups matchstick-size pieces dry-packed sun-dried tomatoes

8 cups fat-free, no-salt-added beef broth

¼ cup no-salt-added tomato paste

1 teaspoon crushed red pepper flakes

½ teaspoon salt

Pinch of cayenne, or to taste

1 cup uncooked wild rice

Finely chopped green onions or chives (optional)

In a large pot, heat the oil over medium-high heat. Cook the onions until golden brown, about 8 minutes, stirring occasionally. Stir in the garlic; cook for 2 minutes. Stir in the mushrooms and celery; cook for 5 minutes, stirring occasionally. Stir in the tomatoes. Reduce the heat to medium-low. Add the beef broth, tomato paste, red pepper flakes, salt, and cayenne. Cook for 1 hour, reducing the heat to low when the soup starts to boil, stirring occasionally.

Meanwhile, cook the wild rice using the package directions, omitting the salt and margarine. Be careful not to overcook.

Just before serving, stir the rice into the soup. Garnish with green onions.

Calories 155	Cholesterol 0 mg
Total Fat 2.0 g	Sodium 204 mg
Saturated 0.5 g	Carbohydrate 27 g
Polyunsaturated 0.5 g	Fiber 5 g
Monounsaturated 1.0 g	Protein 10 g

salads
and
salad
dressings

Lotsa Layers Salad

Greek Salad with Lemon-Oregano
    Vinaigrette

Herbed Salad of Baby Mixed Greens

A to Z Vegetable Salad
    with Lime Dressing

Green Bean Salad
    with Roasted Garlic Dressing

Jícama Coleslaw
    with Mustard-Fennel Vinaigrette

Cucumber Coleslaw with Mint Dressing

Tomatillo and Chile Pepper Salsa Salad
    ❖ Tomato and Bell Pepper Salsa Salad

Sliced Tomatoes with Avocado Salsa

Cinnamon-Kissed Fruit Salad
    ❖ Cinnamon-Kissed Fruit Salad
    with Honeydew Slices

Caribbean Fruit Salad

Sweet and Tangy Pear
    and Blueberry Salad

Nectarine and Cherry Chutney

Brown Rice and Mixed Vegetable Salad

Wild Rice and Dried Apricot Salad

Tricolor Pasta Salad
    with Creamy Balsamic Vinaigrette

Minted Bean Salad

Grilled Shrimp and Watercress Salad
    with Green Goddess Dressing

Tuna and Pasta Salad with Fresh Basil

Warm Chicken Salad

Chicken Salad with Chutney
    and Apricots

Chicken and Fruit Salad with Mint

Chicken Potato Salad
    with Creamy Dressing

Turkey Taco Salad in Phyllo Shells

Mexican Flank Steak Salad

Asian-Style Beef Tenderloin Salad

Honey Mustard Dressing with Cumin

Citrus Vinaigrette

lotsa layers salad

Colorful sugar snap peas add a sweet crunch to this version of a popular layered salad. Unlike many other lettuce-based salads, this one will retain its crispness if tightly covered and refrigerated overnight.

- **4 cups water**
- **4 ounces fresh or frozen no-salt-added sugar snap peas, trimmed if fresh**

dressing

- **3 ounces fat-free or low-fat buttermilk**
- **⅜ cup nonfat or light sour cream**
- **2 tablespoons plus ¾ teaspoon Dijon mustard**
- **½ to 1 medium garlic clove, minced, or ¼ to ½ teaspoon bottled minced garlic**
- **⅛ teaspoon salt**

  ❖ ❖ ❖

- **2 cups packed shredded romaine**
- **⅓ cup thinly sliced red onion**
- **½ cup thinly sliced cucumber**
- **2 cups packed shredded romaine**
- **½ cup shredded fat-free sharp Cheddar cheese**
- **¼ teaspoon pepper, or to taste (coarsely ground preferred)**

In a medium saucepan, bring the water to a boil over high heat. Cook the peas for 1 minute, or until just tender-crisp.

Meanwhile, fill a large bowl with ice water. Remove the peas with a large slotted spoon or skimmer; plunge the peas into the ice water to stop the cooking process. Let stand for 2 minutes, or until completely cooled. Drain well; spread on paper towels and pat dry.

In a small bowl, whisk together all the dressing ingredients until well blended.

Arrange 2 cups romaine in a medium salad bowl or 9-inch glass deep-dish pie pan. Top with the onion, then the cucumber. Spoon the dressing over the cucumber; spread evenly. Top with the peas and the remaining 2 cups romaine. Sprinkle with the cheese and pepper.

Calories 74	Cholesterol 2 mg
Total Fat 0.5 g	Sodium 356 mg
Saturated 0 g	Carbohydrate 9 g
Polyunsaturated 0 g	Fiber 2 g
Monounsaturated 0 g	Protein 7 g

greek salad with lemon-oregano vinaigrette

serves 4; 1½ cups salad and 2 tablespoons dressing per serving

Vivid red and yellow tomatoes, shavings of reddish-purple onions, plump black olives, and tangy crumbled feta cheese nest on crisp, cool greens. Lemon-oregano vinaigrette drizzled on top completes this boldly colored and flavored feast of a salad.

4 cups torn romaine

½ large yellow tomato, sliced

1 large Italian plum tomato, sliced or quartered

1 cup quartered and sliced cucumber, unpeeled (English, or hothouse, preferred)

½ medium red onion, very thinly sliced

8 kalamata olives

2 ounces fat-free or reduced-fat feta cheese, rinsed, drained, and crumbled

lemon-oregano vinaigrette

⅓ cup pineapple juice

½ to 1 teaspoon grated lemon zest

3 tablespoons fresh lemon juice

1 tablespoon finely chopped fresh oregano or 1 teaspoon dried, crumbled

1 medium garlic clove, minced, or ½ teaspoon bottled minced garlic

⅛ teaspoon pepper

For each serving, arrange the romaine, tomato, cucumber, onion, and olives on a salad plate. Sprinkle each salad with feta.

In a medium bowl, stir together all the vinaigrette ingredients. Drizzle 2 tablespoons dressing over each salad. Serve immediately.

Calories 77	Cholesterol 0 mg
Total Fat 2.5 g	Sodium 356 mg
Saturated 0.5 g	Carbohydrate 11 g
Polyunsaturated 0.5 g	Fiber 2 g
Monounsaturated 1.5 g	Protein 5 g

herbed salad of
baby mixed greens

serves 4; 1½ cups per serving

This light salad simply explodes with fresh flavor.

6 cups packed mixed greens (baby greens preferred)
1 small red onion, thinly sliced
¼ cup chopped fresh parsley
1½ tablespoons chopped fresh basil
2 to 3 tablespoons balsamic vinegar (white preferred)
2 ounces fat-free or reduced-fat feta cheese, rinsed, drained, and crumbled
2 tablespoons capers, rinsed and drained

In a large salad bowl, toss the mixed greens, onion, parsley, and basil. Sprinkle with the vinegar; toss gently. Add the cheese and capers; toss gently. Serve immediately.

COOK'S TIP ON CHOPPING PARSLEY

Dry parsley and a sharp knife are the keys to success in chopping parsley. Rinse the parsley under cold water, then shake off the excess water. Pat the parsley dry between two or three layers of paper towels, or use a salad spinner. An 8-inch chef's knife is a handy tool for chopping parsley. The large size allows you to cover more surface area while chopping, saving you time.

Calories 70	Cholesterol 13 mg
Total Fat 3.5 g	Sodium 302 mg
Saturated 2.0 g	Carbohydrate 7 g
Polyunsaturated 0 g	Fiber 3 g
Monounsaturated 0.5 g	Protein 4 g

a to z vegetable salad with lime dressing

Lime dressing with a touch of dillweed complements a medley of vegetables from artichokes to zucchini. Make vegetable substitutions or additions to suit your preferences.

3 medium carrots, cut into matchstick-size strips

½ medium zucchini, seeds removed, cut into matchstick-size strips

16 snow peas, trimmed and cut lengthwise into matchstick-size strips

14-ounce can artichoke hearts (5 to 7 count), rinsed, drained, and quartered, or hearts of 5 to 7 steamed fresh artichokes, quartered

lime dressing

¾ cup nonfat or light sour cream

3 tablespoons fresh lime juice

2 tablespoons fat-free evaporated milk

1 tablespoon sugar

¼ teaspoon salt

¼ teaspoon dried dillweed, crumbled

⅛ teaspoon cayenne

Set a steamer basket in a small amount of simmering water in a medium saucepan. Put the carrots in the basket. Cook, covered, for 2 minutes, or until crisp-tender. While the carrots cook, partially fill a medium bowl with cold water. Plunge the steamed carrots into the cold water to stop the cooking process. Drain well. Transfer the carrots to a large bowl.

Steam the zucchini and snow peas for 1½ to 2 minutes, or until crisp-tender. Prepare another cold water bath. Plunge the vegetables into the cold water. Drain well. Add to the carrots.

Add the artichoke hearts; stir gently but thoroughly. Cover and refrigerate for 1½ hours to two days.

At serving time, in a medium bowl, whisk together all the dressing ingredients. Pour over the chilled vegetables and toss gently, coating all the vegetables.

Calories 86	Cholesterol 3 mg
Total Fat 0 g	Sodium 250 mg
Saturated 0 g	Carbohydrate 17 g
Polyunsaturated 0 g	Fiber 2 g
Monounsaturated 0 g	Protein 4 g

green bean salad with roasted garlic dressing

Whether you use this salad as part of a buffet (the recipe doubles beautifully), as a side dish to complement almost any dinner entrée, or around a mound of chilled tuna salad or chicken salad, you'll appreciate its vibrant colors and its versatility. Although there may seem to be an abundance of onion, the slices are paper-thin and the flavor is sweet, not overpowering.

roasted garlic dressing

1 medium garlic bulb
Vegetable oil spray
1 tablespoon olive oil
1½ to 2 tablespoons balsamic vinegar
⅛ cup fat-free, reduced-sodium chicken broth
1 tablespoon chopped fresh oregano or 1 teaspoon dried, crumbled
½ tablespoon chopped chives or green onions (green part only)
⅛ teaspoon salt
⅛ teaspoon pepper

salad

8 ounces thin green beans, trimmed
½ small or medium sweet onion (Vidalia preferred), sliced paper-thin
½ pint cherry tomatoes or grape tomatoes, halved lengthwise
Chive buds or sliced green onions (optional)
2½ tablespoons sliced almonds (optional)

Preheat the oven or toaster oven to 400°F.

For the dressing, lightly spray the garlic bulb with vegetable oil spray. Put the garlic in a small baking pan or on an ovenproof plate.

Roast for 20 to 30 minutes, or until the garlic is tender to the touch. Let cool enough to handle comfortably.

with almonds

Calories 49	Cholesterol 0 mg
Total Fat 3.0 g	Sodium 41 mg
Saturated 0.5 g	Carbohydrate 5 g
Polyunsaturated 0.5 g	Fiber 2 g
Monounsaturated 2.0 g	Protein 1 g

Squeeze half the roasted garlic out of the skins into a food processor or blender; reserve the remaining garlic for another use. Add the oil; process until a smooth paste forms. Add the vinegar and broth; process until well blended. Add the oregano and chives; process thoroughly. Stir in the salt and pepper. Set aside.

For the salad, in a large pot of boiling water, cook the green beans for 2 to 5 minutes, or until tender-crisp (cooking time will vary depending on the thickness of the beans).

Meanwhile, fill a large bowl with ice water. Remove the beans with a large slotted spoon or skimmer; plunge the beans into the ice water to stop the cooking process. Drain the beans in a colander. Cut the beans on the diagonal, 4 to 5 slices per bean.

In a medium bowl, gently toss together the green beans, onion, tomatoes, and chive buds. Add the dressing, gently tossing to coat evenly. Sprinkle with the almonds. Serve at room temperature.

COOK'S TIP

One use for the remaining roasted garlic is as a spread. Just squeeze the garlic onto the bread slice, then spread. Refrigerate any remaining garlic on a small dish, or wrap the garlic in plastic wrap or place in a plastic bag and refrigerate.

COOK'S TIP ON CHIVE BUDS

Chive buds are the seasonal buds that open and flower on chives. The buds can be found in herb gardens, at specialty produce stores, and often at Asian markets. They may be in a package or in a bunch and are still attached to the rest of the chives. Add as many buds as you like to this recipe; they're primarily for texture rather than flavor.

without almonds

Calories 37	Cholesterol 0 mg
Total Fat 2.0 g	Sodium 40 mg
Saturated 0 g	Carbohydrate 5 g
Polyunsaturated 0 g	Fiber 2 g
Monounsaturated 1.5 g	Protein 1 g

jícama coleslaw
with mustard-fennel vinaigrette

When you want a change from traditional coleslaw, give this quick and simple salad, spiked with pungent fennel seeds and tangy mustard, a try.

coleslaw

1½ cups packaged coleslaw mix
1 cup peeled matchstick-size jícama strips
¾ cup chopped red bell peppers

dressing

2 tablespoons cider vinegar
2 tablespoons unsweetened apple juice
1 tablespoon honey
1 tablespoon Dijon mustard
1 teaspoon fennel seeds, crushed
⅛ teaspoon cayenne

In a medium bowl, toss together the coleslaw ingredients.

In a small bowl, whisk together the dressing ingredients. Pour the dressing over the coleslaw; toss to coat. Serve immediately.

COOK'S TIP ON JÍCAMA

Jícamas are large, bulbous root vegetables. Their brown skin is easily peeled away, revealing crunchy off-white flesh. The sweetish, crisp flavor of jícama makes a good addition to salads or stir-fries. Strips of jícama are also excellent as dippers. Store whole jícamas in the refrigerator for up to two weeks. Peel and slice jícamas just before using. Leftover jícama tightly wrapped in plastic wrap will keep in the refrigerator for several days. Look for jícamas in the produce section of grocery stores or in Hispanic food markets.

Calories 35	Cholesterol 0 mg
Total Fat 0 g	Sodium 66 mg
Saturated 0 g	Carbohydrate 8 g
Polyunsaturated 0 g	Fiber 2 g
Monounsaturated 0 g	Protein 1 g

cucumber coleslaw
with mint dressing

Aromatic mint and oregano liven up the flavors of this summer coleslaw.

½ medium cucumber
3 cups packaged coleslaw mix
¼ cup chopped red onion
¼ cup white wine vinegar
1 tablespoon honey
1 teaspoon acceptable vegetable oil
1 tablespoon chopped fresh mint or 1 teaspoon dried, crumbled
1 teaspoon chopped fresh oregano or ¼ teaspoon dried, crumbled

Cut the cucumber in half lengthwise. Seed and cut into slices about ¼ inch thick. Put in a medium bowl.

Add the coleslaw and onion. Toss.

In a small bowl, whisk together the remaining ingredients. Pour over the vegetables; toss to coat. Serve immediately.

Calories 55	Cholesterol 0 mg
Total Fat 1.5 g	Sodium 11 mg
Saturated 0 g	Carbohydrate 10 g
Polyunsaturated 0.5 g	Fiber 2 g
Monounsaturated 0.5 g	Protein 1 g

tomatillo and chile pepper salsa salad

serves 4; ½ cup per serving

Try this fresh-tasting, crunchy salsa-style salad with fajitas or grilled chicken or pork. You'll be surprised at how such a little bit of cheese adds such a big flavor change.

- **1 cup finely chopped peeled cucumber**
- **3 ounces tomatillos, finely chopped**
- **1½ ounces reduced-fat Monterey Jack or mozzarella cheese, cut into ¼-inch cubes**
- **1 medium Anaheim pepper, seeded and ribs removed, finely chopped**
- **¼ cup snipped fresh cilantro**
- **2 tablespoons finely chopped green onions (green and white parts)**
- **3 to 4 teaspoons fresh lime juice**
- **⅛ teaspoon salt**

In a medium bowl, combine all the ingredients. Let stand for 10 minutes to allow the flavors to blend. Serve immediately or cover and refrigerate for up to 2 hours.

tomato and bell pepper salsa salad

Substitute tomatoes for tomatillos, ½ medium green bell pepper for Anaheim pepper, and parsley for cilantro.

COOK'S TIP ON TOMATILLOS

Rich in vitamin A and a good source of vitamin C, tomatillos resemble small green tomatoes with thin, parchmentlike coverings. They have a green tomato/lemon-herb-apple taste. When selecting tomatillos, choose firm ones and pull back the papery skin to make sure there are no blemishes or bruises. Tomatillos are available in the produce section of major supermarkets and in Hispanic markets.

tomatillo and chile pepper salsa salad

Calories 48	Cholesterol 6 mg
Total Fat 2.0 g	Sodium 143 mg
Saturated 1.0 g	Carbohydrate 4 g
Polyunsaturated 0.5 g	Fiber 1 g
Monounsaturated 0.5 g	Protein 4 g

tomato and bell pepper salsa salad

Calories 47	Cholesterol 6 mg
Total Fat 2.0 g	Sodium 145 mg
Saturated 1.0 g	Carbohydrate 4 g
Polyunsaturated 0.0 g	Fiber 1 g
Monounsaturated 0.0 g	Protein 4 g

sliced tomatoes
with avocado salsa

serves 5; 1 tomato slice and 3 tablespoons salsa per serving

Avocado salsa mounded on thick slices of tomato makes a towering salad that looks as good as it tastes.

- ½ **large avocado, diced**
- **2 teaspoons fresh lime juice**
- ⅛ **teaspoon salt**
- **1 medium Anaheim or poblano pepper, seeded and ribs removed, finely chopped**
- **2 tablespoons snipped fresh cilantro**
- **1 large tomato, cut into 5 slices**
- 1¼ **teaspoons fresh lime juice**

In a medium bowl, stir together the avocado, 2 teaspoons lime juice, salt, Anaheim pepper, and cilantro. Be sure the avocado is coated with the lime juice to prevent discoloration.

For each serving, place a tomato slice on a salad plate. Sprinkle each slice with lime juice. Mound 3 tablespoons avocado mixture on each slice. Serve immediately for the most pronounced flavor and maximum volume, or cover and refrigerate for up to 30 minutes.

Calories 49	Cholesterol 0 mg
Total Fat 3.5 g	Sodium 67 mg
Saturated 0.5 g	Carbohydrate 5 g
Polyunsaturated 0.5 g	Fiber 2 g
Monounsaturated 2.0 g	Protein 1 g

cinnamon-kissed
fruit salad

Ideal as a hot-weather salad, this dish can also become dessert. Serve it as a quick topper for angel food cake or the fat-free or reduced-fat versions of pound cake, ice cream, or yogurt.

1½ to 2 tablespoons sugar
¼ to ½ teaspoon ground cinnamon
½ teaspoon vanilla extract
1½ cups quartered fresh strawberries or cubed watermelon
½ cup fresh blueberries

In a medium bowl, stir together the sugar, cinnamon, and vanilla. Gently stir in the strawberries and blueberries. Let stand at room temperature for 10 minutes to allow the flavors to blend. Serve immediately or cover and refrigerate for up to 12 hours.

cinnamon-kissed fruit salad
with honeydew slices

Cut half a medium honeydew melon into 16 slices; peel. Arrange 2 slices on each salad plate and top with ¼ cup of the fruit salad. Serves 8.

COOK'S TIP ON BLUEBERRIES

Unlike thawed frozen blueberries, fresh blueberries won't bleed on the other ingredients.

Calories 49	Cholesterol 0 mg
Total Fat 0.5 g	Sodium 2 mg
Saturated 0 g	Carbohydrate 12 g
Polyunsaturated 0 g	Fiber 2 g
Monounsaturated 0 g	Protein 1 g

with honeydew

Calories 56	Cholesterol 0 mg
Total Fat 0 g	Sodium 23 mg
Saturated 0 g	Carbohydrate 14 g
Polyunsaturated 0 g	Fiber 2 g
Monounsaturated 0 g	Protein 1 g

caribbean fruit salad

Going to a cookout? Offer to bring this cool, refreshing salad.

1 medium mango, diced, or 1 cup diced bottled mango slices

1 medium banana, sliced

½ cup cubed fresh pineapple (about ½-inch pieces) or pineapple chunks canned in their own juice, drained

2 tablespoons frozen orange juice concentrate, thawed

1 tablespoon rum or ¼ teaspoon rum extract (optional)

1 teaspoon sugar (optional)

1 teaspoon imitation coconut flavoring

In a medium bowl, stir together all the ingredients. Let stand at room temperature for 10 minutes to allow the flavors to blend. Serve immediately or cover and refrigerate for up to 30 minutes.

Calories 88	Cholesterol 0 mg
Total Fat 0.5 g	Sodium 2 mg
Saturated 0 g	Carbohydrate 22 g
Polyunsaturated 0 g	Fiber 2 g
Monounsaturated 0 g	Protein 1 g

sweet and tangy pear and blueberry salad

serves 4; ½ pear and ¼ cup berries per serving

Impress your guests with this picture-perfect salad. It will definitely generate compliments.

3 tablespoons fresh lemon juice
2½ teaspoons sugar
4 romaine leaves
2 large pears
1 cup fresh blueberries
2 tablespoons chopped fresh mint
1 lemon, quartered (optional)

In a small bowl, stir together the lemon juice and sugar until the sugar has dissolved.

For each serving, place a romaine leaf on a salad plate.

Peel and thinly slice the pears. Arrange the slices in a fan pattern on the romaine. Top each serving with the blueberries, lemon mixture, and mint. Place a lemon quarter on each plate. Serve immediately. Squeeze the lemon over the salad if more tartness is desired.

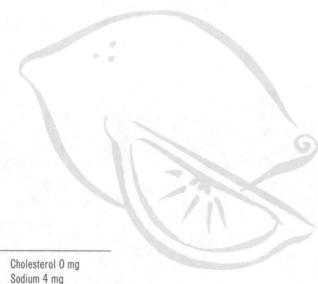

Calories 98	Cholesterol 0 mg
Total Fat 0.5 g	Sodium 4 mg
Saturated 0 g	Carbohydrate 25 g
Polyunsaturated 0 g	Fiber 4 g
Monounsaturated 0 g	Protein 1 g

nectarine and cherry chutney

Whether you want to dress up a ham or a roast or simply want a make-ahead side dish to go with turkey or chicken, this is an attractive solution.

2 medium nectarines, peeled and cut into ½-inch cubes
½ cup dried cherries
¼ teaspoon grated orange zest
½ cup fresh orange juice
¼ cup finely chopped red onion
1 tablespoon sugar
1 tablespoon raspberry vinegar
½ teaspoon ground cinnamon
Dash of salt

Set aside ¼ cup nectarine cubes.

Put all the remaining ingredients in a medium saucepan. Bring to a boil over high heat; stir. Reduce the heat and simmer for 10 minutes, or until the nectarines are just tender, stirring occasionally. Remove from the heat. Stir in the reserved nectarines. Let stand for 5 minutes. Serve hot, warm, or at room temperature.

COOK'S TIP

The very small amount of salt added to this dish takes out the acidity.

Calories 81	Cholesterol 0 mg
Total Fat 0.5 g	Sodium 30 mg
Saturated 0 g	Carbohydrate 22 g
Polyunsaturated 0 g	Fiber 2 g
Monounsaturated 0 g	Protein 1 g

brown rice and mixed vegetable salad

Turn convenience foods—instant brown rice and frozen vegetables—into a different, interesting salad by combining them with basic Asian flavoring ingredients. Add lots of crunchiness with celery, water chestnuts, and almonds.

dressing

2 tablespoons plain rice vinegar

1 tablespoon light brown sugar

2 teaspoons acceptable vegetable oil

2 teaspoons low-salt soy sauce

⅛ teaspoon pepper

❖ ❖ ❖

2 cups cooked instant brown rice

1 cup no-salt-added frozen mixed vegetables, rinsed in warm water and drained

1 medium rib of celery, chopped

½ cup sliced water chestnuts, rinsed and drained

1 tablespoon sliced almonds

In a medium bowl, stir together all the dressing ingredients.

Stir in the remaining ingredients except the almonds. Serve at room temperature or cover and refrigerate until chilled.

Just before serving, sprinkle with the almonds.

Calories 105	Cholesterol 0 mg
Total Fat 2.5 g	Sodium 59 mg
Saturated 0 g	Carbohydrate 18 g
Polyunsaturated 1.0 g	Fiber 2 g
Monounsaturated 1.5 g	Protein 2 g

wild rice and dried apricot salad

This is an ideal year-round salad. It's great with roasted meats and poultry on blustery days and with grilled entrées when the temperature sizzles.

- **2 tablespoons finely chopped pecans**
- **½ cup uncooked wild rice**
- **½ cup chopped dried apricots**
- **¼ cup chopped red bell pepper**
- **½ teaspoon grated orange zest**
- **¼ cup fresh orange juice**
- **2 tablespoons finely chopped red onion**
- **1 teaspoon sugar**
- **1 teaspoon cider vinegar**
- **¼ teaspoon crushed red pepper flakes**
- **⅛ teaspoon salt**

Heat a medium skillet over medium-high heat. Dry-roast the pecans for 3 to 4 minutes, or until they begin to brown and become fragrant, stirring occasionally. Remove from the heat.

Cook the rice using the package directions, omitting the salt and margarine. To cool the rice quickly, spread it on a baking sheet. (Cooling will take about 10 minutes.)

In a medium bowl, stir together all the ingredients. Serve immediately or cover and refrigerate for up to 2 hours.

Calories 152	Cholesterol 0 mg
Total Fat 3.0 g	Sodium 77 mg
Saturated 0.5 g	Carbohydrate 29 g
Polyunsaturated 1.0 g	Fiber 3 g
Monounsaturated 1.5 g	Protein 4 g

tricolor pasta salad with creamy balsamic vinaigrette

serves 4; 1 cup per serving

Excellent warm or cold, any time of year—how much more versatile can a salad be? Spruced up with the bold flavor of fresh dillweed, the creamy dressing coats every inch of pasta, making each bite a taste sensation. Use fresh seasonal produce for unlimited variations.

> **8 ounces dried tricolor pasta, such as rotini**
> **½ cup nonfat or light sour cream or fat-free or low-fat plain yogurt**
> **¼ cup snipped fresh parsley (optional)**
> **¼ cup chopped fresh basil, stems removed (optional)**
> **2 tablespoons snipped fresh dillweed or 2 teaspoons dried, crumbled**
> **2 tablespoons balsamic vinegar**
> **1 tablespoon fresh lemon juice (optional)**
> **½ teaspoon salt**
> **¼ teaspoon pepper**
> **2 small zucchini, grated or halved lengthwise and sliced crosswise into ½-inch-thick slices (about ¼ pound)**
> **1 cup cherry tomatoes**
> **1 medium yellow or red bell pepper, diced**
> **Scant ¼ cup diced red onion**

Cook the pasta until just tender using the package directions, omitting the salt and oil. Drain well. Transfer to a large bowl.

In a small bowl, whisk together the sour cream, parsley, basil, dillweed, vinegar, lemon juice, salt, and pepper. Stir into the pasta. Gently stir in the remaining ingredients. Serve immediately or cover and refrigerate until needed.

COOK'S TIP

Balsamic vinegar adds a sweet and tangy flavor to this dish without overpowering the other ingredients. If you don't have balsamic vinegar, try sherry vinegar or red wine vinegar.

Calories 276	Cholesterol 3 mg
Total Fat 1.0 g	Sodium 327 mg
Saturated 0 g	Carbohydrate 55 g
Polyunsaturated 0.5 g	Fiber 3 g
Monounsaturated 0 g	Protein 10 g

minted bean salad

You can use this satisfying dish as a side salad or part of a relish tray.

15-ounce can low-sodium Great Northern beans, rinsed if desired, drained

1 medium tomato, diced

½ tablespoon chopped fresh mint or ½ teaspoon dried mint, crumbled

½ medium garlic clove, minced or grated, or ¼ teaspoon bottled minced garlic

2½ tablespoons fresh lemon juice

½ tablespoon olive oil

⅛ to ¼ teaspoon salt

⅛ to ¼ teaspoon sugar

Pepper, to taste

Fresh sprig of mint (optional)

In a large bowl, stir together the beans, tomato, chopped mint, and garlic.

In a small bowl, whisk together the remaining ingredients except the sprig of mint. Pour over the beans; stir gently to coat thoroughly (a rubber scraper works well). Cover and refrigerate for at least 3 hours.

To serve, garnish with the mint sprig. Serve chilled or at room temperature.

COOK'S TIP ON JUICING CITRUS FRUIT

To get the most juice out of fresh lemons and other citrus fruit, start with room-temperature fruit. Roll the fruit on a counter or other flat surface, applying gentle pressure, before juicing.

COOK'S TIP ON GRATING GARLIC

A food rasp works well for grating garlic.

Calories 102	Cholesterol 0 mg
Total Fat 2.0 g	Sodium 218 mg
Saturated 0.0 g	Carbohydrate 17 g
Polyunsaturated 0 g	Fiber 4 g
Monounsaturated 1.5 g	Protein 5 g

grilled shrimp and watercress salad with green goddess dressing

serves 4; 3 ounces shrimp and 1 cup salad per serving

Fresh herbs provide vibrant color and delightful flavor to the dressing in this pretty salad. Watercress, a cruciferous vegetable, adds a peppery bite. If you can't find watercress, substitute other greens, such as leaf lettuce, spinach, or romaine.

Vegetable oil spray

1 pound peeled, large shrimp or 1¼ pounds large shrimp in shells, peeled

2 bunches watercress

½ English, or hothouse, cucumber or 2 small pickling cucumbers, such as Kirby

2 medium tomatoes

green goddess dressing

¼ cup light silken tofu, drained if necessary

2 tablespoons minced green onions (green part only) or chives

2 tablespoons minced fresh Italian, or flat-leaf, parsley

3 tablespoons plain rice vinegar

2 tablespoons fat-free, cholesterol-free or light, reduced-calorie mayonnaise dressing

1 tablespoon minced fresh tarragon or 1 teaspoon dried, crumbled

1 small garlic clove, crushed, or ¼ teaspoon bottled minced garlic

½ teaspoon anchovy paste (optional)

4 small green onions, cut into ½-inch pieces (white parts only)

with anchovy paste

Calories 127	Cholesterol 162 mg
Total Fat 1.5 g	Sodium 384 mg
Saturated 0.5 g	Carbohydrate 7 g
Polyunsaturated 0.5 g	Fiber 2 g
Monounsaturated 0 g	Protein 21 g

Heat a large indoor grill pan over high heat. Remove the pan from the heat and lightly spray with vegetable oil spray (being careful not to spray near a gas flame). Return the pan to the heat. When the pan starts to smoke, 4 to 5 minutes, reduce the heat to medium; carefully place the shrimp on the ridges, making sure the shrimp don't touch one another. Remove from the heat and lightly spray the top side of the shrimp with vegetable oil spray. Cook the shrimp until they start to curl and look pink on the underside, about 2 minutes. Turn the shrimp over; cook until opaque and firm to the touch, 2 to 3 minutes. (To prepare the shrimp on an outdoor grill, preheat the grill on medium-high. Grill the shrimp for 2 to 3 minutes on each side, or until opaque and firm to the touch.) Transfer the shrimp to a plate and let cool.

Discard the large stems of the watercress. Peel and thinly slice the cucumber. Dice the tomatoes. Combine in a medium bowl and refrigerate, covered, until ready to serve.

In a food processor or blender, process all the dressing ingredients until smooth. Transfer to a small serving bowl or cover and refrigerate until serving time, up to 24 hours.

To assemble, place the watercress mixture on each plate. Top with the shrimp, spoon about 2 tablespoons dressing over each serving, and sprinkle with the cut green onions. Serve immediately.

without anchovy paste

Calories 123	Cholesterol 161 mg
Total Fat 1.5 g	Sodium 279 mg
Saturated 0.5 g	Carbohydrate 7 g
Polyunsaturated 0.5 g	Fiber 2 g
Monounsaturated 0 g	Protein 20 g

tuna and pasta salad
with fresh basil

Lots of basil and a light vinaigrette distinguish this refreshing pasta salad. Adding a salt-free seasoning to pasta or rice during cooking, as in this recipe, is a good way to keep in the flavor when lowering the sodium in the food you prepare.

8 ounces dried whole-wheat pasta, such as rotini

2 tablespoons salt-free garlic and herb seasoning

vinaigrette

¼ cup plain rice vinegar

1 tablespoon sugar (optional)

1 tablespoon acceptable vegetable oil

1 tablespoon frozen unsweetened apple juice concentrate

1 tablespoon Dijon mustard

2 teaspoons white wine Worcestershire sauce

3 medium garlic cloves, crushed, or ½ tablespoon bottled minced garlic

¼ teaspoon salt

Pepper to taste

❖ ❖ ❖

12-ounce can albacore tuna in distilled or spring water

1 large cucumber

2 medium tomatoes

1 cup loosely packed fresh basil, stems removed

3 to 6 green onions (green and white parts)

In a large pot, cook the pasta using the package directions, substituting the garlic and herb seasoning for the salt and omitting the oil. Drain, rinse with cold water, and drain again. Put in a very large bowl.

In a small bowl, whisk together all the vinaigrette ingredients. Pour over the pasta; stir well.

Calories 257	Cholesterol 24 mg
Total Fat 5.0 g	Sodium 399 mg
Saturated 1.0 g	Carbohydrate 35 g
Polyunsaturated 1.5 g	Fiber 5 g
Monounsaturated 2.0 g	Protein 20 g

Drain and flake the tuna. Stir into the pasta. Cover and refrigerate until serving time, 30 minutes to 24 hours.

To serve, peel, seed, and dice the cucumber; dice the tomatoes; mince or very thinly slice the basil; and slice the onions. Stir into the tuna mixture.

COOK'S TIP ON RICE VINEGAR

Rice vinegar is also known as rice wine vinegar because it is made from rice wine. The Chinese variety is sharp and sour, and a mellow, sweet flavor denotes the Japanese version. Avoid seasoned rice vinegar; it may be high in sodium.

warm chicken salad

A soothing, tangy blend of red wine vinegar and chicken broth is the base for the warm dressing for this salad. The combination also serves as the poaching liquid for the chicken. Chicken strips top a mound of shredded napa cabbage and radicchio, which is surrounded by red onion, zucchini, and tomatoes.

2 cups fat-free, low-sodium chicken broth

⅔ cup red wine vinegar

2 medium garlic cloves or 1 teaspoon bottled minced garlic

1 bay leaf

6 whole peppercorns or ¼ teaspoon pepper

1 pound boneless, skinless chicken breasts, all visible fat removed, cut into ¼-inch-wide slices

1 small red onion, very thinly sliced

1 large zucchini, thinly sliced

2 medium Italian plum tomatoes, thinly sliced

15 ounces napa cabbage, shredded

1 small head radicchio, shredded

1 large carrot, grated

1 teaspoon Dijon mustard

¼ cup toasted unsalted soy nuts (optional)

In a medium saucepan, stir together the broth, vinegar, garlic, bay leaf, and peppercorns. Bring to a boil over high heat. Reduce the heat and simmer for 10 minutes. Add the chicken. Simmer for 5 minutes, or until the chicken is no longer pink in the center, stirring occasionally.

Meanwhile, separate the onion slices into rings; arrange the onion rings around the edges of four plates. In a slightly smaller circle, add a ring of zucchini slices so they just overlap the onion. Add a slightly smaller ring of tomato slices so they just overlap the zucchini slices. The center of the plates should remain uncovered.

without soy nuts

Calories 181	Cholesterol 66 mg
Total Fat 2.0 g	Sodium 144 mg
Saturated 0.5 g	Carbohydrate 13 g
Polyunsaturated 0.5 g	Fiber 6 g
Monounsaturated 0.5 g	Protein 30 g

Remove the chicken from the broth. Set the chicken aside. Strain the broth, reserving 1 cup. Discard any remaining broth.

In a large bowl, toss together the cabbage, radicchio, and carrot.

Whisk the mustard into the reserved broth until smooth. Pour over the cabbage mixture; toss to coat. Mound the cabbage mixture in the center of each of the plates, reserving any liquid. Top each salad with the chicken.

Drizzle the salads, including the vegetables ringing the plates, with the dressing reserved from the cabbage mixture. Sprinkle 1 tablespoon toasted soy nuts on each salad. Serve immediately.

COOK'S TIP ON SOY NUTS

Many gourmet markets, health food stores, and Asian markets carry toasted soy nuts, which are about the size of pine nuts. Look for the unsalted variety. High in protein, soy nuts are crunchy and have a mild, nutty taste.

with soy nuts

Calories 229	Cholesterol 66 mg
Total Fat 4.0 g	Sodium 144 mg
Saturated 1.0 g	Carbohydrate 16 g
Polyunsaturated 2.0 g	Fiber 6 g
Monounsaturated 1.0 g	Protein 34 g

chicken salad with chutney and apricots

For a festive but light lunch, pair this curried chicken salad with a cup of your favorite soup. The chicken salad mixture is also delightful as a filling for finger sandwiches made with whole-wheat bread.

¼ cup plus 2 tablespoons mango chutney

2 ounces fat-free or reduced-fat cream cheese, softened

¼ cup fat-free or low-fat plain yogurt

½ teaspoon curry powder

2 cups diced cooked chicken or turkey, white meat only, skin and all visible fat removed (about 12 ounces, cooked weight)

½ cup drained diced apricots canned in extra-light syrup

2 tablespoons chopped walnuts

4 cups mixed salad greens

In a small bowl, stir together the chutney, cream cheese, yogurt, and curry powder. Stir in the chicken, apricots, and walnuts.

For each serving, place 1 cup mixed salad greens on a plate and top with ½ cup chicken salad.

Calories 259	Cholesterol 61 mg
Total Fat 6.0 g	Sodium 154 mg
Saturated 1.0 g	Carbohydrate 25 g
Polyunsaturated 2.5 g	Fiber 2 g
Monounsaturated 1.5 g	Protein 26 g

chicken and fruit salad with mint

With its perfect balance of sweet figs, juicy melon, tart vinegar, and aromatic mint, this recipe will make an unusual addition to your chicken salad repertoire.

4 boneless, skinless chicken breast halves (about 4 ounces each), all visible fat removed

¼ cup fresh mint leaves

3 tablespoons sherry vinegar

2 tablespoons honey

1½ tablespoons fat-free or low-fat plain yogurt (optional)

2 cups cubed honeydew melon

1 cup peeled, diced cucumber

⅓ cup sliced dried Mission figs, sliced dates, or raisins

Put the chicken in a medium saucepan. Pour in enough water to cover. Bring to a boil over medium-high heat. Reduce the heat to medium-low; cook for 10 minutes, or until the chicken is no longer pink in the center.

Meanwhile, chop or very thinly slice the mint.

When the chicken is cooked, drain well and pat dry with paper towels. Cut the chicken into 1-inch cubes.

In a large bowl, whisk together the vinegar, honey, and yogurt. Stir in the chicken and the remaining ingredients. Serve immediately or cover and refrigerate until ready to serve, or up to two days.

with yogurt

Calories 239	Cholesterol 66 mg
Total Fat 2.0 g	Sodium 91 mg
Saturated 0.5 g	Carbohydrate 30 g
Polyunsaturated 0.5 g	Fiber 3 g
Monounsaturated 0.5 g	Protein 28 g

without yogurt

Calories 236	Cholesterol 66 mg
Total Fat 2.0 g	Sodium 87 mg
Saturated 0.5 g	Carbohydrate 29 g
Polyunsaturated 0.5 g	Fiber 3 g
Monounsaturated 0.5 g	Protein 28 g

chicken potato salad
with creamy dressing

You can serve this traditional salad as a light lunch, or for a new twist, substitute uncooked chopped kohlrabi or more potato for the chicken and serve it as a side dish. Be sure to allow time for the yogurt to drain.

16 ounces fat-free or low-fat plain yogurt, no gelatin added

12 ounces boneless, skinless chicken breasts, all visible fat removed

1 pound red potatoes (about 6 medium)

½ cup frozen green peas, thawed

½ cup shredded celery root or ½ cup chopped celery

dressing

¼ cup chopped red onion

¼ cup fat-free, cholesterol-free or light, reduced-calorie mayonnaise dressing

1 tablespoon Dijon mustard

1 tablespoon plus 1 teaspoon capers, rinsed and drained

1 tablespoon plus 1 teaspoon chopped dill pickle

1 teaspoon grated lemon zest

1 tablespoon fresh lemon juice

1 teaspoon sugar

¾ teaspoon dried dillweed, crumbled

¼ teaspoon white pepper

8 red-leaf lettuce leaves (optional)

2 medium Italian plum tomatoes, cut into thin slices (optional)

8 thin slices red onion (optional)

Calories 265	Cholesterol 51 mg
Total Fat 1.5 g	Sodium 468 mg
Saturated 0.5 g	Carbohydrate 36 g
Polyunsaturated 0.5 g	Fiber 4 g
Monounsaturated 0.5 g	Protein 29 g

Line a rustproof colander or large strainer with two layers of cheesecloth or an unused coffee filter. Pour the yogurt into the colander and cover. Put the colander in a deep bowl. Refrigerate for 6 to 8 hours, or until most of the whey (yellowish liquid) has drained off and the yogurt has thickened. Discard the whey; set the yogurt aside.

Meanwhile, put the chicken in a small saucepan with enough water to cover by 1 inch. Bring to a simmer over medium-high heat. Reduce the heat; simmer for 20 to 30 minutes, or until the chicken is no longer pink in the center. Drain well. Let cool for 5 to 10 minutes, or until cool enough to handle. Cut into ½-inch cubes.

While the chicken is cooking, cut the potatoes into ½-inch cubes. Put them in a medium saucepan with enough water to cover by 1 inch. Bring the water to a boil over high heat. Reduce the heat and simmer, covered, for 10 to 15 minutes, or until tender. Drain well. Transfer to a large bowl, cover, and refrigerate.

Add the chicken to the cooked potatoes; cover and refrigerate.

When the yogurt is ready, stir into the potatoes and chicken. Stir in the peas and celery root.

In a small bowl, whisk together all the dressing ingredients. Stir into the potato mixture.

To serve, line a bowl with the lettuce. Spoon the salad into the bowl; garnish with the tomato and red onion slices.

COOK'S TIP ON DRAINING YOGURT

When draining yogurt to thicken it, use a yogurt that contains no gelatin. Gelatin holds in the liquid, or whey, so the yogurt can't drain to the thick, creamy consistency you want.

turkey taco salad in phyllo shells

serves 4; 1 filled phyllo shell per serving

Flaky baked phyllo shells are the perfect edible bowls. Here they're filled with ground turkey, black beans, and lots of accompaniments.

Vegetable oil spray

4 sheets frozen phyllo dough, thawed

6 ounces lean ground turkey breast or ground skinless chicken

¾ teaspoon chili powder

¾ teaspoon garlic powder

3 tablespoons nonfat or light sour cream

¼ teaspoon fresh lime juice

1 cup canned no-salt-added black beans, rinsed if desired, drained

1 cup shredded iceberg lettuce

¼ cup fat-free or reduced-fat shredded Cheddar or Monterey Jack cheese, or a combination

1 tablespoon plus 1 teaspoon sliced black olives

½ cup salsa

Preheat the oven to 375° F. Lightly spray four 5-ounce custard cups or 4½-inch aluminum pie tins with vegetable oil spray.

Stack the phyllo sheets on a cutting board. Cut the stacked sheets crosswise into quarters. Keeping unused phyllo covered with a damp cloth or damp paper towels to prevent drying, place 1 piece of phyllo in a custard cup. Lightly spray with vegetable oil spray. Repeat with 3 more pieces of phyllo, the second perpendicular to the first, and the third and fourth crisscrossing to fill in the spaces. Repeat for the other custard cups. Place the custard cups on an ungreased baking sheet.

Bake for 8 to 10 minutes, or until the phyllo is golden brown. Leaving the shells in the custard cups on the baking sheet, let the shells cool on a cooling rack for at least 10 minutes.

Calories 197	Cholesterol 26 mg
Total Fat 2.0 g	Sodium 357 mg
Saturated 0.5 g	Carbohydrate 24 g
Polyunsaturated 0.5 g	Fiber 3 g
Monounsaturated 1.0 g	Protein 18 g

In a medium nonstick skillet, cook the turkey over medium-high heat for 6 to 7 minutes, or until cooked through, stirring occasionally to turn and break into small pieces. Stir in the chili powder and garlic powder.

Meanwhile, in a small bowl, whisk together the sour cream and lime juice.

To assemble each salad, layer the ingredients in the phyllo cups in the following order: beans, turkey, lettuce, cheese, olives, sour cream mixture, and salsa. Serve immediately.

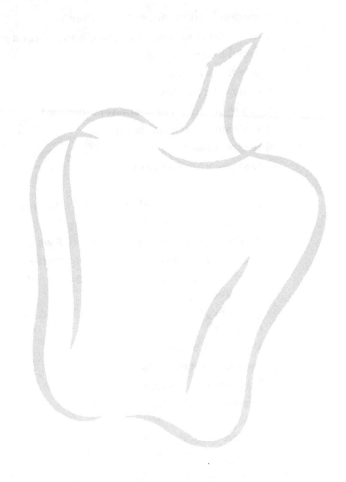

mexican flank steak salad

Chunks of hearty whole-grain bread go well with this meat-lover's salad. You can grill them for 2 to 3 minutes while the steak sets. Be sure to allow plenty of time for the meat to marinate.

marinade

½ medium red onion, cut into chunks

3 large garlic cloves or 2¼ teaspoons bottled minced garlic

¼ cup balsamic vinegar

¼ cup fresh lime juice

¼ cup barbecue sauce

1½ tablespoons dried oregano, crumbled

1 tablespoon vegetable oil

½ teaspoon salt

1 teaspoon ground cumin

❖ ❖ ❖

1 pound flank steak, all visible fat removed

2 medium ears of corn

2 medium red onions, each cut into 8 wedges

3 medium zucchini, quartered lengthwise

1 medium red bell pepper, quartered lengthwise, seeds and ribs removed

1 medium yellow bell pepper, quartered lengthwise, seeds and ribs removed

Vegetable oil spray

4 cups torn mixed salad greens

Tomato wedges (optional)

Fresh cilantro sprigs (optional)

In a food processor or blender, process ½ red onion and the garlic until coarsely chopped. Add the remaining marinade ingredients and process until smooth. Remove ⅓ cup for the marinade; cover and refrigerate the remainder for the salad dressing.

Calories 289	Cholesterol 47 mg
Total Fat 10.0 g	Sodium 400 mg
Saturated 3.5 g	Carbohydrate 28 g
Polyunsaturated 1.0 g	Fiber 6 g
Monounsaturated 4.0 g	Protein 24 g

With a sharp knife, make four or five slashes about ¼ inch deep against the grain of the meat; turn the meat over and repeat. Put the meat in an airtight plastic bag or glass baking dish; pour in the reserved marinade and turn to coat. Seal and refrigerate for 6 to 12 hours, turning occasionally.

Preheat the grill to medium-high.

Remove the meat from the marinade. Discard the marinade. Grill the meat 4 to 6 inches from the heat for 10 minutes, or until the desired doneness, turning once. Remove from the heat and cover loosely with aluminum foil. Let stand for 10 to 15 minutes.

Meanwhile, husk and desilk the corn. Wrap each ear of corn separately in aluminum foil. Insert metal skewers into the remaining onion pieces. Lightly spray the onion, zucchini, and bell peppers with vegetable oil spray. Grill with the corn for 10 to 15 minutes, or until the desired doneness, turning frequently. Or lightly spray a perforated grill pan with vegetable oil spray; put the corn, onions, zucchini, and bell peppers in the pan and grill for 10 to 15 minutes, turning frequently.

To assemble, arrange the salad greens on four plates. When cool enough to handle, cut the corn from the cob. Cut the onions, zucchini, and bell peppers into uniform pieces about ¾ inch long. In a large bowl, toss the corn and other vegetables with the marinade reserved for salad dressing. Cut the meat diagonally across the grain into thin slices. Arrange the vegetables and steak slices over the salad greens.

asian-style beef tenderloin salad

serves 4; 1½ cups salad and 2 tablespoons dressing per serving

Rainbow-colored vegetables and tender beef strips, topped with lime-flavored dressing, make an elegant salad.

marinade

1 tablespoon low-sodium soy sauce

1 teaspoon toasted sesame oil

¼ teaspoon pepper

❖ ❖ ❖ ❖

1 pound beef tenderloin, all visible fat removed

¼ cup water

¼ cup fresh lime juice

3 tablespoons sugar

Vegetable oil spray

8 to 10 medium spears of asparagus, trimmed

3.3-ounce package fresh shiitake mushrooms, stems removed and caps sliced

½ medium yellow bell pepper, thinly sliced

1 cup shredded red cabbage

1 cup shredded carrot

4 to 6 fresh mint sprigs (optional)

In an airtight plastic bag or glass baking dish, combine the marinade ingredients.

Slice the beef crosswise into four pieces. Add the meat to the marinade and turn to coat. Seal and refrigerate for 20 minutes to 12 hours, turning occasionally.

Calories 265	Cholesterol 71 mg
Total Fat 8.5 g	Sodium 168 mg
Saturated 3.0 g	Carbohydrate 20 g
Polyunsaturated 0.5 g	Fiber 3 g
Monounsaturated 3.0 g	Protein 26 g

In a small saucepan, stir together the water, lime juice, and sugar. Bring to a boil over high heat, stirring until the sugar has dissolved. Reduce the heat and simmer for 5 minutes, or until the mixture is the consistency of thin syrup. Set aside.

Lightly spray the grill rack or the broiler pan and rack with vegetable oil spray. Preheat the grill on medium-high or preheat the broiler.

Drain the meat. Discard the marinade. Grill or broil 5 to 6 inches from the heat for 6 to 7 minutes per side for medium-well, or until desired doneness (5 to 6 minutes per side for medium-rare to medium). Cut into thin strips.

Meanwhile, fill a large skillet with water to a depth of 1 inch. Bring to a boil over high heat. Cook the asparagus for 2 to 3 minutes, or until tender-crisp. Drain well.

In a medium salad bowl, stir together the mushrooms, bell pepper, cabbage, and carrot. Arrange the beef slices and asparagus on top. Garnish with the mint sprigs. Serve the dressing on the side.

honey mustard dressing with cumin

serves 4; 2 tablespoons per serving

Adding cumin to honey mustard dressing gives it a bit of distinction.

¼ cup fat-free or low-fat plain yogurt

2 tablespoons honey

2 tablespoons prepared mustard

2 teaspoons cider vinegar

2 teaspoons sugar

¼ teaspoon ground cumin

⅛ teaspoon cayenne

In a small bowl, whisk together all the ingredients. Serve immediately or refrigerate in an airtight container for up to two weeks.

Calories 55	Cholesterol 0 mg
Total Fat 0.5 g	Sodium 100 mg
Saturated 0 g	Carbohydrate 13 g
Polyunsaturated 0 g	Fiber 0 g
Monounsaturated 0 g	Protein 1 g

citrus vinaigrette

This tangy dressing is equally good with fruit or vegetable salads or with a combination of the two. It contains only a fraction of the amount of oil found in most vinaigrettes.

1 teaspoon grated orange or grapefruit zest

¼ cup fresh orange juice

¼ cup fresh grapefruit juice

2 tablespoons balsamic or red wine vinegar

2 to 3 teaspoons finely chopped shallots

2 teaspoons acceptable vegetable oil

1 teaspoon honey

1 teaspoon Dijon mustard

¼ teaspoon pepper

Combine all the ingredients by whisking in a small bowl or shaking in a small jar with a tight-fitting lid. Serve immediately or cover and refrigerate for up to five days.

COOK'S TIP ON CITRUS ZEST

The colored part of the rind on citrus fruits is the zest. An inexpensive and indispensable kitchen tool to have on hand is the zester, which easily removes the zest. More expensive but ever so handy is the kitchen rasp. Whichever you use, be careful to grate only the zest, not the bitter white part underneath (the pith). Make sure to zest the whole fruit before cutting it in half to juice it. You can wrap any extra zest in plastic wrap or aluminum foil and freeze it. The zest of various citrus fruits—lemons, oranges, limes, and grapefruit—frequently is interchangeable in recipes. That knowledge not only may save rush trips to the grocery when you're cooking but also could open up new taste adventures.

Calories 33	Cholesterol 0 mg
Total Fat 1.5 g	Sodium 22 mg
Saturated 0 g	Carbohydrate 5 g
Polyunsaturated 0.5 g	Fiber 0 g
Monounsaturated 1.0 g	Protein 0 g

seafood

Herbed Cod with Root Vegetables

Cod with Lemon-Wine Sauce

Fish and Chips with Malt Vinegar and Green Onion Sauce

Halibut with Horseradish and Herb Crust

Citrus-Poached Fish Fillets

Herbed Salmon

Grilled Lemon-Ginger Salmon

Fresh Salmon Cakes with Lemon and Capers

Red Snapper with Tomato-Caper Sauce and Orzo

Sea Bass with Ginger-Tomato Sauce

Asparagus-Stuffed Sole with Horseradish Cream

Swordfish Topped with Tomatillo Sauce
   ❖ Chicken Topped with Tomatillo Sauce

Citrus-Stuffed Trout

Tuna with Cilantro-Lime Glaze and Quinoa

Broiled Tuna Steak
   with Lemongrass-Chamomile Glaze

Tuna Cakes with Cucumber Yogurt Sauce

Grilled Tuna with Tomato Salsa

Sea Scallops with Snow Peas

Caribbean Shrimp and Black Beans

herbed cod
with root vegetables

serves 6; 3 ounces fish and ½ cup vegetables per serving

After a long day, seafood dishes are convenient because they are usually quick to prepare and to cook. This one spotlights firm-textured, mild-flavored cod, enhanced with lemon, thyme, and marjoram.

Vegetable oil spray

1½ pounds cod fillets

2 slices light whole-wheat bread, cubed

2 medium carrots, 2 medium parsnips, or 1 medium carrot and 1 medium parsnip, diced

2 medium onions, chopped

2 medium ribs of celery, finely chopped

2 teaspoons grated lemon zest

2 tablespoons fresh lemon juice

1 teaspoon dried thyme, crumbled

1 teaspoon dried marjoram, crumbled

¼ teaspoon pepper

½ cup fat-free, low-sodium chicken broth

Preheat the oven to 375° F. Lightly spray a 13 × 9 × 2-inch baking dish with vegetable oil spray.

Rinse the fish and pat dry with paper towels. Put the fish in the prepared dish.

In a medium bowl, stir together the remaining ingredients except the broth. Spoon over the cod. Pour the broth over all.

Bake, covered, for 20 minutes, or until the fish flakes easily when tested with a fork and the vegetables are tender. Bake, uncovered, for 5 minutes.

Calories 136	Cholesterol 49 mg
Total Fat 1.0 g	Sodium 126 mg
Saturated 0.0 g	Carbohydrate 10 g
Polyunsaturated 0.5 g	Fiber 3 g
Monounsaturated 0.0 g	Protein 22 g

cod with lemon-wine sauce

serves 4; 3 ounces fish and 1 tablespoon sauce per serving

A light cornstarch coating adds a bit of crispness to the fish fillets in this dish. Try sugar snap peas and orzo, a rice-shaped pasta, as accompaniments.

3 tablespoons cornstarch

1 teaspoon chopped fresh lemon thyme or regular thyme,
   or ½ teaspoon dried lemon thyme or regular thyme, crumbled

¼ to ½ teaspoon grated lemon zest

½ teaspoon salt

¼ teaspoon pepper

4 cod fillets or other mild fish fillets, such as haddock, flounder, or scrod (about 4 ounces each)

2 teaspoons acceptable vegetable oil

½ cup dry white wine (regular or nonalcoholic)

1 tablespoon fresh lemon juice

In a shallow dish or pie pan, combine the cornstarch, lemon thyme, zest, salt, and pepper.

Rinse the fish and pat dry with paper towels. Lightly dust both sides of the fish, shaking off the excess.

Heat a medium nonstick skillet over medium heat. Pour the oil into the skillet and swirl to coat the bottom. Cook the fish for 6 to 8 minutes, or until it is golden brown on both sides and flakes easily when tested with a fork, turning once.

Add the remaining ingredients. Increase the heat to medium-high; bring to a boil. Cook for about 1 minute, or until the sauce is reduced slightly, scraping up any browned bits on the bottom of the pan.

To serve, spoon the sauce over the fish.

Calories 158	Cholesterol 49 mg
Total Fat 3.0 g	Sodium 354 mg
Saturated 0.5 g	Carbohydrate 6 g
Polyunsaturated 1.0 g	Fiber 0 g
Monounsaturated 1.5 g	Protein 20 g

fish and chips with malt vinegar and green onion sauce

serves 4; 3 ounces fish, ½ cup potatoes, and
2 tablespoons sauce per serving

Fish and chips is traditionally served in newspapers to absorb the fat from deep frying. You won't need newspaper for our heart-healthy version, however. Mild fish nuggets are coated in a buttermilk, cracker crumb, and cornflake mixture, then baked with crinkle-cut red potatoes until crispy. A sweet-and-sour malt vinegar sauce tops both.

Vegetable oil spray

¼ cup nonfat or low-fat buttermilk

½ teaspoon garlic powder

½ teaspoon onion powder

1 pound white fish fillets, such as orange roughy, tilapia, cod, or sole, cut into 1½- to 2-inch cubes

1 pound red potatoes (about 4 small)

Vegetable oil spray

½ teaspoon salt-free lemon pepper

½ teaspoon paprika

½ cup crushed cornflake cereal

¼ cup cracker meal

⅓ cup malt vinegar

4 medium green onions, thinly sliced (green and white parts)

1 tablespoon sugar

Preheat the oven to 400°F. Lightly spray a large nonstick baking sheet with vegetable oil spray.

In a large airtight plastic bag or glass baking dish, combine the buttermilk, garlic powder, and onion powder.

Calories 239	Cholesterol 23 mg
Total Fat 1.0 g	Sodium 191 mg
Saturated 0 g	Carbohydrate 38 g
Polyunsaturated 0 g	Fiber 3 g
Monounsaturated 0.5 g	Protein 21 g

Rinse the fish and pat dry with paper towels. Add the fish to the buttermilk mixture and turn to coat. Seal and refrigerate for 10 minutes to 3 hours, turning occasionally.

With a crinkle cutter or sharp knife, cut the potatoes crosswise into ¼-inch slices. Arrange the potato slices in a single layer on half the baking sheet. Lightly spray the tops of the potatoes with vegetable oil spray. Sprinkle with lemon pepper and paprika.

Bake for 20 minutes.

Meanwhile, in a shallow bowl, stir together the cereal and cracker meal. Using a slotted spoon or tongs, remove the fish from the marinade and coat in the crumb mixture, turning gently. Discard the marinade.

When the potatoes have baked for 20 minutes, arrange the fish in a single layer on the empty half of the baking sheet. Lightly spray the fish with vegetable oil spray.

Bake for about 15 minutes, or until the fish flakes easily when tested with a fork.

Meanwhile, in a small bowl, stir together the remaining ingredients. Spoon 2 tablespoons sauce over each serving or serve on the side as a dipping sauce.

COOK'S TIP ON CRACKER MEAL

A very low sodium crumb mixture made from finely crushed crackers, cracker meal is usually found near the bread crumbs.

COOK'S TIP ON CRINKLE CUTTERS

Crinkle cutters are wavy-edged metal implements often used for making garnishes. Gourmet shops and some supermarkets carry them.

halibut with horseradish and herb crust

Silky halibut combines with fresh bread crumbs and spicy horseradish to make an elegant dish for family or company.

Vegetable oil spray

1 pound halibut or other firm white fish

½ teaspoon salt

½ cup fat-free, cholesterol-free or light, reduced-calorie mayonnaise dressing

1½ tablespoons grated horseradish (fresh preferred)

1 tablespoon fresh rosemary or thyme, minced, or 1 teaspoon dried, crushed or crumbled (fresh preferred)

¼ cup plain soft bread crumbs (about ½ slice light bread), divided use

1 teaspoon fresh rosemary, minced, or ¼ to ½ teaspoon dried, crushed (optional)

Preheat the oven to 400°F. Lightly spray a broilerproof 12 × 8 × 2-inch or 1½-quart glass baking dish with vegetable oil spray.

Rinse the fish and pat dry with paper towels. Place the fish in the prepared dish. Bake for 6 minutes. Sprinkle with salt.

Meanwhile, in a small bowl, stir together the mayonnaise, horseradish, 1 tablespoon rosemary, and 2 tablespoons bread crumbs.

Remove the halibut from the oven; spread the mayonnaise mixture evenly over the top. Sprinkle with the remaining bread crumbs.

Preheat the broiler. Broil the fish about 4 inches from the heat for 3 to 4 minutes, or until the top is golden brown and the fish flakes easily when tested with a fork.

Sprinkle with the remaining rosemary.

Calories 150	Cholesterol 36 mg
Total Fat 2.5 g	Sodium 340 mg
Saturated 0.5 g	Carbohydrate 5 g
Polyunsaturated 1.0 g	Fiber 0 g
Monounsaturated 1.0 g	Protein 24 g

citrus-poached fish fillets

Grapefruit juice and orange juice infused with lemony crushed coriander seeds are used to gently poach fish fillets. For an extra burst of flavor, squeeze a seasoned lime wedge over the finished dish.

- ¾ **cup fresh grapefruit juice**
- ¾ **cup fresh orange juice**
- 2 **teaspoons coriander seeds, crushed**
- ¼ **teaspoon pepper**
- 4 **sole or tilapia fillets (about 4 ounces each)**
- ½ **teaspoon chili powder**
- 1 **medium lime, quartered**

In a large, shallow saucepan, combine the grapefruit juice and orange juice.

Add the coriander and pepper to the saucepan. Bring to a simmer over medium-high heat.

Place the fish in a single layer in the simmering liquid. Reduce the heat to medium-low and cook, covered, for about 10 minutes, or until the fish flakes easily when tested with a fork, turning once.

Meanwhile, put the chili powder on a small plate. Dip one edge of each lime wedge into the chili powder to coat lightly.

To serve, remove the fish from the poaching liquid. Discard the poaching liquid. Garnish each serving with a lime wedge.

COOK'S TIP ON CORIANDER SEEDS

Crush the coriander seeds using a mortar and pestle, or put them in an airtight plastic bag and crush with a rolling pin or the flat side of a meat mallet.

COOK'S TIP ON CANNED JUICES

Keep 6-ounce cans of unsweetened grapefruit, orange, and pineapple juices in your pantry. When you need a small amount of juice for cooking and don't have fresh on hand, you're prepared.

Calories 92	Cholesterol 53 mg
Total Fat 1 g	Sodium 82 mg
Saturated 0.5 g	Carbohydrate 0 g
Polyunsaturated 0.5 g	Fiber 0 g
Monounsaturated 0 g	Protein 19 g

herbed salmon

Add a spinach or romaine salad and some whole-wheat pasta for a delicious, attractive, and quick meal.

- 2 tablespoons Dijon mustard
- 1 tablespoon chopped fresh thyme, rosemary, or basil or 1 teaspoon dried, crumbled or crushed
- ⅛ teaspoon pepper
- 1 pound salmon fillet with skin, about 1 inch thick
- Vegetable oil spray
- Fresh herb sprigs (optional)
- 1 medium or large orange, cut into 8 wedges (optional)

In a cup or small bowl, stir together the mustard, thyme, and pepper.

Rinse the fish and pat dry with paper towels. Spread the mustard mixture over the flesh side of the fish.

Heat a large, heavy nonstick skillet over high heat. Remove from the heat and lightly spray with vegetable oil spray (being careful not to spray near a gas flame). When the skillet is very hot, lower the temperature to medium-high. Cook the fish with the mustard side down for 3 to 5 minutes, or until the mustard browns and becomes crusty—don't move the fish around. Carefully turn the fish over (a spatula works well); cook for 4 to 5 minutes, or until the fish flakes easily when tested with a fork. (If the mustard crust sticks to the spatula, place the crust back on the fish.) If the fish needs more cooking time, put a piece of aluminum foil loosely over the skillet and reduce the heat to low; continue cooking until the fish is done. Or transfer the fish to a microwave-safe dish and microwave it, uncovered, for 1 minute on 100 percent power (high). (This method keeps the fish moist without overcooking it.)

To serve, cut the fish into four pieces. Serve warm or at room temperature. Garnish with the fresh herbs or orange wedges.

Calories 140	Cholesterol 59 mg
Total Fat 4.0 g	Sodium 256 mg
Saturated 0.5 g	Carbohydrate 0 g
Polyunsaturated 1.5 g	Fiber 0 g
Monounsaturated 1.0 g	Protein 23 g

grilled lemon-ginger salmon

Salmon offers a double bonus—it tastes delicious and is rich in omega-3 acids. Omega-3s are polyunsaturated fatty acids that may be beneficial to your heart.

marinade

2 tablespoons snipped fresh parsley (Italian, or flat-leaf, preferred)

2 to 2½ tablespoons fresh lemon juice

2 tablespoons low-salt soy sauce (see Cook's Tip on Soy Sauce, page 95)

2 teaspoons grated peeled gingerroot

¼ teaspoon pepper

❖ ❖ ❖

4 salmon fillets (about 4 ounces each)

Vegetable oil spray

In a large airtight plastic bag or glass baking dish, combine the marinade ingredients.

Rinse the fish and pat dry with paper towels. Add the fish to the marinade and turn to coat. Seal and refrigerate for 15 minutes to 1 hour. Remove the fish from the marinade; pat dry with paper towels. Discard the marinade.

Lightly spray a ridged stovetop grill pan or large nonstick skillet with vegetable oil spray. Grill the fish with the flesh side down over medium-high heat for 4 minutes. Turn and grill for 3 to 4 minutes, or until the fish flakes easily when tested with a fork.

Calories 137	Cholesterol 59 mg
Total Fat 4.0 g	Sodium 271 mg
Saturated 0.5 g	Carbohydrate 1 g
Polyunsaturated 1.5 g	Fiber 0 g
Monounsaturated 1.0 g	Protein 23 g

fresh salmon cakes
with lemon and capers

serves 4; 1 salmon cake per serving

Fresh salmon chunks—delicately bound with cornmeal and seasoned with a creamy mix of capers, green peppercorns, and lemon zest—sizzle to perfection in just a few minutes. Serve with a half-portion of 10-Minute Fettuccine in Tomato Broth (page 196) or on top of your favorite green salad, perhaps tossed with Citrus Vinaigrette (page 69).

- 1 tablespoon grated lemon zest
- 2 teaspoons capers, rinsed and drained
- 1 teaspoon black or green peppercorns
- 1 medium garlic clove, coarsely chopped, or ½ teaspoon bottled chopped or minced garlic
- ¼ teaspoon pepper
- 1 tablespoon fresh lemon juice
- Whites of 2 large eggs
- ¼ cup fat-free, cholesterol-free or light, reduced-calorie mayonnaise dressing
- ¼ cup cornmeal
- 12 ounces salmon fillet, skin removed
- Vegetable oil spray

With a mortar and pestle (see Cook's Tip on Mortar and Pestle, page 24), crush and grind together the lemon zest, capers, peppercorns, garlic, and pepper. Transfer to a medium bowl. If you don't have a mortar and pestle, use the blade of a chef's knife to crush the capers and peppercorns against a cutting board; put the mixture in a medium bowl and stir in the zest, garlic, and pepper, mashing with a fork.

Add the lemon juice; using the mortar or the back of a wooden spoon, make a paste. Stir in the egg whites, mayonnaise, and cornmeal.

Rinse the fish and pat dry with paper towels. Cut the fish into about ¼-inch squares. (The pieces don't have to be uniform size.) Stir into the egg white mixture.

Calories 160	Cholesterol 44 mg
Total Fat 3.0 g	Sodium 245 mg
Saturated 0.5 g	Carbohydrate 11 g
Polyunsaturated 1.0 g	Fiber 1 g
Monounsaturated 1.0 g	Protein 20 g

Preheat a large nonstick skillet over medium heat. Remove the skillet from the heat and lightly spray with vegetable oil spray (being careful not to spray near a gas flame).

Using your hands, form four soft patties from the fish mixture. Place the patties in the skillet; press down gently but firmly, shaping each into a circle about ¾ inch thick. Cook for 3 to 4 minutes on each side, turning only once, until the patties are a dappled mixture of pink, light brown, and dark brown and are cooked through.

red snapper with tomato-caper sauce and orzo

serves 4; 3 ounces fish, ¼ cup tomato sauce, and ½ cup orzo per serving

Smothered in a sweet and tangy sauce, these tender snapper fillets are infused with the bold flavors of tomatoes, capers, and oregano.

Vegetable oil spray

6 ounces dried orzo

4 slightly firm fish fillets, such as red snapper, grouper, bass, sole, or tilapia (about 4 ounces each)

½ teaspoon pepper

14.5-ounce can no-salt-added diced tomatoes, undrained

½ cup fresh basil, stems removed, leaves chopped

3 to 4 tablespoons rinsed and drained capers

2 tablespoons no-salt-added tomato paste

1 teaspoon dried oregano, crumbled

Preheat the oven to 400°F. Lightly spray a large roasting pan with vegetable oil spray.

Cook the orzo using the package directions, omitting the salt and oil. Drain well.

Meanwhile, rinse the fish and pat dry with paper towels. Season both sides of the fish with the pepper. Place the fish with skin side down in the prepared pan.

In a medium bowl, stir together the remaining ingredients. Spoon over the fish.

Bake for 15 minutes, or until the fish flakes easily when tested with a fork.

To serve, spoon the orzo to the side on each plate. Place the fish beside the orzo, and spoon any remaining sauce over both.

Calories 303	Cholesterol 42 mg
Total Fat 2.5 g	Sodium 299 mg
Saturated 0.5 g	Carbohydrate 39 g
Polyunsaturated 1.0 g	Fiber 3 g
Monounsaturated 0.5 g	Protein 30 g

sea bass with ginger-tomato sauce

serves 4; 3 ounces fish and ½ cup sauce per serving

When coriander seeds are planted, the herb that sprouts is called cilantro or fresh coriander. The marinade here incorporates both the seed and the fresh form, with added flavor dimension from soy sauce and mandarin orange juice.

- **2 tablespoons snipped fresh cilantro**
- **2 tablespoons fresh mandarin orange, tangerine, or orange juice**
- **1 tablespoon low-salt soy sauce**
- **2 teaspoons coriander seeds, crushed**
- **4 white fish fillets, such as sea bass, halibut, orange roughy, or sole (about 4 ounces each)**
- **Vegetable oil spray**
- **14.5-ounce can no-salt-added diced tomatoes, undrained, pureed**
- **½ cup fat-free, low-sodium chicken broth**
- **1 teaspoon grated peeled gingerroot**
- **¼ teaspoon salt**
- **⅛ teaspoon pepper**

In an airtight plastic bag or baking dish, combine the cilantro, orange juice, soy sauce, and coriander seeds.

Rinse the fish and pat dry with paper towels. Add the fish to the marinade and turn to coat. Seal and refrigerate for 10 minutes to 2 hours, turning occasionally.

Heat a large nonstick skillet over medium-high heat. Remove from the heat and lightly spray with vegetable oil spray (being careful not to spray near a gas flame). Drain the fish. Discard the marinade. Cook the fish for 2 to 4 minutes, or until lightly browned, turning once.

Add the remaining ingredients around the fish, stirring gently to combine. Bring to a simmer. Reduce the heat to low; cook, covered, for 6 to 8 minutes, or until the fish flakes easily when tested with a fork.

Calories 134	Cholesterol 47 mg
Total Fat 2.5 g	Sodium 338 mg
Saturated 0.5 g	Carbohydrate 5 g
Polyunsaturated 1.0 g	Fiber 1 g
Monounsaturated 0.5 g	Protein 22 g

asparagus-stuffed sole with horseradish cream

You won't soon forget the taste of delicate sole combined with pencil-thin asparagus and rich (but not so sinful) cream sauce.

1 cup water

1 medium carrot, sliced

1 medium rib of celery, sliced

2 medium green onions, sliced (green and white parts)

⅛ teaspoon pepper

8 sole fillets (Dover preferred) (about 4 ounces each)

1 pound asparagus (pencil-thin size preferred), trimmed

¼ cup nonfat or light sour cream

1 tablespoon all-purpose flour

1 teaspoon prepared horseradish

½ teaspoon paprika (optional)

In a large skillet, bring the water, carrot, celery, green onions, and pepper to a simmer over high heat. Reduce the heat to low; cook, covered, for 5 minutes. Set aside.

Rinse the fish and pat dry with paper towels. Place 5 or 6 stalks of asparagus across one end of a fillet (the asparagus will overhang the fillet by 2 to 3 inches on each side). Roll the fillet around the asparagus and secure with a wooden toothpick. Repeat with the remaining asparagus and fillets.

Return the carrot mixture to a simmer over medium-high heat. Add the fillets. Reduce the heat and simmer, covered, for 10 minutes, or until the fish flakes easily when tested with a fork and the asparagus is tender.

Meanwhile, in a small bowl, whisk together the remaining ingredients except the paprika. Set aside.

Carefully transfer the fish to a serving platter; cover the platter with aluminum foil to keep the fish warm.

Calories 131	Cholesterol 54 mg
Total Fat 1.5 g	Sodium 101 mg
Saturated 0.5 g	Carbohydrate 5 g
Polyunsaturated 0.5 g	Fiber 1 g
Monounsaturated 0.5 g	Protein 23 g

Using a slotted spoon, remove the vegetables from the skillet. Discard the vegetables. Whisk about 1 tablespoon strained liquid into the sour cream mixture; whisk into the remaining liquid in the saucepan. Bring to a simmer over medium heat. Reducing the heat if necessary, simmer for 2 to 3 minutes, or until the mixture thickens, stirring occasionally.

To serve, remove the toothpicks from the fish, ladle the sauce over each fillet, and sprinkle with paprika.

swordfish topped with tomatillo sauce

serves 4; 3 ounces fish and 3 tablespoons sauce per serving

Tomatillo sauce turns ordinary grilled fish into a spicy taste treat. Leave the seeds and ribs of the pepper in only if you like things really hot. Fluffy rice laced with saffron or turmeric makes an attractive accompaniment.

tomatillo sauce

8 medium tomatillos, quartered (see Cook's Tip on Tomatillos, page 42)

½ cup fat-free, low-sodium chicken broth

¼ cup coarsely snipped fresh cilantro

½ to 1 medium jalapeño or habañero pepper, seeded and ribs removed, if desired

1½ teaspoons olive oil

½ small onion, finely chopped

2 medium garlic cloves, minced, or 1 teaspoon bottled minced garlic

¼ teaspoon salt

Dash red hot-pepper sauce (optional)

❖ ❖ ❖

Vegetable oil spray

2 swordfish steaks or mahimahi fillets (about 8 ounces each)

½ medium lime

1 medium lime, quartered (optional)

For the sauce, in a food processor or blender, process the tomatillos, broth, cilantro, and jalapeño until smooth except for the seeds.

Heat a large nonstick skillet over medium heat. Pour the oil into the skillet and swirl to coat the bottom. Cook the onion until lightly browned, about 5 minutes, stirring occasionally. Stir in the garlic. Reduce the heat to low. Stir in the tomatillo puree; simmer for 10 to 15 minutes, or until most of the liquid

swordfish topped
with tomatillo sauce

Calories 185	Cholesterol 44 mg
Total Fat 7.0 g	Sodium 258 mg
Saturated 1.5 g	Carbohydrate 6 g
Polyunsaturated 1.5 g	Fiber 2 g
Monounsaturated 3.0 g	Protein 24 g

has evaporated. After the sauce has thickened, stir in the salt and red hot-pepper sauce. Set aside.

Lightly spray the grill rack with vegetable oil spray. Preheat the grill to medium-high.

Rinse the fish and pat dry with paper towels. Lightly spray the fish with vegetable oil spray. Put the fish on the grill; squeeze the juice of ½ lime over the fish.

Cook for 9 to 10 minutes, or to the desired doneness, turning once. The fish should flake easily when tested with a fork.

To serve, cut each piece of fish into four slices. Place two slices on each plate. Spoon the sauce over the fish. Serve with the lime quarters.

chicken topped with tomatillo sauce
Serve the tomatillo sauce over grilled chicken breasts.

COOK'S TIP

For a quick and zesty appetizer, serve the tomatillo sauce over a block of fat-free cream cheese. Spread the combination on fat-free, low-sodium crackers.

chicken topped with tomatillo sauce

Calories 172	Cholesterol 66 mg
Total Fat 4.0 g	Sodium 230 mg
Saturated 0.5 g	Carbohydrate 6 g
Polyunsaturated 1.0 g	Fiber 2 g
Monounsaturated 1.5 g	Protein 28 g

citrus-stuffed trout

This is such an impressive entrée, you won't believe how easy it is to prepare. Try the same technique with any favorite whole fish, or grill fillets between layers of lemon or lime slices. Serve with Green Bean Salad with Roasted Garlic Dressing (page 38).

- **2 whole trout (12 to 14 ounces each)**
- **2 medium lemons or limes, each cut into 4 slices**
- **4 sprigs of fresh summer savory or 1 teaspoon dried, crumbled**
  - **Vegetable oil spray**
- **1 medium lemon or lime, halved**
  - **Lemon or lime wedges (optional)**

Rinse the fish and pat dry with paper towels. (Keep the heads on so the fish doesn't fall apart on the grill.) Put 4 lemon slices and 2 sprigs of savory in each fish.

Lightly spray the grill rack with vegetable oil spray. Preheat the grill to medium-high. Put the fish on the grill; squeeze ½ lemon over the fish. Grill the fish, covered if possible, for 10 minutes; carefully turn the fish over, keeping the stuffing intact. Squeeze the remaining lemon half over the fish. Cook for 10 minutes, or until the fish flakes easily when tested with a fork.

Carefully place the fish on a serving platter. Cut each fish in half, opening so that the skin side of each half is down. Remove the lemon slices. Gently lift the tail of each fish and pull the skeleton away. Garnish with the lemon wedges.

COOK'S TIP ON FRESH FISH

If the fish is fresh, the eyes should be clear and there should be no odor.

Calories 104	Cholesterol 83 mg
Total Fat 3.5 g	Sodium 58 mg
Saturated 1.0 g	Carbohydrate 0 g
Polyunsaturated 0.5 g	Fiber 0 g
Monounsaturated 1.0 g	Protein 17 g

tuna with cilantro-lime glaze and quinoa

serves 4; 3 ounces tuna, ½ cup quinoa, and ⅓ cup sauce per serving

The combination of cilantro and lime juice adds a wonderful freshness to the rich taste of tuna.

¾ cup uncooked quinoa
Vegetable oil spray
4 tuna, salmon, or swordfish steaks (about 4 ounces each)
¼ to ½ teaspoon pepper

glaze

1 cup fat-free, low-sodium chicken broth
½ cup fresh cilantro, finely snipped
¼ cup fresh lime juice
1 tablespoon cornstarch

Prepare the quinoa using the package instructions, omitting the salt and oil. Set aside.

Meanwhile, lightly spray the grill rack with vegetable oil spray and preheat the grill on high, or lightly spray a broiler pan and rack with vegetable oil spray and preheat the broiler. If broiling, set the rack about 5 inches from the heat.

Rinse the fish and pat dry with paper towels. Season both sides of the fish with the pepper.

Grill or broil the fish for 8 to 12 minutes, or until it flakes easily when tested with a fork, turning once.

In a small saucepan, whisk together all the glaze ingredients. Cook over medium heat for 2 to 3 minutes, or until the sauce thickens, whisking constantly.

To serve, spoon the quinoa to the side on each plate. Arrange the tuna steaks alongside. Spoon the glaze over both.

COOK'S TIP ON QUINOA

Quinoa's protein is considered complete because it contains all essential amino acids. This highly nutritious grain is mild in taste, so it teams nicely with many flavors and has many uses, including as a breakfast cereal.

Calories 252	Cholesterol 53 mg
Total Fat 3.0 g	Sodium 70 mg
Saturated 0.5 g	Carbohydrate 26 g
Polyunsaturated 1.0 g	Fiber 2 g
Monounsaturated 0.5 g	Protein 30 g

broiled tuna steak with lemongrass-chamomile glaze

serves 4; 3 ounces tuna and 2 tablespoons glaze per serving

Fragrant chamomile and lemongrass combined with hints of ginger and pepper glaze these tuna steaks. Unforgettable! Although it might sound like an unlikely pairing, Sesame-Dusted Collard Greens (page 232) and this Asian-flavored tuna are delicious together.

glaze

2 medium stalks lemongrass

1½ cups water

2 chamomile tea bags, strings and tags removed

1 tablespoon dark brown sugar

1 tablespoon coarsely chopped peeled gingerroot

⅛ teaspoon pepper

1 teaspoon cornstarch

¼ cup water

❖ ❖ ❖

1 tablespoon olive oil

1 teaspoon wasabi powder

⅛ teaspoon pepper

4 tuna steaks (about 4 ounces each), about 1 inch thick

For the glaze, discard any discolored lemongrass leaves. Coarsely chop the lemongrass; put it in a small saucepan. Add 1½ cups water, tea bags, brown sugar, gingerroot, and ⅛ teaspoon pepper; stir. Bring to a boil over high heat. Boil, uncovered, until reduced to ¼ cup, 12 to 15 minutes (no stirring needed). Discard the tea bags.

Put the cornstarch in a small bowl. Add the remaining water, stirring to dissolve. Whisk into the reduced glaze. Reduce the heat to medium-low; cook

Calories 174	Cholesterol 51 mg
Total Fat 4.5 g	Sodium 47 mg
Saturated 0.5 g	Carbohydrate 5 g
Polyunsaturated 0.5 g	Fiber 0 g
Monounsaturated 2.5 g	Protein 27 g

until the glaze starts to thicken and coats the back of a spoon, 2 to 3 minutes, whisking constantly. Remove from the heat. Set aside.

Meanwhile, preheat the broiler.

In a cup, stir together the remaining ingredients except the fish. Rinse the fish and pat dry with paper towels. Rub the glaze on both sides of the fish, retaining the remaining glaze. Put the fish on a small baking sheet.

Broil 5 to 6 inches from the heat for about 3½ minutes for medium-rare, 4½ minutes for medium. Remove from the oven; turn the fish over and rub each with ½ tablespoon glaze. Broil for about 3 minutes for medium-rare, 4 minutes for medium.

To serve, drizzle the tuna with the remaining glaze.

COOK'S TIP ON WASABI

Wasabi powder is dried ground horseradish root and is used in Japanese cooking. Mixed with water, it becomes the green paste served as a condiment with sushi. Look for this fiery seasoning in the Asian section of your supermarket or at Asian markets.

tuna cakes with cucumber yogurt sauce

serves 6; 1 tuna cake and 2 tablespoons sauce per serving

For great brown-bag lunches, make a double batch of these delicious tuna cakes and use the extras for pita sandwiches during the week.

cucumber yogurt sauce

½ cup peeled, seeded, and finely chopped cucumber

½ cup nonfat or low-fat plain yogurt

2 tablespoons snipped fresh dillweed or 2 teaspoons dried, crumbled

2 teaspoons fresh lemon juice

⅛ to ¼ teaspoon pepper

tuna cakes

2 6-ounce cans albacore tuna in distilled or spring water, drained and flaked

Egg substitute equivalent to 2 eggs, or 2 large eggs

⅓ cup crushed fat-free, no-salt-added whole-wheat crackers

¼ cup chopped green onions (green and white parts)

2 teaspoons Dijon mustard

1 teaspoon prepared horseradish

¼ teaspoon salt

¼ teaspoon pepper

❖ ❖ ❖

1 tablespoon acceptable vegetable oil

In a small bowl, stir together the sauce ingredients. Cover and refrigerate.

Meanwhile, in a medium bowl, combine all the tuna cake ingredients. Shape into 6 cakes about 2½ inches in diameter.

Heat a large nonstick skillet over medium heat. Pour the oil into the skillet and swirl to coat the bottom. Cook the tuna cakes for 6 to 8 minutes, or until golden brown on both sides, turning once. Serve with the sauce on the side.

Calories 133	Cholesterol 24 mg
Total Fat 4.0 g	Sodium 416 mg
Saturated 0.5 g	Carbohydrate 6 g
Polyunsaturated 1.5 g	Fiber 1 g
Monounsaturated 2.0 g	Protein 17 g

grilled tuna with tomato salsa

serves 4; 3 ounces fish and 2 tablespoons salsa per serving

Glorious summer tomatoes from farm stands or your own garden make excellent salsa.

salsa

- **1 large tomato, chopped**
- **¼ cup coarsely snipped fresh cilantro or fresh Italian, or flat-leaf, parsley**
- **¼ cup sliced green onions (green and white parts)**
- **1 tablespoon fresh lime juice**
- **1 small fresh or canned jalapeño, seeded and ribs removed, chopped, or ½ teaspoon bottled pickled jalapeño juice**
- **1 large garlic clove, minced, or 1 teaspoon bottled minced garlic**

seasoned oil

- **2 teaspoons acceptable vegetable oil**
- **¼ teaspoon dried oregano, crumbled**
- **¼ teaspoon paprika**
- **¼ teaspoon salt**
- **¼ teaspoon pepper**

❖ ❖ ❖

- **4 tuna fillets or steaks (about 4 ounces each)**
- **Vegetable oil spray**

In a medium bowl, stir together the salsa ingredients.

If using an outdoor grill, lightly spray the grill rack with vegetable oil spray. Preheat the grill to medium-high. If grilling indoors, lightly spray a ridged stovetop grill pan with vegetable oil spray.

In a small bowl, combine the seasoned oil ingredients.

Rinse the fish and pat dry with paper towels. Brush the oil on both sides of the fish.

Grill over medium-high heat for 4 to 6 minutes, or until firm to the touch and cooked to the desired doneness, turning once.

To serve, spoon the salsa over the fish.

Calories 164	Cholesterol 51 mg
Total Fat 3.5 g	Sodium 195 mg
Saturated 0.5 g	Carbohydrate 5 g
Polyunsaturated 1.0 g	Fiber 1 g
Monounsaturated 1.5 g	Protein 27 g

sea scallops
with snow peas

serves 4; 1½ cups per serving

Cooking snow peas in apple juice increases their sweetness and provides a contrast to the spiciness of the garlic and ginger. Serve with a scoop of brown rice for a quick but sophisticated dinner.

Vegetable oil spray

12 ounces sea scallops, rinsed and patted dry with paper towels

2 tablespoons grated peeled gingerroot

3 to 4 medium garlic cloves, minced, or 1½ to 2 teaspoons bottled minced garlic

¼ cup unsweetened apple juice

1 large red or yellow bell pepper, or a combination, cut into ½-inch cubes

¼ cup unsweetened apple juice (plus more as needed)

1 pound fresh snow peas or sugar snap peas, trimmed

4 medium green onions, chopped (white parts only)

1 tablespoon low-salt soy sauce

1 teaspoon toasted sesame oil

1 teaspoon dry-roasted sesame seeds

Heat a large skillet over medium-high heat. Remove the skillet from the heat and lightly spray with vegetable oil spray (being careful not to spray near a gas flame). Place the scallops in the skillet so the scallops are not touching. Cook without stirring for 2 minutes. Turn the scallops over and cook for 1 to 2 minutes, or until opaque. (Be careful not to overcook; smaller scallops will be done sooner.) Transfer to a plate and cover with aluminum foil to keep warm.

Remove the skillet from the heat and lightly spray with vegetable oil spray (being careful not to spray near a gas flame). Cook the gingerroot and garlic for 2 minutes, gradually adding ¼ cup apple juice, stirring constantly. Stir in the bell peppers; cook for 2 minutes, gradually adding some of the remaining apple juice as needed to keep the food from sticking, stirring constantly. Add

Calories 170	Cholesterol 28 mg
Total Fat 2.5 g	Sodium 243 mg
Saturated 0.5 g	Carbohydrate 19 g
Polyunsaturated 1.0 g	Fiber 4 g
Monounsaturated 0.5 g	Protein 18 g

the snow peas; cook until tender, 3 to 4 minutes, adding apple juice as needed to keep the food from sticking, stirring constantly. Add the green onions and soy sauce; cook until all the liquid has evaporated, stirring constantly.

To serve, spoon the bell pepper mixture onto each plate. Top with the scallops. Drizzle the sesame oil over the scallops. Sprinkle the scallops with the sesame seeds.

COOK'S TIP FOR DRY-ROASTING SESAME SEEDS

Preheat the oven to 400° F. Spread the sesame seeds in a single layer on a baking sheet or pan. Dry-roast for 3 minutes, stir, and dry-roast for 2 to 3 minutes more. Watch carefully; the sesame seeds will burn easily. Refrigerate or freeze any extra sesame seeds for later use. Sprinkle half a teaspoon on a green salad for added crunch.

COOK'S TIP ON SOY SAUCE

When shopping for soy sauce, be sure to read the nutrition label and choose the sauce with the least amount of sodium.

caribbean shrimp
and black beans

When you want a light, colorful dish that boasts an incredible flavor combination—cumin, thyme, and fresh lime juice—here's just the thing. For a stunning presentation, spoon the salad into a hollowed-out pineapple half or onto red-leaf lettuce. Serve with steamed asparagus and thick slices of juicy tomatoes.

1 pound medium shrimp in shells or 12 ounces shelled medium shrimp

2 teaspoons olive oil or acceptable vegetable oil

1 cup chopped red onion

1 medium green bell pepper, chopped

2 teaspoons ground cumin

½ teaspoon dried thyme, crumbled

¼ teaspoon pepper

15-ounce can no-salt-added black beans, rinsed and drained well

2 tablespoons fresh lime juice

¼ teaspoon salt

3 medium green onions, chopped (green and white parts)

¼ cup finely snipped fresh cilantro

Shell the shrimp if in the shell. Devein the shrimp if desired.

Heat a large nonstick skillet or wok over medium-high heat. Pour the oil into the skillet and swirl to coat. Cook the onion and bell pepper for 2 minutes, stirring occasionally. Stir in the cumin, thyme, and pepper. Stir in the shrimp; cook for 3 to 4 minutes, or until bright pink and almost cooked through, stirring frequently. Stir in the beans, lime juice, and salt. Cook for 2 minutes, or until heated through. Remove from the heat. Gently stir in the green onions. Sprinkle with the cilantro.

Calories 211	Cholesterol 135 mg
Total Fat 3.5 g	Sodium 306 mg
Saturated 0.5 g	Carbohydrate 24 g
Polyunsaturated 0.5 g	Fiber 6 g
Monounsaturated 2.0 g	Protein 21 g

COOK'S TIP ON MAKING PINEAPPLE BOATS

Cut a ripe pineapple, including the leaves, in half lengthwise; remove the core. Using a large spoon, cut out enough of the flesh in the center to make a 2-inch-deep bowl in each half. Fill the hollowed bowl with cubed pineapple, mixed fruit, or a poultry or seafood salad, such as this one.

COOK'S TIP ON CILANTRO

A staple of Mexican, Chinese, Thai, and Indian cooking, cilantro is also known as fresh coriander or Mexican or Chinese parsley. It looks a lot like Italian, or flat-leaf, parsley but has a distinctive aroma and flavor. To store cilantro, trim the stems, remove the rubber band or twist tie, and put the unwashed bunch in a glass with a couple of inches of water. Place a plastic bag over the cilantro, secure with a rubber band, and refrigerate for up to a week. Change the water every two or three days and discard any leaves that have begun to spoil.

poultry

One-Dish Roast Chicken Dinner

Cantonese Chicken
   ❖ Cantonese Pork

Spicy Korean Chicken Breasts

Chicken Kiev

Chicken Breast Pockets with Lentil,
   Leek, and Water Chestnut
   Stuffing

Chicken Breasts with Swiss Chard,
   Walnuts, and Goat Cheese

Spinach-Stuffed Chicken
   with Sun-Dried Tomato
   and Basil Sauce

Kiwifruit and Pineapple Marinated
   Chicken

Grilled Chicken and Pineapple
   Sandwich

Chicken Satay with Cucumber Slaw
   and Peanut Dipping Sauce

Chicken Mole

Crispy Baked Chicken Strips
   with Spicy-Sweet
   Mustard Sauce

Creole-Crusted Chicken Breasts
   with Polenta

Rustic Stuffed Potatoes

Cheesy Chicken Vermicelli

Ginger Chicken with Whole-Wheat
   Spaghetti and Green Beans

Stovetop Chicken Lasagna Stew

Lemony Chicken with Broccoli

Chicken and Vegetable Meal-in-One

Chicken Marsala

Chicken Paprikash

Greek Chicken with Capers

Cumin Chicken with Onions
   and Squash

Spicy Seared Chicken
   with Chipotle Salsa
   ❖ Seared Chicken with Basil-Caper
   Salsa

Savory Chicken with Bell Pepper
   and Mushrooms

Beefy Chicken with Mushrooms

Gourmet Pizza with Chicken
   and Vegetables

Chicken and Noodles

Zucchini Boats

Turkey "Filet Mignon"
   with Leek Ribbons

Turkey Lo Mein

Grilled Turkey Breast
   with Fresh Herb Sauce

Turkey Meatballs
   with Mushroom Gravy

Turkey and Okra Gumbo

Turkey and Vegetable Pie

Cornish Game Hens with Plum Glaze

one-dish roast chicken dinner

serves 8; 3 ounces chicken and ½ cup apple and vegetables per serving
(plus 12 ounces chicken reserved)

Here's a very simple way to prepare a fine meal-in-one for eight people and have leftovers as well. The extra chicken will come in handy for sandwiches, salads, or casseroles. Feel free to add other vegetables, such as carrots, celery, and parsnips, when you put the potatoes, apples, and onion in the roasting pan.

6-pound roasting chicken, giblets removed and discarded
2 tablespoons chopped fresh rosemary or 2 teaspoons dried, crushed
2 tablespoons chopped fresh thyme or 2 teaspoons dried, crumbled
½ teaspoon pepper
1 pound Yukon gold or red potatoes, cut into 2-inch chunks
2 medium McIntosh or Granny Smith apples, cored and each cut into 8 wedges
1 large red onion, cut into 2-inch pieces
½ cup fat-free, low-sodium chicken broth

Preheat the oven to 450°F.

Coat the chicken all over with rosemary, thyme, and pepper. Place in a shallow roasting pan. Arrange the potatoes, apples, and onion around the chicken. Pour the broth over the vegetables and apples. Insert a meat thermometer deep into the thickest part of a thigh, next to the body and not touching the bone.

Put the chicken in the oven and immediately reduce the oven temperature to 325°F. Roast, uncovered, for 2 hours (20 minutes per pound), or until the thermometer reads 180°F to 185°F, basting every 30 minutes. Remove from the oven; let the chicken stand for 10 minutes before carving.

To serve, remove the skin and carve the chicken. Arrange two-thirds of the chicken slices on a platter, with the vegetables and apple wedges on the side. Wrap and refrigerate or freeze the remaining chicken.

Calories 196	Cholesterol 74 mg
Total Fat 3.0 g	Sodium 90 mg
Saturated 1.0 g	Carbohydrate 18 g
Polyunsaturated 1.0 g	Fiber 3 g
Monounsaturated 1.0 g	Protein 25 g

cantonese chicken

serves 4; 3 ounces chicken and ½ cup noodles per serving

The combination of sweet mandarin oranges and savory hoisin sauce creates a wonderfully tangy sweet-and-sour sauce.

Vegetable oil spray
4 skinless chicken breast halves with bone, all visible fat removed
¼ teaspoon pepper
10.5- or 11-ounce can mandarin oranges in light syrup
2 tablespoons hoisin sauce
2 teaspoons toasted sesame oil
6 ounces dried Chinese noodles

Preheat the oven to 400°F. Lightly spray an 11 × 7 × 2-inch baking pan with vegetable oil spray.

Season both sides of the chicken with the pepper. Arrange in a single layer in the baking pan.

Drain the mandarin oranges, reserving ¼ cup juice. Put the oranges and reserved juice in a small bowl. Stir in the hoisin sauce and sesame oil. Pour over the chicken.

Bake for 35 minutes, or until the chicken is no longer pink in the center.

Meanwhile, cook the noodles using the package directions, omitting the salt and oil. Drain well.

To serve, place the chicken on dinner plates. Arrange the noodles beside the chicken. Spoon the sauce over all.

cantonese pork

Substitute 1 pound of pork tenderloin, cut crosswise into ½-inch pieces, for the chicken.

COOK'S TIP ON CHINESE NOODLES

You may find these called "mein" instead of Chinese noodles. Pale yellow and about ⅛ inch thick, they look somewhat like curly spaghetti. You can substitute unseasoned ramen noodles or vermicelli if you can't easily find Chinese noodles.

---

cantonese chicken

Calories 343	Cholesterol 66 mg
Total Fat 4.5 g	Sodium 118 mg
Saturated 0.5 g	Carbohydrate 47 g
Polyunsaturated 1.5 g	Fiber 6 g
Monounsaturated 1.5 g	Protein 31 g

cantonese pork

Calories 338	Cholesterol 74 mg
Total Fat 6.0 g	Sodium 75 mg
Saturated 1.5 g	Carbohydrate 45 g
Polyunsaturated 1.0 g	Fiber 6 g
Monounsaturated 2.0 g	Protein 29 g

spicy korean chicken breasts

The trick to ensuring a perfect coating is to lightly dust the chicken with flour before rolling it in the honey mixture. The result here is a tangy crust with a slight bite. This dish is particularly good with jasmine rice.

Vegetable oil spray

¼ **cup all-purpose flour**

2 **tablespoons low-salt soy sauce**

2 **tablespoons honey**

2 **teaspoons chili oil or toasted sesame oil**

½ **teaspoon garlic powder**

½ **teaspoon crushed red pepper flakes**

4 **skinless chicken breast halves with bone (about 6 ounces each), all visible fat removed**

Preheat the oven to 400° F. Lightly spray a shallow roasting pan with vegetable oil spray.

Put the flour in a shallow dish.

In another shallow dish, whisk together the remaining ingredients except the chicken.

Line up the dish with the flour, the dish with the honey mixture, and the roasting pan. Roll each piece of chicken in the flour. Shake off the excess flour. Roll the chicken in the honey mixture. Put the chicken in the roasting pan; pour any remaining honey mixture over the chicken.

Bake for 35 minutes, or until the chicken is no longer pink in the center.

COOK'S TIP ON CHILI OIL

Also known as hot chili oil, hot pepper oil, hot oil, and red oil, this spicy oil is available in Asian markets and in the Asian section of grocery stores. The oil gets its red color from the fiery hot red chiles that flavor it.

Calories 212	Cholesterol 66 mg
Total Fat 4.0 g	Sodium 270 mg
Saturated 0.5 g	Carbohydrate 16 g
Polyunsaturated 1.0 g	Fiber 0 g
Monounsaturated 1.5 g	Protein 28 g

chicken kiev

Traditionally deep-fried, chicken Kiev is usually high in fat. Baking it instead helps make it more healthful.

Vegetable oil spray

4 boneless, skinless chicken breast halves (about 4 ounces each), all visible fat removed

2 tablespoons light stick margarine, softened

1 tablespoon dried parsley, crumbled

1 tablespoon chopped green onions (green part only) or chives

1 medium garlic clove, minced, or ½ teaspoon bottled minced garlic

Egg substitute equivalent to 2 eggs, or 2 large eggs, or whites of 4 large eggs

½ cup plain dry bread crumbs

2 teaspoons onion powder

1 teaspoon garlic powder

⅛ teaspoon salt

⅛ to ¼ teaspoon cayenne (optional)

⅛ teaspoon black pepper

Preheat the oven to 375°F. Lightly spray a 9-inch square baking dish with vegetable oil spray. Set aside.

Place the breasts with the smooth side up between two pieces of plastic wrap. Using a tortilla press, the smooth side of a meat mallet, or a rolling pin, lightly flatten to ¼-inch thickness, being careful not to tear the meat.

In a small bowl, combine the margarine, parsley, green onions, and garlic.

To assemble, spread one-fourth of the margarine mixture down the center of a breast, almost to each end. Fold the sides of the breast toward the center. Starting from one long end, roll the chicken jelly-roll style, until the margarine mixture is completely enclosed. Repeat with the remaining breasts.

Pour the egg substitute into a shallow bowl. In another shallow bowl, stir together the remaining ingredients. Dip each stuffed breast in the egg substitute, roll it in the bread crumb mixture, then dip it in the egg substitute again. Place the coated breasts with the seam side down in the baking dish.

Bake for 50 minutes, or until the chicken is no longer pink in the center.

Calories 261	Cholesterol 66 mg
Total Fat 5.5 g	Sodium 455 mg
Saturated 1.0 g	Carbohydrate 18 g
Polyunsaturated 1.5 g	Fiber 1 g
Monounsaturated 1.5 g	Protein 34 g

chicken breast pockets with lentil, leek, and water chestnut stuffing

serves 4; 1 stuffed chicken breast half per serving

Moroccan-influenced spices, red lentils, leeks, and tomato chutney give this chicken a savory-sweet richness.

1 cup fat-free, low-sodium chicken broth

½ cup split red lentils, sorted for stones or shriveled lentils, but not rinsed

1 tablespoon olive oil

1 large leek, coarsely chopped (white part only)

¼ cup diced water chestnuts, rinsed and drained

1 medium garlic clove, minced, or ½ teaspoon bottled minced garlic

¼ teaspoon ground cinnamon

¼ teaspoon ground cumin

¼ teaspoon ground coriander

¼ teaspoon pepper, or to taste

Vegetable oil spray

4 boneless, skinless chicken breast halves (about 4 ounces each), all visible fat removed

2 tablespoons tomato chutney, tomato jelly, or mango chutney

In a small saucepan, bring the broth to a boil over high heat.

Rinse the lentils; add to the broth. (If you rinse the lentils in advance, they will stick to each other.) Reduce the heat to medium-low; cook until the lentils are tender, about 10 minutes, stirring occasionally. Increase the heat to high; cook until all the liquid is absorbed, about 2 minutes, stirring constantly. Set aside.

Heat a large nonstick skillet over medium-high heat. Pour the olive oil into the skillet and swirl to coat the bottom. Cook the leeks until translucent, 4 to 5 minutes, stirring constantly. Stir in the water chestnuts, garlic, cinnamon,

Calories 275	Cholesterol 66 mg
Total Fat 5.0 g	Sodium 103 mg
Saturated 1.0 g	Carbohydrate 24 g
Polyunsaturated 0.5 g	Fiber 4 g
Monounsaturated 3.0 g	Protein 33 g

cumin, coriander, and pepper. Cook for 1 minute, stirring constantly. Remove from the heat. Stir in the lentil mixture.

Preheat the oven to 375°F. Lightly spray a baking sheet with vegetable oil spray.

Put a chicken breast half on a cutting board. Using a boning knife or other long, thin knife, make a pocket by cutting a slit along a long side in the thickest part of the chicken. Gradually work the knife into the breast, making a pocket about 3 inches long and being careful not to cut all the way through the breast. Try to keep the knife blade parallel to the cutting board. Repeat with the remaining chicken.

Using your fingers, fill the pockets with the lentil stuffing. Place the stuffed breasts on the baking sheet. Spread ½ tablespoon tomato chutney on each breast.

Bake for 20 minutes, or until a small amount of clear juice appears on the baking sheet and the chicken is no longer pink in the center.

COOK'S TIP ON RED LENTILS

As they cook, red lentils will change color from a vibrant to a slightly faded orange. At that point, they're nearly cooked. Taste a few to test for doneness, keeping in mind that it takes only a few minutes for the lentils to go from nearly cooked to mushy.

COOK'S TIP ON TOMATO CHUTNEY

Excellent as a condiment served with beef or lamb, tomato chutney is available in many gourmet grocery stores and Indian markets.

chicken breasts with swiss chard, walnuts, and goat cheese

A bit of goat cheese, a hint of lemon, and a few nuts flavor the chard that is tucked inside tender chicken breasts in this elegant dish.

> **Vegetable oil spray**
> **1 pound fresh green Swiss chard or spinach, unwashed**
> **¼ cup plus 1 tablespoon fat-free, low-sodium chicken broth**
> **3 tablespoons minced onion**
> **2 tablespoons coarsely chopped dry-roasted walnuts**
> **2 tablespoons goat cheese**
> **1 teaspoon minced lemon zest**
> **¼ teaspoon pepper**
> **Scant ⅛ teaspoon cayenne**
> **Dash of ground nutmeg**
> **4 boneless, skinless chicken breast halves (about 1½ pounds), all visible fat removed**
> **½ teaspoon olive oil**

Preheat the oven to 400°F. Lightly spray a 13 × 9 × 2-inch baking dish with vegetable oil spray.

Remove the thick white stems from the chard. Wash the chard, but don't dry it. With the water still clinging to its leaves, cook the chard in a large nonstick skillet over medium heat for 2 minutes, or until wilted, stirring constantly. Drain the chard in a colander, pressing to remove as much water as possible. Finely chop the chard.

In the same skillet, bring the broth to a simmer over low heat. Stir in the onion. Simmer for 2 minutes, or until translucent. Remove from the heat. Add the walnuts, goat cheese, lemon zest, black pepper, cayenne, and nutmeg, stirring until the cheese melts. Set aside.

Calories 131	Cholesterol 51 mg
Total Fat 3.5 g	Sodium 191 mg
Saturated 1.0 g	Carbohydrate 3 g
Polyunsaturated 1.0 g	Fiber 1 g
Monounsaturated 1.0 g	Protein 22 g

Put the chicken with the smooth side up between two pieces of plastic wrap. Using a tortilla press, the smooth side of a meat mallet, or a rolling pin, lightly flatten the breasts to a thickness of ¼ inch, being careful not to tear the meat.

To assemble, put the chicken on a piece of wax paper about 24 inches long. Put ½ cup filling, shaped in an oval, on each piece of chicken. Starting with a long side and using the wax paper as a helper, roll each piece jelly-roll style. Place the chicken with the seam side down in the prepared dish. Brush the tops with the olive oil.

Bake for 20 to 25 minutes, or until no longer pink in the center. Let cool for about 5 minutes so the filling will set slightly.

To serve, cut the chicken crosswise into 1-inch slices. Arrange overlapping slices on a serving platter so the chicken and filling are visible.

COOK'S TIP

Use green chard in this recipe because the colors from ruby or rainbow chard tend to bleed into the chicken.

COOK'S TIP ON DRY-ROASTING WALNUTS

Put the nuts in a medium skillet over medium heat and dry-roast until fragrant and lightly browned, 5 to 7 minutes, stirring occasionally. Or put the nuts on the tray of a toaster oven. Set the temperature to 400°F and toast for 5 to 10 minutes, or until fragrant and lightly browned, stirring occasionally.

spinach-stuffed chicken with sun-dried tomato and basil sauce

serves 4; 1 stuffed chicken breast half and ½ cup sauce per serving

You'll love how quick and easy this tomato-basil sauce is to prepare. Since this recipe makes a generous amount of the sauce, you'll have enough to top a side dish of pasta. If you prefer, use one-fourth cup of sauce per serving now and the rest over grilled fish later in the week.

Vegetable oil spray

10-ounce package frozen chopped spinach, thawed and squeezed dry

¼ cup fat-free or light ricotta cheese

¼ teaspoon ground nutmeg

4 boneless, skinless chicken breast halves (about 4 ounces each), all visible fat removed

sun-dried tomato and basil sauce

14.5-ounce can fat-free, low-sodium chicken broth

1 cup dry-packed sun-dried tomatoes, diced

1 cup packed fresh basil, stems removed

2 medium garlic cloves or 1 teaspoon bottled minced garlic

Preheat the oven to 375°F. Lightly spray an 11 × 7 × 2-inch baking dish with vegetable oil spray. Set aside.

In a medium bowl, stir together the spinach, ricotta, and nutmeg.

Place the chicken with the smooth side up between two pieces of plastic wrap. Using a tortilla press, the smooth side of a meat mallet, or a rolling pin, lightly flatten the chicken to about ¼ inch thick, being careful not to tear the meat. Put with the smooth side down on a flat surface. Spoon the spinach mixture onto each piece, leaving ¼ inch around the edges. Starting from a short end, roll up the chicken pieces jelly-roll style. Place the rolls with the seam side down in the prepared dish.

Calories 207	Cholesterol 67 mg
Total Fat 2.0 g	Sodium 188 mg
Saturated 0.5 g	Carbohydrate 12 g
Polyunsaturated 0.5 g	Fiber 4 g
Monounsaturated 0.5 g	Protein 34 g

In a food processor or blender, process all the sauce ingredients until the mixture is thick; pour over the chicken.

Bake for 40 minutes, or until the chicken is no longer pink in the center.

To serve, place 1 breast half with sauce on each plate; or for an impressive presentation, cut the chicken crosswise into rounds to reveal the spinach filling. Arrange the slices in a fan pattern on each plate and top with the sauce.

kiwifruit and pineapple marinated chicken

serves 4; 3 ounces chicken, 2 slices kiwifruit, and 2 cherry tomatoes per serving

Kiwifruit is the surprise tenderizing ingredient in this recipe.

marinade

1 medium green kiwifruit, peeled, sliced, and slightly mashed

¼ cup pineapple juice

2 teaspoons acceptable vegetable oil

½ teaspoon paprika

¼ teaspoon salt

⅛ teaspoon pepper

❖ ❖ ❖

4 boneless, skinless chicken breast halves (about 4 ounces each), all visible fat removed

1 medium green kiwifruit and 1 medium gold kiwifruit, or 2 medium green kiwifruit, peeled and sliced

8 cherry tomatoes, halved

In an airtight plastic bag or glass baking dish, combine marinade ingredients.

Put the chicken with the smooth side up between two pieces of plastic wrap. Using a tortilla press, the smooth side of a meat mallet, or a rolling pin, lightly flatten, being careful not to tear the meat. Add to the marinade and turn to coat. Seal and refrigerate for 30 minutes to 2 hours, turning occasionally.

Preheat the grill on medium-high. Drain the chicken. Discard the marinade. Pat the chicken dry with paper towels.

Grill the chicken for 8 to 10 minutes, or until no longer pink in the center, turning once. Watch the chicken carefully to keep it from burning.

To serve, garnish with the remaining kiwifruit and cherry tomatoes.

Calories 157	Cholesterol 66 mg
Total Fat 2.0 g	Sodium 222 mg
Saturated 0.5 g	Carbohydrate 8 g
Polyunsaturated 0.5 g	Fiber 1 g
Monounsaturated 0.5 g	Protein 27 g

grilled chicken and pineapple sandwich

serves 4; 1 sandwich per serving

This recipe uses the same marinade as the Kiwifruit and Pineapple Marinated Chicken (facing page). Then the dish takes on a new life in a classy sandwich, complete with grilled pineapple slices.

marinade

- **1 medium green kiwifruit, peeled, sliced, and slightly mashed**
- **¼ cup pineapple juice**
- **2 teaspoons acceptable vegetable oil**
- **½ teaspoon paprika**
- **¼ teaspoon salt**
- **⅛ teaspoon pepper**

❖ ❖ ❖

- **2 boneless, skinless chicken breast halves (about 4 ounces each), all visible fat removed**
- **4 medium slices pineapple, fresh or canned in its own juice**
- **Butter-flavored vegetable oil spray**
- **8 slices light whole-wheat bread**
- **¼ cup honey mustard**
- **2 cups torn lettuce leaves, such as romaine or green leaf**
- **¼ cup plus 2 tablespoons imitation bacon-flavored bits**

Marinate and grill the chicken as directed on page 110. Cut each chicken breast into 8 strips.

Meanwhile, lightly spray pineapple with butter-flavored vegetable oil spray. Grill over medium-high heat for 2 to 4 minutes, or until the pineapple is warmed through and has golden-brown grill marks, turning once.

When the chicken and pineapple are ready, lightly toast the bread.

To assemble, spread the honey mustard on 4 slices of toast. Top each with lettuce, chicken strips, pineapple, and bacon-flavored bits. Top with the remaining toast.

Calories 222	Cholesterol 33 mg
Total Fat 2.0 g	Sodium 368 mg
Saturated 0.5 g	Carbohydrate 34 g
Polyunsaturated 0 g	Fiber 4 g
Monounsaturated 0.5 g	Protein 19 g

chicken satay with cucumber slaw and peanut dipping sauce

serves 5; 2 skewers, ⅓ cup slaw, and 2 tablespoons sauce per serving

Sweetly tangy chicken is served with a subtle dipping sauce and savory, crunchy slaw. The result is a fine example of the layering of flavors and textures that Southeast Asian cuisines feature.

1 pound boneless, skinless chicken breast tenders, all visible fat removed

marinade

¼ cup mirin or sweet vermouth

2 tablespoons chopped green onions (green and white parts)

2 tablespoons fresh lime juice

1 tablespoon grated peeled gingerroot

1 tablespoon sugar

1 tablespoon low-salt soy sauce

1 teaspoon toasted sesame oil

1 medium garlic clove, minced, or ½ teaspoon bottled minced garlic

½ teaspoon pepper

slaw

2 medium Kirby or other pickling cucumbers or ½ English, or hothouse, cucumber, sliced paper-thin (about 1 cup)

3 tablespoons plain rice vinegar

1 large shallot, sliced paper-thin and separated into rings

2 tablespoons sugar

⅛ teaspoon crushed red pepper flakes

Vegetable oil spray

Calories 228	Cholesterol 53 mg
Total Fat 6.5 g	Sodium 233 mg
Saturated 1.5 g	Carbohydrate 17 g
Polyunsaturated 2.0 g	Fiber 2 g
Monounsaturated 3.0 g	Protein 26 g

dipping sauce

¼ cup snipped fresh cilantro

1 peeled, seeded, and coarsely chopped small Italian plum tomato

¼ cup plus 1 tablespoon reduced-fat creamy peanut butter

2 medium green onions, minced (green and white parts)

2 to 3 tablespoons fresh lime juice

1 tablespoon light brown sugar

1 teaspoon grated lemon zest

1 medium garlic clove, minced, or ½ teaspoon bottled minced garlic

¼ teaspoon white pepper

2 tablespoons fat-free, low-sodium chicken broth (optional)

Soak ten 8-inch wooden skewers in cold water for at least 10 minutes to keep them from charring.

Meanwhile, place the chicken tenders between two pieces of plastic wrap. Using a tortilla press, the smooth side of a meat mallet, or a rolling pin, lightly flatten the tenders, being careful not to tear the meat. The pieces should be about 6 × 1½ inches. Thread onto skewers.

In a glass baking dish, combine all the marinade ingredients. Add the chicken and turn to coat. Cover the dish and let stand at room temperature for 30 minutes or refrigerate for up to 1 hour, turning occasionally.

Meanwhile, in a small bowl, combine all the slaw ingredients. Cover and refrigerate until ready to serve.

Lightly spray the grill rack with vegetable oil spray. Preheat the grill on medium-high.

In a food processor or blender, process all the dipping sauce ingredients except the broth until smooth. For a thinner sauce, stir in the chicken broth. Pour into a serving bowl. Set aside.

Remove the chicken from the marinade. Discard the marinade. Grill the chicken about 6 inches from the heat for about 6 minutes, or until no longer pink in the center, turning once.

To serve, arrange the skewers on a serving platter. Serve with the slaw and dipping sauce.

COOK'S TIP ON KIRBY CUCUMBERS

Usually used for pickling, Kirby cucumbers are quite crisp when chilled. Kirbies have very small seeds and dark, thin skin.

COOK'S TIP ON MIRIN

A Japanese rice wine, mirin adds a touch of sweetness to Asian sauces and glazes. When shopping, be sure to purchase regular mirin, not cooking mirin, which has added salt.

chicken mole

Chipotle chiles, cocoa, and almonds give this mole (*MO-lay*) its intense depth of flavor.

1 tablespoon olive oil

1 small onion, coarsely chopped

1 medium garlic clove, minced, or ½ teaspoon bottled minced garlic

4- to 4.5-ounce can diced green chiles, rinsed and drained

¼ cup sliced almonds, finely chopped

1 to 3 chipotle peppers canned in adobo sauce, plus 1 tablespoon sauce

2 tablespoons unsweetened cocoa powder

1 tablespoon dark brown sugar

10½-ounce can fat-free, low-sodium chicken broth

8-ounce can no-salt-added tomato sauce

4 8-inch reduced-fat flour tortillas, cut into ½-inch strips

2 pounds chicken tenders or boneless, skinless chicken breasts, all visible fat removed, cut into ½-inch cubes

½ cup light or nonfat sour cream

2 tablespoons chopped green onions (green part only) (optional)

Heat a stockpot over medium-high heat. Pour the oil into the pot and swirl to coat the bottom. Cook the onion and garlic for about 1½ minutes, stirring occasionally. Stir in the green chiles, almonds, chipotle peppers, adobo sauce, cocoa powder, and brown sugar. Stir in the broth and tomato sauce.

Using a hand blender, puree the mixture in the stockpot. Or puree in a food processor or blender, in batches if necessary; return the mixture to the stockpot. Bring to a boil over high heat; reduce the heat and simmer for 5 minutes.

Meanwhile, preheat the broiler. Put the tortilla strips on a baking sheet.

Broil the tortilla strips about 6 inches from the heat for 2 minutes; stir. Broil for 1 minute; stir. Broil for 1 to 2 minutes, or until the strips start to turn crisp and golden. Remove from the broiler. (Some strips will be partly soft.)

Stir the chicken into the stockpot. Reduce the heat; simmer for about 8 minutes, or until no longer pink in the center, stirring occasionally.

Put a few tortilla strips and about ¾ cup mole in each small bowl. Top with the remaining tortilla strips, sour cream, and green onions.

Calories 272	Cholesterol 71 mg
Total Fat 6.5 g	Sodium 373 mg
Saturated 2.0 g	Carbohydrate 20 g
Polyunsaturated 1.0 g	Fiber 3 g
Monounsaturated 2.5 g	Protein 31 g

crispy baked chicken strips with spicy-sweet mustard sauce

serves 4; 3 ounces chicken and 2 tablespoons sauce per serving

Serve mashed potatoes and steamed green beans with this classic dinner standby.

Vegetable oil spray

2 tablespoons all-purpose flour

2 teaspoons salt-free lemon pepper

1 pound chicken breast tenders, all visible fat removed

Egg substitute equivalent to 1 egg, or 1 large egg

½ cup crumbled cornflake cereal (about 1¼ cups flakes)

½ cup soft light whole-wheat bread crumbs or ¼ cup plain dry bread crumbs

spicy-sweet mustard sauce

¼ cup all-purpose flour

2 tablespoons dry mustard

3 tablespoons honey

2 tablespoons water

1 tablespoon white wine vinegar

⅛ teaspoon paprika

Preheat the oven to 350° F. Lightly spray a baking sheet with vegetable oil spray.

In a large airtight plastic bag, combine the flour and lemon pepper. Add the chicken and shake to coat. Add the egg substitute and shake gently to coat.

In a shallow bowl, stir together the cornflake crumbs and bread crumbs. Add the chicken, turning gently to coat. Arrange the chicken in a single layer on the baking sheet. Lightly spray the chicken with vegetable oil spray.

Bake for 30 minutes, or until the chicken is no longer pink in the center and the outside coating is crispy.

Meanwhile, in a small bowl, whisk together all the sauce ingredients.

Serve the chicken strips with the sauce on the side or spooned on top.

Calories 293	Cholesterol 66 mg
Total Fat 3.5 g	Sodium 228 mg
Saturated 0.5 g	Carbohydrate 34 g
Polyunsaturated 0.5 g	Fiber 2 g
Monounsaturated 0.5 g	Protein 32 g

creole-crusted chicken breasts with polenta

serves 4; 4 polenta slices and ¾ cup chicken mixture per serving

It's hard to say what's better about this Creole-crusted chicken with basil-scented tomato sauce and soft slices of polenta—its quickness or its simplicity.

> **Vegetable oil spray**
>
> **12 ounces fat-free, ready-to-eat polenta (half a 24-ounce package, halved lengthwise), cut crosswise into 16 slices**
>
> **1 pound boneless, skinless chicken breasts, all visible fat removed, cut into 2-inch cubes**
>
> **2 teaspoons salt-free Creole seasoning (see Cook's Tip on Cajun/Creole Seasoning, page 147)**
>
> **1 teaspoon dried oregano, crumbled**
>
> **¼ cup packed fresh basil, stems removed**
>
> **14.5-ounce can no-salt-added diced tomatoes, undrained**
>
> **2 tablespoons shredded or grated Parmesan cheese**

Preheat the oven to 400° F.

Lightly spray an 11 × 7 × 2-inch baking pan with vegetable oil spray. Arrange the polenta slices in a single layer in the pan.

In a medium bowl, stir together the chicken, Creole seasoning, and oregano, coating the chicken.

Chop the basil leaves. Add with the undrained tomatoes to the chicken mixture; stir well. Spoon over the polenta; sprinkle with the Parmesan.

Bake for 30 minutes, or until the chicken is no longer pink in the center.

COOK'S TIP

You can replace the raw chicken breasts with leftover cooked chicken or fish (such as tuna, cod, sole, or snapper). The baking time remains the same.

COOK'S TIP ON POLENTA

Sold in tube-shaped packages similar to refrigerated cookie dough packages, polenta is cooked and ready to heat. It's usually found in the Italian or produce section of the grocery store. To

Calories 225	Cholesterol 68 mg
Total Fat 2.5 g	Sodium 290 mg
Saturated 1.0 g	Carbohydrate 19 g
Polyunsaturated 0.5 g	Fiber 3 g
Monounsaturated 0.5 g	Protein 29 g

store the polenta not used in this recipe, wrap it in plastic wrap and refrigerate it for up to one week, or wrap it in plastic wrap and aluminum foil and freeze it for up to one month. One way to use up the leftover portion is to top ½-inch-thick slices with no-salt-added tomato sauce and part-skim mozzarella cheese; broil until the cheese melts. Another combination is to top slices of polenta with goat cheese mixed with fresh herbs, then broil until the goat cheese turns golden. Or lightly brush rounds with olive oil, sprinkle with Parmesan cheese, broil until golden, dice, and stir into soups and stews.

rustic stuffed potatoes

serves 4; 1 potato and about ½ cup chicken mixture per serving

Barbecue and potatoes go hand in hand. For a different way to pair them, mound barbecued chicken, Cheddar cheese, and green onions on red potatoes.

4 medium red potatoes (about 6 ounces each)

½ cup bottled barbecue sauce

2 to 3 teaspoons cider vinegar

¼ teaspoon cayenne

Vegetable oil spray

12 ounces boneless, skinless chicken breasts, all visible fat removed, cut into bite-size pieces

Fat-free, no-calorie liquid margarine spray

2 ounces shredded reduced-fat sharp Cheddar cheese

¼ to ½ cup finely chopped green onions (green and white parts)

Pierce the potatoes in several places with a fork. Microwave on 100 percent power (high) for 10 minutes, or until tender when pierced to the center with a fork, turning once.

Meanwhile, in a small measuring cup or bowl, stir together the barbecue sauce, vinegar, and cayenne.

Heat a large nonstick skillet over medium-high heat. Remove the skillet from the heat and lightly spray with vegetable oil spray (being careful not to spray near a gas flame). Cook the chicken for 2 minutes, or until no longer pink on the outside, stirring constantly. Increase the heat to high. Add the barbecue sauce mixture; cook for 1½ minutes, or until the sauce has thickened slightly and the chicken is no longer pink in the center, stirring constantly. Remove from the heat.

Cut the potatoes in half; fluff with a fork. Place 2 potato halves on each plate. Lightly spray each half with 2 pumps of liquid margarine spray. Sprinkle with the cheese. Spoon the chicken mixture over the potatoes. Sprinkle with the green onions.

Calories 277	Cholesterol 57 mg
Total Fat 4.0 g	Sodium 403 mg
Saturated 2.0 g	Carbohydrate 35 g
Polyunsaturated 0.5 g	Fiber 4 g
Monounsaturated 1.0 g	Protein 29 g

cheesy chicken vermicelli

If comfort food is what you need, a serving of tender noodles, chunks of chicken, and slowly melting cheese will do the job.

Vegetable oil spray

12 ounces boneless, skinless chicken breasts, all visible fat removed, cut into 1-inch pieces

1 teaspoon dried oregano, crumbled

1 large red bell pepper, chopped

14.5-ounce can fat-free, low-sodium chicken broth

½ cup water

6 ounces dried vermicelli, broken in half

1 cup frozen green peas, thawed

¼ teaspoon salt

¼ teaspoon pepper

¾ cup shredded reduced-fat sharp Cheddar cheese

Heat a Dutch oven over medium-high heat. Remove from the heat and lightly spray with vegetable oil spray (being careful not to spray near a gas flame). Cook the chicken and oregano for 5 minutes, or until the chicken is no longer pink in the center, stirring frequently. Transfer to a plate.

Lightly spray the same Dutch oven with vegetable oil spray. Cook the bell peppers for 3 minutes, or until the edges just begin to brown. Add to the chicken. Set aside.

Increase the heat to high; add the broth and water. Bring to a boil. Stir in the vermicelli; return to a boil. Reduce the heat and simmer, covered, for 9 minutes, or until just tender. Stir in the peas, chicken mixture with any accumulated juices, salt, and pepper. Remove from the heat. Sprinkle with the Cheddar, cover tightly, and let stand for 3 to 4 minutes, or until the cheese melts.

Calories 357	Cholesterol 67 mg
Total Fat 6.0 g	Sodium 408 mg
Saturated 3.0 g	Carbohydrate 40 g
Polyunsaturated 0.5 g	Fiber 4 g
Monounsaturated 1.0 g	Protein 34 g

ginger chicken with whole-wheat spaghetti and green beans

Instead of the rice so often found in Asian dishes, whole-wheat spaghetti is featured in this meal-in-one.

1 pound boneless, skinless chicken breasts, all visible fat removed

marinade

3 tablespoons low-salt soy sauce

3 tablespoons dry sherry or 2 tablespoons white wine vinegar

2 teaspoons sugar

1 teaspoon minced peeled gingerroot

❖ ❖ ❖

4 ounces dried whole-wheat spaghetti

2 teaspoons toasted sesame oil

2 cups frozen no-salt-added green beans

2 medium green onions (green and white parts), thinly sliced

½ teaspoon grated orange zest

Cut the chicken into thin strips about 2 inches long. Put the chicken in an airtight plastic bag or glass baking dish. Add the marinade ingredients. Seal the bag and turn to coat. Refrigerate for 15 minutes to 8 hours, turning occasionally.

Prepare the spaghetti using the package directions, omitting the salt and oil. Drain well. Return the spaghetti to the pot and stir in the sesame oil. Cover and set aside.

Meanwhile, cook the beans using the package directions, omitting the salt and margarine. Stir the beans into the spaghetti.

Calories 289	Cholesterol 66 mg
Total Fat 4.0 g	Sodium 372 mg
Saturated 1.0 g	Carbohydrate 29 g
Polyunsaturated 1.5 g	Fiber 6 g
Monounsaturated 1.5 g	Protein 32 g

Heat a nonstick wok or large nonstick skillet over medium-high heat. Cook the chicken and marinade for 2 to 3 minutes, or until the chicken is no longer pink in the center, stirring constantly. Cook for 5 minutes, stirring occasionally. Stir in the spaghetti mixture, green onions, and orange zest. Cook for about 3 minutes, or until most of the liquid has evaporated and forms a glaze on the chicken, stirring occasionally.

stovetop chicken lasagna stew

serves 4; 1½ cups per serving

The flavors that mingle in this one-dish meal are traditional for lasagna. However, this recipe provides a new (and quick) way to enjoy the old favorite. This lasagna stew is cooked on the stovetop, and the ricotta, mozzarella, and Parmesan cheeses aren't added until the dish is about to be served.

1 pound boneless, skinless chicken breasts or turkey breast tenderloins, all visible fat removed

1 teaspoon acceptable vegetable oil

8 ounces fresh mushrooms, sliced

2 cups shredded carrots

½ cup sliced onion

1 to 2 medium garlic cloves, minced, or ½ to 1 teaspoon bottled minced garlic

3 cups water

14.5-ounce can no-salt-added tomatoes, undrained, pureed

8-ounce can no-salt-added tomato sauce

1 teaspoon salt-free Italian seasoning, crumbled

1 teaspoon dried basil, crumbled

¼ teaspoon salt

¼ to ⅛ teaspoon crushed red pepper flakes

⅛ teaspoon black pepper

4 dried lasagna noodles or 6 dried no-boil lasagna noodles, broken into 1-inch pieces

¾ cup fat-free or low-fat ricotta cheese

¼ cup plus 2 tablespoons shredded part-skim mozzarella cheese

1 tablespoon plus 1 teaspoon shredded or grated Parmesan cheese

Cut the chicken into ¾-inch cubes.

Heat a nonstick Dutch oven over medium-high heat. Pour the oil into the pot and swirl to coat the bottom. Cook the chicken for 3 to 4 minutes, or until browned and almost cooked through, stirring occasionally.

Calories 365	Cholesterol 77 mg
Total Fat 5.5 g	Sodium 444 mg
Saturated 2.0 g	Carbohydrate 36 g
Polyunsaturated 1.0 g	Fiber 5 g
Monounsaturated 1.5 g	Protein 42 g

122   american heart association low-calorie cookbook

Stir in the mushrooms, carrots, onion, and garlic. Cook for 4 to 5 minutes, or until the vegetables are tender, stirring occasionally. Stir in the water, tomatoes, tomato sauce, Italian seasoning, basil, salt, red pepper flakes, and black pepper. Increase the heat to high; bring the mixture to a boil, stirring occasionally. Reduce the heat to medium-low; cook, covered, for 5 minutes. Increase the heat to medium-high and return to a boil, uncovered.

Stir in the pasta. Cook for about 20 minutes, or until the noodles are tender, stirring occasionally.

To serve, spoon the stew into shallow bowls. Top each portion with 3 tablespoons ricotta, 2 tablespoons mozzarella, and 1 teaspoon Parmesan.

lemony chicken
with broccoli

Cumin, lemon, and cilantro are the flavor boosters in this stovetop meal-in-one. Real lemon-lovers may want to squeeze the lemon-wedge garnish over their portions.

- ¾ cup uncooked rice
- ½ cup water
- 3 cups fresh or 10-ounce package no-salt-added frozen broccoli florets
- Vegetable oil spray
- 1¼ pounds boneless, skinless chicken breasts, all visible fat removed, cut into bite-size pieces
- 2 to 3 tablespoons fresh lemon juice
- ¼ to ½ teaspoon ground cumin
- ¼ teaspoon salt
- ⅛ teaspoon cayenne
- 2 tablespoons snipped fresh cilantro or parsley
- 1 medium or large lemon, cut into 6 wedges (optional)

Cook the rice using the package directions, omitting the salt and margarine.

Meanwhile, in a large skillet, bring the water to a boil over high heat. Add the broccoli. Reduce the heat and simmer, covered, for 3 minutes, or until tender-crisp. Drain well.

Dry the skillet with paper towels. Heat the skillet over medium-high heat. Remove from the heat and lightly spray with vegetable oil spray (being careful not to spray near a gas flame). Cook the chicken for 3 to 4 minutes, or until no longer pink on the outside, stirring frequently. Stir in the broccoli, lemon juice, cumin, salt, and cayenne. Reduce the heat and simmer, covered, for 5 minutes, or until the chicken is no longer pink in the center.

Spread the rice on a serving platter. Spoon the chicken mixture over the rice. Sprinkle with the cilantro. Arrange the lemon wedges around the edge of the platter.

Calories 200	Cholesterol 55 mg
Total Fat 1.5 g	Sodium 170 mg
Saturated 0.5 g	Carbohydrate 21 g
Polyunsaturated 0.5 g	Fiber 1 g
Monounsaturated 0.5 g	Protein 25 g

chicken and vegetable meal-in-one

serves 8; 1 cup per serving

While the vegetables are cooking, you'll have time to cut the chicken and roll it in a mixture of rosemary, lemon, and cornstarch. Then combine all the ingredients and, in minutes, this stove-top meal-in-one will be ready.

10 ounces red potatoes

16 ounces frozen no-salt-added baby green bean and carrot mixture, other frozen vegetable mixture, or mixture of fresh carrots and green beans

12 ounces boneless, skinless chicken breasts, all visible fat removed

3 tablespoons cornstarch

¼ to ½ teaspoon dried rosemary, crushed

½ teaspoon grated lemon zest

½ teaspoon salt

¼ teaspoon pepper

2 teaspoons acceptable vegetable oil

½ cup dry white wine (regular or nonalcoholic)

1 tablespoon fresh lemon juice

Steam, boil, or microwave the potatoes until tender. Peel and cut into ½-inch cubes.

Meanwhile, in a medium saucepan, cook the frozen vegetables using the package directions. Drain well. Set aside.

Cut the chicken into thin strips.

In a shallow dish or pie pan, combine the cornstarch, rosemary, lemon zest, salt, and pepper. Roll the chicken in the cornstarch mixture; shake off the excess.

Heat a large nonstick skillet over medium-high heat. Add the oil and swirl to coat the bottom of the skillet. Cook the chicken for about 4 minutes, stirring and turning until golden outside and no longer pink inside.

Stir in the vegetable mixture, potatoes, wine, and lemon juice. Bring to a boil. Cook for about 1 minute, or until the sauce is reduced slightly, using a spoon to scrape up any browned bits on the bottom of the skillet.

Calories 126	Cholesterol 25 mg
Total Fat 1.5 g	Sodium 192 mg
Saturated 0 g	Carbohydrate 13 g
Polyunsaturated 0.5 g	Fiber 2 g
Monounsaturated 1.0 g	Protein 11 g

chicken marsala

Tarragon, balsamic vinegar, capers, and—of course—the marsala it is named for team up to provide rich flavor for this classic dish.

4 boneless, skinless chicken breast halves (about 4 ounces each), all visible fat removed

3 tablespoons all-purpose flour

1 teaspoon dried tarragon, crumbled

¼ teaspoon pepper

1 tablespoon acceptable vegetable oil

¼ cup dry marsala or dry red wine (regular or nonalcoholic)

¼ cup fat-free, low-sodium chicken broth

1 tablespoon balsamic vinegar

2 teaspoons capers, rinsed and drained

Place the chicken with the smooth side up between two pieces of plastic wrap. Using a tortilla press, the smooth side of a meat mallet, or a rolling pin, lightly flatten the breasts to ¼-inch thickness, being careful not to tear the meat.

In a shallow dish or pie pan, combine the flour, tarragon, and pepper. Lightly dust both sides of the chicken, shaking off the excess flour.

Heat a large nonstick skillet over medium-high heat. Pour the oil into the skillet and swirl to coat the bottom. Cook the chicken for 6 to 8 minutes, or until lightly browned and no longer pink in the center, turning once. Transfer the chicken to a plate; cover with aluminum foil to keep warm.

Stir in the remaining ingredients. Bring to a boil; cook for 1 minute, or until the sauce is reduced slightly, using a wooden spoon to scrape up any browned bits on the bottom of the pan. Spoon the sauce over the chicken.

Calories 205	Cholesterol 66 mg
Total Fat 5.0 g	Sodium 119 mg
Saturated 0.5 g	Carbohydrate 8 g
Polyunsaturated 1.5 g	Fiber 0 g
Monounsaturated 2.5 g	Protein 27 g

chicken paprikash

Hungarian paprika gives this dish pizzazz by providing rich color and adding great flavor as well. Be creative—use a colorful combination of bell peppers. You can pick from green, red, yellow, orange, purple, and white. Serve this lightened version of paprikash with noodles or rice.

1 teaspoon acceptable vegetable oil

6 boneless, skinless chicken breast halves (about 4 ounces each), all visible fat removed

1 teaspoon acceptable vegetable oil

1 medium onion, chopped

1 medium garlic clove, minced, or ½ teaspoon bottled minced garlic

1 tablespoon all-purpose flour

1 cup fat-free, low-sodium chicken broth

1 teaspoon paprika (Hungarian preferred)

1 cup chopped bell pepper, any color or combination

½ cup nonfat or light sour cream

Heat a large nonstick skillet over medium-high heat. Pour 1 teaspoon oil into the skillet and swirl to coat the bottom. Cook the chicken for about 6 minutes, or until lightly browned on each side, turning once. Remove from the skillet. Set aside. Wipe the skillet with paper towels.

Reduce the heat to medium. Pour 1 teaspoon oil into the same skillet and swirl to coat the bottom. Cook the onion and garlic for 3 to 4 minutes, or until the onion is translucent, stirring occasionally.

Add the flour; cook for 30 seconds, stirring constantly. Add the broth, paprika, and chicken. Bring to a simmer. Reduce the heat and simmer, covered, for 10 minutes. Add the bell pepper; simmer, covered, for 5 minutes. Reduce the heat to low.

Stir some of the hot liquid into the sour cream (to prevent curdling); stir the sour cream mixture into the skillet. Cook for 2 to 3 minutes, or until the desired consistency. Don't let the mixture boil.

COOK'S TIP

You can reheat the sauce in this recipe, but it may separate slightly. If you plan to make it ahead, for best results add room-temperature sour cream after you have reheated the sauce.

Calories 183	Cholesterol 66 mg
Total Fat 3.0 g	Sodium 102 mg
Saturated 0.5 g	Carbohydrate 9 g
Polyunsaturated 1.0 g	Fiber 1 g
Monounsaturated 1.0 g	Protein 29 g

greek chicken with capers

serves 4; 3 ounces chicken and 2 tablespoons sauce per serving

This lemony chicken is equally good when served alone or over hot, fluffy rice.

¾ cup fat-free, low-sodium chicken broth

¼ cup capers, rinsed and drained

2 tablespoons dry white wine (regular or nonalcoholic)

1½ tablespoons fresh lemon juice

1 tablespoon dried oregano, crumbled

2 medium garlic cloves, minced, or 1 teaspoon bottled minced garlic

⅛ teaspoon pepper

Vegetable oil spray

4 boneless, skinless chicken breast halves (about 4 ounces each), all visible fat removed

½ tablespoon olive oil (extra virgin preferred)

In a medium bowl, stir together the broth, capers, wine, lemon juice, oregano, garlic, and pepper.

Heat a large nonstick skillet over medium-high heat. Remove the skillet from the heat and lightly spray with vegetable oil spray (being careful not to spray near a gas flame). Cook the chicken with the smooth side down for 4 minutes, or until just beginning to lightly brown; turn the chicken over. Increase the heat to high. Add the broth mixture; bring to a boil. Reduce the heat; simmer, covered, for 8 minutes, or until the chicken is no longer pink in the center. Transfer the chicken to a serving plate.

Increase the heat to high; bring the sauce to a boil. Boil until the liquid is reduced to ½ cup. Remove from the heat; stir in the olive oil.

To serve, spoon the sauce over the chicken.

Calories 156	Cholesterol 66 mg
Total Fat 3.0 g	Sodium 320 mg
Saturated 0.5 g	Carbohydrate 2 g
Polyunsaturated 0.5 g	Fiber 1 g
Monounsaturated 1.5 g	Protein 27 g

cumin chicken
with onions and squash

serves 4; 1 cup per serving

For complementary color and flavor, choose Sliced Tomatoes with Avocado Salsa (page 44) as an accompaniment to this tasty dish.

1 pound boneless, skinless chicken breasts, all visible fat removed, cut into 1-inch pieces

1 teaspoon chili powder

1 teaspoon ground cumin

Vegetable oil spray

1 large onion, cut in eighths, layers separated

2 medium yellow summer squash, quartered lengthwise and cut into 1-inch cubes

½ teaspoon salt

Put the chicken in a large, shallow bowl or baking dish. Sprinkle with the chili powder and cumin; stir well.

Heat a large nonstick skillet over high heat. Remove the skillet from the heat; lightly spray with vegetable oil spray (being careful not to spray near a gas flame). Cook the chicken for 2 minutes, or until browned, stirring constantly. Transfer to a medium bowl.

Reduce the heat to medium. Lightly spray the skillet again with vegetable oil spray. Cook the onion and squash for 10 minutes, or until they are tender-crisp and the edges of the onion are richly browned, stirring frequently. Stir in the salt and the chicken with any accumulated juices. Cook for 1 minute, or until the mixture is heated thoroughly and the chicken is no longer pink in the center, stirring constantly.

Calories 167	Cholesterol 66 mg
Total Fat 1.5 g	Sodium 373 mg
Saturated 0.5 g	Carbohydrate 9 g
Polyunsaturated 0.5 g	Fiber 3 g
Monounsaturated 0.5 g	Protein 28 g

spicy seared chicken with chipotle salsa

serves 4; 3 ounces chicken and ¼ cup salsa per serving

Here's a quick and easy way to prepare chicken that packs a wallop of flavor.

½ **teaspoon paprika**
½ **teaspoon ground cumin**
4 **boneless, skinless chicken breast halves (about 4 ounces each), all visible fat removed**
Vegetable oil spray

salsa

½ **to** 1 **chipotle pepper canned in adobo sauce**
½ **cup finely chopped tomato**
⅓ **cup finely chopped green bell pepper**
2 **tablespoons finely chopped green onions (green and white parts)**
2 **tablespoons snipped fresh cilantro**
2 **tablespoons fresh lime juice**
2 **teaspoons olive oil**
¼ **teaspoon salt**

In a cup or small bowl, stir together the paprika and cumin. Rub evenly over both sides of the chicken.

Heat a large nonstick skillet over high heat. Remove the skillet from the heat and lightly spray with vegetable oil spray (being careful not to spray near a gas flame). Cook the chicken with the smooth side down for 1 minute. Reduce the heat to medium; cook for 5 minutes. Turn the chicken over; cook for 7 minutes, or until no longer pink in the center.

Meanwhile, put the chipotle pepper on a flat surface. Using a fork, mash the pepper to a paste consistency. Transfer to a small bowl. Stir in the remaining salsa ingredients.

To serve, spoon the salsa over the chicken, or serve the salsa on the side.

with chipotle salsa

Calories 160	Cholesterol 66 mg
Total Fat 4.0 g	Sodium 247 mg
Saturated 0.5 g	Carbohydrate 3 g
Polyunsaturated 0.5 g	Fiber 1 g
Monounsaturated 2.0 g	Protein 27 g

seared chicken
with basil-caper salsa

½ teaspoon paprika

½ teaspoon dried basil, crumbled

4 boneless, skinless chicken breast halves (about 4 ounces each), all visible fat removed

Vegetable oil spray

salsa

¼ teaspoon crushed red pepper flakes

½ cup finely chopped tomato

⅓ cup finely chopped green bell pepper

2 tablespoons finely chopped green onions (green and white parts)

2 tablespoons snipped fresh parsley

1 tablespoon red wine vinegar

2 teaspoons dried basil, crumbled

2 teaspoons olive oil

1½ tablespoons capers, rinsed and drained

Prepare the chicken as directed, rubbing with paprika and basil. In a small bowl, stir together all the salsa ingredients. Serve as directed.

COOK'S TIP ON HOT CHILE PEPPERS

Be careful when handling chile peppers. They can cause skin burns. Use rubber gloves when touching peppers, and wash your hands well with soap and water immediately afterward.

COOK'S TIP ON CHIPOTLE PEPPERS

Chipotle peppers are smoked jalapeño peppers. Some come in plastic bags and are ready to be rehydrated; others are canned in adobo sauce. To store leftover canned chipotles, refrigerate them in an airtight container for up to three weeks.

with basil-caper salsa

Calories 159	Cholesterol 66 mg
Total Fat 4.0 g	Sodium 196 mg
Saturated 1.0 g	Carbohydrate 4 g
Polyunsaturated 1.0 g	Fiber 1 g
Monounsaturated 2.0 g	Protein 27 g

savory chicken with bell pepper and mushrooms

serves 4; 3 ounces chicken and ½ cup vegetables per serving

Balsamic vinegar, caramelized onion, bell pepper, and mushrooms enhance the sauce that smothers golden-brown chicken in this flavorful dish.

4 boneless, skinless chicken breast halves (about 4 ounces each), all visible fat removed

Vegetable oil spray

1 teaspoon acceptable vegetable oil

1 medium onion, thinly sliced

8 ounces fresh mushrooms, sliced

1 medium red bell pepper, thinly sliced

1 cup fat-free, low-sodium chicken broth

1 tablespoon balsamic vinegar

½ teaspoon dried oregano, crumbled

⅛ teaspoon pepper

1 teaspoon cornstarch

1 teaspoon water

Put the breasts with the smooth side up between two sheets of plastic wrap. Using a tortilla press, the smooth side of a meat mallet, or a rolling pin, lightly flatten the breasts to ¼-inch thickness, being careful not to tear the meat.

Heat a large nonstick skillet over medium-high heat. Remove from the heat and lightly spray with vegetable oil spray (being careful not to spray near a gas flame). Cook the chicken for 4 to 6 minutes, or until lightly golden brown, turning once. Transfer to a plate.

Reduce the heat to medium. Pour the oil into the skillet and swirl to coat the bottom. Cook the onion until light golden brown, 5 to 6 minutes, stirring constantly. Stir in the mushrooms and bell pepper. Cook for 2 to 3 minutes, or until the vegetables are tender, stirring occasionally. Reduce the heat to medium-low.

Calories 181	Cholesterol 66 mg
Total Fat 3.0 g	Sodium 94 mg
Saturated 0.5 g	Carbohydrate 9 g
Polyunsaturated 1.0 g	Fiber 2 g
Monounsaturated 1.0 g	Protein 29 g

Stir in the chicken, broth, vinegar, oregano, and pepper. Cook for 10 minutes, or until the chicken is no longer pink in the center, turning once. Transfer the chicken to a platter. Cover with aluminum foil to keep warm.

Increase the heat to high. Cook until the liquid is reduced by half, 3 to 4 minutes.

Put the cornstarch in a small bowl. Add the water, stirring to dissolve. Stir into the liquid mixture in the skillet. Cook for 1 to 2 minutes, or until the mixture is thickened, stirring occasionally.

To serve, pour the vegetables and sauce over the chicken.

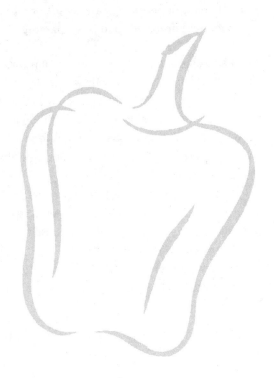

beefy chicken with mushrooms

The unusual addition of beef granules to chicken gives this dish a rich brown color and deep flavor.

> **Vegetable oil spray**
>
> **4 boneless, skinless chicken breast halves (about 4 ounces each), all visible fat removed**
>
> **8 ounces fresh mushrooms, sliced**
>
> **1 medium garlic clove, minced, or ½ teaspoon bottled minced garlic**
>
> **½ cup chopped green onions (green and white parts)**
>
> **3 tablespoons dry red wine (regular or nonalcoholic)**
>
> **1 tablespoon very low sodium beef bouillon granules**
>
> **⅛ to ¼ teaspoon pepper (coarsely ground preferred)**
>
> **2 tablespoons snipped fresh parsley**

Heat a large nonstick skillet over medium-high heat. Remove the skillet from the heat and lightly spray with vegetable oil spray (being careful not to spray near a gas flame). Cook the chicken with the smooth side down for 4 minutes, or until lightly browned. Transfer with the browned side up to a plate.

In the same skillet, cook the mushrooms for 4 minutes, stirring frequently. Add the garlic; cook for 1 minute, or until the mushrooms are limp, stirring frequently. Stir in the green onions.

Make a well in the center of the skillet. Put the chicken, browned side up, with any accumulated juices in the well. Sprinkle the wine, bouillon granules, and pepper evenly over the chicken. Reduce the heat to medium; cook, covered, for 6 minutes, or until the chicken is no longer pink in the center.

To serve, transfer the chicken to a platter. Stir the mushroom mixture, then spoon it around the chicken. Sprinkle the parsley over all.

Calories 161	Cholesterol 66 mg
Total Fat 1.5 g	Sodium 84 mg
Saturated 0.5 g	Carbohydrate 5 g
Polyunsaturated 0.5 g	Fiber 1 g
Monounsaturated 0.5 g	Protein 28 g

gourmet pizza with chicken and vegetables

A sprinkle of zesty blue cheese adds an extra flavor boost to this sensational pizza.

- **12-inch prepared pizza crust (use the brand with the lowest fat and sodium)**
- **8-ounce can no-salt-added tomato sauce**
- **1 teaspoon dried oregano, crumbled**
- **½ teaspoon garlic powder**
- **⅛ teaspoon salt**
- **2 ounces shredded part-skim mozzarella cheese**
- **1 cup sliced fresh mushrooms**
- **1 cup diced cooked skinless chicken breast (about 4 ounces)**
- **½ 9-ounce package frozen artichoke hearts, thawed, or ½ 14-ounce can artichokes, quartered and rinsed, well drained**
- **1 ounce blue cheese or goat cheese, crumbled**

Preheat the oven to 425°F.

Put the pizza crust on an ungreased nonstick baking sheet.

In a small bowl, stir together the tomato sauce, oregano, garlic powder, and salt. Spread over the crust. Sprinkle with the remaining ingredients.

Bake for 10 to 12 minutes, or until the crust is light golden brown and the cheese has melted.

Calories 229	Cholesterol 29 mg
Total Fat 6.5 g	Sodium 447 mg
Saturated 3.0 g	Carbohydrate 25 g
Polyunsaturated —	Fiber 2 g
Monounsaturated —	Protein 17 g

chicken and noodles

Hard to resist on a winter day, chicken and noodles is one of America's favorite comfort foods. We've included ingredients and instructions for making your own noodles. When you're pressed for time, though, you can substitute store-bought fresh pasta. With so many different vegetable combinations available, you can easily vary this dish.

noodles

½ cup all-purpose flour, plus more as needed

2 tablespoons egg substitute, or ½ large egg, beaten with a fork

2 tablespoons fat-free milk

❖ ❖ ❖

3 cups fat-free, low-sodium chicken broth

1 cup diced cooked chicken, white meat only, skin and all visible fat removed (6 to 8 ounces cooked)

1½ cups no-salt-added frozen mixed vegetables, thawed

¼ teaspoon dried thyme, crumbled

¼ teaspoon salt

¼ teaspoon pepper

⅓ cup water

3 tablespoons all-purpose flour

For the noodles, put the flour in a medium bowl; in the center, make a well about the size of an egg. Pour the egg substitute and milk into the well. Using a fork, stir until the mixture forms a ball. Lightly flour a cutting board. Lightly knead the dough for 1 to 2 minutes, or until the dough is fairly smooth and slightly elastic. Cover with a dry dish towel and let rest for 15 minutes.

Lightly flour the cutting board. Roll the dough to a 9 × 6-inch rectangle. Using a knife or pizza cutter, cut the dough into strips about 3 inches long and ½ inch wide. Cover with the dish towel. Set aside.

In a medium saucepan, stir together the broth, chicken, mixed vegetables, thyme, salt, and pepper. Cover and bring to a boil over high heat. Reduce the

Calories 235	Cholesterol 40 mg
Total Fat 2.5 g	Sodium 328 mg
Saturated 0.5 g	Carbohydrate 29 g
Polyunsaturated 0.5 g	Fiber 3 g
Monounsaturated 1.0 g	Protein 22 g

heat to medium-high. Add the noodles; cook for 4 to 5 minutes, stirring occasionally. The noodles should be tender to the bite and no longer appear chalky in the center when cut in half.

In a small bowl, whisk together the water and 3 tablespoons flour. Stir into the chicken mixture. Cook for 2 to 3 minutes, or until the mixture thickens, stirring occasionally.

COOK'S TIP

Uncooked noodles will keep in an airtight container (in a single layer) in the refrigerator for up to 24 hours or in the freezer for up to one month. (The noodles can be stacked after they are frozen.) Do not thaw the noodles before cooking; increase the cooking time by 1 to 2 minutes.

zucchini boats

Delightfully seasoned stuffed zucchini is almost a meal in itself. By the time the zucchini emerge hot and bubbly from the oven, you can have a salad ready to complete the meal.

½ cup water

¼ cup uncooked bulgur

2 large or 4 medium zucchini (about 16 ounces)

    Vegetable oil spray

2 teaspoons acceptable vegetable oil

1 small onion, chopped

1 large garlic clove, minced, or ¾ teaspoon bottled minced garlic

½ pound lean ground chicken breast, skin removed before grinding

½ cup no-salt-added tomato sauce

½ cup fat-free, low-sodium chicken broth

2 tablespoons chopped fresh basil or 2 teaspoons dried, crumbled

2 tablespoons snipped fresh parsley

1 teaspoon ground cumin

¼ teaspoon pepper

2 tablespoons shredded or grated Parmesan cheese

In a small saucepan, combine the water and bulgur. Bring to a boil over high heat. Reduce the heat and simmer, covered, for 13 to 16 minutes, or until the liquid is absorbed.

Trim the ends from the zucchini; cut the zucchini in half lengthwise. Scoop out the flesh and seeds, leaving about a ½-inch shell. Save the flesh and seeds for another use, such as vegetable soup, or discard.

Heat a large nonstick skillet over medium heat. Pour the oil into the skillet and swirl to coat the bottom. Cook the onion and garlic for 3 to 4 minutes, or until the onion is translucent, stirring occasionally. Add the chicken. Cook for 5 to 7 minutes, or until browned and cooked through, using a wooden spoon to stir frequently and break up the chicken into small pieces. Stir in the cooked

Calories 177	Cholesterol 35 mg
Total Fat 4.0 g	Sodium 108 mg
Saturated 1.0 g	Carbohydrate 18 g
Polyunsaturated 1.0 g	Fiber 5 g
Monounsaturated 2.0 g	Protein 18 g

bulgur and the remaining ingredients except the Parmesan. Cook until the liquid is reduced by about half, about 5 minutes, stirring constantly.

Meanwhile, preheat the oven to 350°F. Lightly spray an 11 × 7 × 2-inch pan with vegetable oil spray.

Lightly pack each zucchini half with the chicken and bulgur mixture. Place the zucchini boats in the pan. Sprinkle with the Parmesan.

Bake for about 30 minutes, or until the boats can be easily pierced with the tip of a knife or a fork and the tops are browned. If the cheese begins to get too brown, cover the pan lightly with aluminum foil.

turkey "filet mignon" with leek ribbons

serves 4; 3 ounces turkey plus ¼ cup leeks per serving

Tie strips of leek leaves around pieces of turkey tenderloin for a dramatic presentation. With cooked sweet potato slices and cranberry sauce, this becomes Thanksgiving dinner for four.

2 medium leeks

2 8-ounce turkey tenderloins, all visible fat removed

2 tablespoons finely chopped fresh rosemary or 2 teaspoons dried, crushed

¼ teaspoon pepper

1 teaspoon olive oil

½ cup fat-free, low-sodium chicken broth

2 teaspoons very low sodium or low-sodium Worcestershire sauce

1 teaspoon crushed pink or black peppercorns (optional)

Fill a medium saucepan halfway with water; bring to a boil over high heat. Remove and cook 4 leek leaves for 1 to 2 minutes, or until tender. Transfer leaves to a cutting board and let cool for 5 minutes.

Meanwhile, thinly slice the white part of the leeks. Set aside.

Cut each turkey tenderloin in half crosswise. Butterfly each of the four pieces by cutting almost in half, parallel to the cutting surface; be careful and don't cut all the way through (you'll still have four pieces). Take one piece and turn the cut ends outward, away from each other, to form a round fillet about 1½ inches thick. Repeat with the remaining pieces.

Cut the cooked leek leaves into strips about ¼ inch wide and 6 to 8 inches long. You may need to tie two strips together with a single knot to make a strip long enough to go around a turkey fillet. Snugly tie a leek "string" around each fillet. (The leek encircles the turkey much like the bacon encircles the beef in filet mignon.)

Sprinkle both sides of the turkey with rosemary and pepper.

Heat a large skillet over medium-high heat. Pour the oil into the skillet and swirl to coat the bottom. Cook the turkey for 4 to 6 minutes, or until golden brown, turning once. Reduce heat to medium.

Calories 174	Cholesterol 82 mg
Total Fat 2.0 g	Sodium 71 mg
Saturated 0.5 g	Carbohydrate 7 g
Polyunsaturated 0.5 g	Fiber 1 g
Monounsaturated 1.0 g	Protein 31 g

Add the white part of the leeks; cook for 2 to 3 minutes, or until tender, stirring occasionally. Add the remaining ingredients except the peppercorns. Reduce the heat to low and cook, covered, for 20 to 25 minutes, or until the turkey is no longer pink in the center (no stirring needed). Transfer the turkey to a platter. Cover with aluminum foil to keep warm.

Increase the heat to high and cook without stirring until the liquid is reduced by half, about 2 to 3 minutes. Spoon the leeks and sauce around the turkey. Sprinkle the turkey with the peppercorns. Remind diners to remove the leek strings; they're too tough to eat.

COOK'S TIP

If you prefer not to tie the fillets with leeks, you can use kitchen twine instead.

COOK'S TIP ON WASHING LEEKS

Leeks tend to be gritty, so you'll want to rinse them thoroughly. Leaving about an inch of green leaves attached, cut off the dark green part. Next, cut the roots from the whites and remove any tough outer leaves. Cut the whites in half lengthwise. Fanning the leaves, rinse the leeks under cold running water. If any dirt remains, swish the leeks in a bowl of cold water, changing the water until it stays clear.

turkey lo mein

Chunks of turkey and vegetables, crunchy water chestnuts, and noodles flavored with soy and hoisin sauces combine for a very filling and satisfying entrée. Complete your dinner with a bowl of chilled mandarin orange slices.

- 1 tablespoon low-salt soy sauce
- 1 tablespoon dry sherry or plain rice vinegar
- 1 teaspoon cornstarch
- 1 pound boneless, skinless turkey breast tenderloins or chicken breast tenders, all visible fat removed
- 3 cups cooked linguine or other flat pasta (7 ounces dried, uncooked)
- 1 cup fat-free, low-sodium chicken broth
- ¼ cup hoisin sauce
- 1 teaspoon toasted sesame oil
- 8-ounce can sliced water chestnuts
- 8-ounce can sliced bamboo shoots
- 4 medium green onions
- 1 teaspoon acceptable vegetable oil
- 2 to 3 teaspoons crushed red pepper flakes
- ½ medium red bell pepper, sliced
- 1 medium carrot, shredded
- 2 medium ribs bok choy (stalks and leaves), sliced
- 1 cup sliced fresh mushrooms, such as oyster or button

In an airtight plastic bag or glass baking dish, combine the soy sauce, sherry, and cornstarch. Cut the turkey into ¾-inch cubes. Add the turkey to the marinade and turn to coat. Seal and refrigerate for 10 minutes to 8 hours, turning occasionally.

Meanwhile, cook the pasta using the package directions, omitting the salt and oil. Drain and set aside.

In a small bowl, stir together the broth, hoisin sauce, and toasted sesame oil. Set aside.

Calories 377	Cholesterol 82 mg
Total Fat 4.0 g	Sodium 273 mg
Saturated 0.5 g	Carbohydrate 46 g
Polyunsaturated 1.5 g	Fiber 5 g
Monounsaturated 1.5 g	Protein 38 g

Rinse and drain the water chestnuts and bamboo shoots. Slice the green onions (green and white parts).

Heat a wok or large nonstick skillet over medium-high heat. Pour in the vegetable oil and swirl to coat the bottom. Add the red pepper flakes and the turkey with marinade; cook for 5 minutes, stirring occasionally. Stir in the bell peppers and carrots; cook for 2 to 3 minutes, or until the vegetables are tender-crisp, stirring occasionally. Stir in the bok choy; cook for 1 minute, or until the stems are just tender-crisp and the greens are slightly wilted, stirring occasionally. Stir in the mushrooms, water chestnuts, bamboo shoots, and green onions; cook for 1 to 2 minutes, or until the mixture is warmed through, stirring occasionally. Stir in the linguine and reserved broth mixture. Reduce the heat to medium; cook for 2 to 3 minutes, or until warmed through.

COOK'S TIP ON HOISIN SAUCE

This rich, thick brown sauce is made of garlic, ginger, soy sauce, and spices. It could almost be called Chinese ketchup because it is delicious with so many foods, from stir-fry sauces to dipping sauce for Crispy Baked Chicken Strips (page 117), or even brushed on your favorite heart-healthy meat loaf halfway through baking. Look for hoisin sauce in Asian markets or the Asian section of your supermarket.

COOK'S TIP ON BOK CHOY

The most common type of bok choy has creamy white stalks and dark green leaves and grows in a bunch like celery. Although usually associated with Asian stir-fries, bok choy can be steamed or sautéed and served as a side dish for other cuisines as well. Add strips of bok choy to soup during the last 5 minutes of cooking time, or toss a few slices of raw bok choy into salads for a nice crunch.

COOK'S TIP ON TOASTED SESAME OIL

Also known as fragrant toasted sesame oil or oriental sesame oil, this oil has a darker color and fuller flavor than the sesame oil stocked with cooking oils. Look instead in the Asian section for this nutty, fragrant oil, made from roasted sesame seeds. It has a low smoking point, so it is not meant for sautéing or browning foods. Add ½ teaspoon to a serving of chicken noodle soup or ½ cup cooked noodles or rice, stir 1 to 2 tablespoons into a heart-healthy meatball recipe, incorporate some into any Asian sauce or marinade, or add to a marinade for grilled pork, chicken, or beef. A little goes a long way, so you may want to buy just a small bottle. You can store it in the refrigerator for up to six months.

grilled turkey breast with fresh herb sauce

serves 4; 3 ounces turkey and about 2½ tablespoons sauce per serving

Fresh basil and parsley combine in a delectable sauce to top grilled turkey, as here, or fish.

Vegetable oil spray

1 pound boneless, skinless turkey breast, all visible fat removed, cut crosswise into 4 slices

herb sauce

1 cup chopped fresh basil, stems removed

¾ cup fresh parsley

3 to 4 tablespoons balsamic vinegar (white or regular)

2 medium green onions (green and white parts), chopped

1½ tablespoons dry white wine (regular or nonalcoholic)

1 tablespoon capers, rinsed and drained

1 tablespoon olive oil

¼ teaspoon salt

⅛ teaspoon white pepper

Lightly spray the grill rack with vegetable oil spray. Preheat the grill to medium-high.

Lightly spray the turkey slices with vegetable oil spray. Grill the turkey, covered if possible, for 16 to 20 minutes, or until the turkey is no longer pink in the center, turning once.

Meanwhile, in a food processor or blender, process the sauce ingredients until smooth, about 1 minute. Spoon the sauce over the turkey.

COOK'S TIP

Freeze any remaining sauce in an ice cube tray. Transfer the frozen cubes to a plastic freezer bag for storage. When you make soup or stew, pop out a cube and add it for some interesting flavor. Another way to enjoy leftover sauce is to add it to fat-free or low-fat cream cheese. Puree the mixture in a food processor or blender to create a zesty dip. Start with two parts sauce to one part cream cheese and adjust to suit your preferences.

Calories 188	Cholesterol 82 mg
Total Fat 4.5 g	Sodium 267 mg
Saturated 0.5 g	Carbohydrate 5 g
Polyunsaturated 0.5 g	Fiber 1 g
Monounsaturated 2.5 g	Protein 31 g

turkey meatballs
with mushroom gravy

serves 4; 4 meatballs and ¼ cup gravy per serving

So you can soak up the incredible mushroom gravy, serve these moist, flavor-packed meatballs over mashed potatoes or brown rice.

1 pound lean ground turkey breast, skin removed before grinding

½ cup chopped onion

¼ cup plain dry bread crumbs

¼ cup fresh parsley, snipped

½ teaspoon dried basil, crumbled

½ teaspoon dried oregano, crumbled

½ teaspoon salt

¼ teaspoon pepper

Vegetable oil spray

8 ounces fresh mushrooms, stems trimmed, caps thinly sliced

½ tablespoon dried thyme, crumbled

1 cup fat-free, no-salt-added beef broth, divided use

2 teaspoons cornstarch

In a large bowl, stir together the turkey, onion, bread crumbs, parsley, basil, oregano, salt, and pepper. Shape into 16 meatballs.

Heat a large nonstick skillet over medium-high heat. Remove from the heat and lightly spray with vegetable oil spray (being careful not to spray near a gas flame). Cook the meatballs for about 5 minutes, or until golden brown on all sides, turning frequently. Using tongs or a slotted spoon, transfer to a plate.

In the same skillet, cook the mushrooms and thyme for 3 minutes, or until the mushrooms release their liquid, stirring frequently.

Return the meatballs to the skillet. Pour in ¾ cup broth. Reduce the heat to medium; cook, covered, for 6 to 8 minutes, or until the meatballs are cooked through, turning once.

Put the cornstarch in a small bowl. Add the remaining ¼ cup broth, stirring to completely dissolve. Add to the skillet; stir well. Simmer for 1 minute, or until the sauce thickens to the consistency of gravy.

Calories 188	Cholesterol 77 mg
Total Fat 1.5 g	Sodium 423 mg
Saturated 0.5 g	Carbohydrate 11 g
Polyunsaturated 0.5 g	Fiber 2 g
Monounsaturated 0.5 g	Protein 31 g

turkey and okra gumbo

serves 6; 1 cup gumbo and ½ cup rice per serving

Many traditional Cajun and Creole dishes start with a roux, a flour and fat combination that is browned to add flavor and color. In our heart-healthy version, you brown the flour by itself, then mix it with chicken broth to produce the same effect. A real time and fat saver!

½ cup all-purpose flour

1 cup uncooked rice

1 pound lean ground turkey breast, skin removed before grinding

1 teaspoon acceptable vegetable oil

1½ cups chopped red, yellow, or green bell peppers, or any combination

1 medium onion, chopped

3 medium ribs of celery, diced

2 medium garlic cloves, minced, or 1 teaspoon bottled minced garlic

3 cups fat-free, low-sodium chicken broth

10-ounce package no-salt-added sliced okra or no-salt-added green beans

1 tablespoon no-salt-added Cajun/Creole seasoning

1 cup fat-free, low-sodium chicken broth

Put the flour in a nonstick Dutch oven or large nonstick saucepan over medium-high heat. Cook for 3 to 6 minutes, or until the flour turns a light, golden brown, stirring occasionally. Watch carefully; don't let the flour burn. Transfer the flour to a small bowl to cool. Wipe the Dutch oven with paper towels.

In a medium saucepan, cook the rice using the package directions, omitting the salt and margarine.

Meanwhile, heat the Dutch oven over medium-high heat. Cook the turkey for 7 to 8 minutes, or until no longer pink, stirring frequently. Remove the turkey. Wipe the Dutch oven with paper towels.

Heat the Dutch oven over medium heat. Pour the oil into the pot and swirl to coat the bottom. Cook the bell peppers, onion, celery, and garlic for 4 to 5 minutes, or until the vegetables are tender, stirring occasionally.

Calories 290	Cholesterol 51 mg
Total Fat 2.0 g	Sodium 290 mg
Saturated 0.5 g	Carbohydrate 42 g
Polyunsaturated 0.5 g	Fiber 3 g
Monounsaturated 0.5 g	Protein 24 g

Stir in the turkey, 3 cups broth, okra, and Cajun/Creole seasoning. Bring to a boil over high heat. Reduce the heat; simmer for 10 to 15 minutes, or until the flavors are blended, stirring occasionally.

Whisk 1 cup broth into the browned flour. Pour into the gumbo. Increase the heat to medium-high; cook until the mixture thickens, 1 to 2 minutes, stirring occasionally.

To serve, put about ½ cup cooked rice in each bowl. Top each serving with about 1 cup gumbo.

COOK'S TIP

Okra releases a rather sticky substance when it is cooked. Sometimes known as "roping," the substance helps thicken food, such as this gumbo. If you're planning to freeze the gumbo, substitute 2½ cups sliced fresh okra for the frozen okra, and add it with the bell peppers and onions. Refreezing frozen okra often yields mushy results.

COOK'S TIP ON CAJUN/CREOLE SEASONING

Many traditional Cajun and Creole recipes feature a zesty blend of herbs and spices. No-salt-added versions may be challenging to find, but it's easy to make your own. In a small bowl, combine 1 tablespoon each of chili powder, ground cumin, garlic powder, onion powder, and paprika with 2 teaspoons ground thyme, crumbled; 2 teaspoons ground oregano, crumbled; and ½ teaspoon pepper. Cover tightly and store at room temperature for up to six months.

turkey and vegetable pie

Different textures and flavors abound in this delicious dish, encased in flaky phyllo. Fruit sorbet makes an easy, very refreshing dessert.

Olive oil spray

12 ounces lean ground turkey breast, skin removed before grinding

2 teaspoons salt-free Italian seasoning, crumbled

1 teaspoon olive oil

½ medium onion, sliced

8 ounces fresh mushrooms, sliced

2 medium zucchini, shredded

1 medium yellow summer squash, diced

¼ cup roasted red bell pepper, rinsed and drained if bottled, chopped (see Cook's Tip on Grilling Vegetables, page 215)

½ teaspoon salt-free Italian seasoning, crumbled

1 medium garlic clove, minced, or ½ teaspoon bottled minced garlic

6 sheets frozen phyllo dough, thawed

Olive oil spray

½ cup fat-free or low-fat ricotta cheese

2 ounces fat-free or reduced-fat feta cheese, rinsed, drained, and crumbled

Preheat the oven to 375°F. Lightly spray a 9-inch glass pie pan with olive oil spray.

In a large nonstick skillet, cook the turkey and 2 teaspoons Italian seasoning over medium-high heat for 6 to 8 minutes, or until no longer pink, stirring occasionally to break into small pieces. Transfer to a plate. Set aside.

Reduce the heat to medium. Pour the olive oil into the skillet and swirl to coat the bottom. Cook the onion for 3 to 4 minutes, or until translucent, stirring occasionally. Stir in the mushrooms, zucchini, and summer squash. Cook for 3 to 4 minutes, or until tender, stirring occasionally. Stir in the bell pepper, ½ teaspoon Italian seasoning, and garlic. Cook for 1 to 2 minutes, or until the mixture is warmed through, stirring occasionally. Remove from the heat.

Calories 185	Cholesterol 40 mg
Total Fat 2.5 g	Sodium 317 mg
Saturated 0.5 g	Carbohydrate 18 g
Polyunsaturated 0.5 g	Fiber 3 g
Monounsaturated 1.5 g	Protein 22 g

Keeping the unused phyllo covered with a damp cloth or damp paper towels to prevent drying, place 1 phyllo sheet in the pie pan (the ends will overhang the pan). Lightly spray with vegetable oil spray. Crisscross the second phyllo sheet over the first sheet; lightly spray with vegetable oil spray. Repeat with the remaining sheets of phyllo, making a pie shell and covering the pie pan.

Drain any turkey juices that accumulated. Spread the turkey in the pie shell. Arrange the vegetable mixture on top. Spread the ricotta over the vegetables. Sprinkle with the feta. Fold the edges of the phyllo toward the center to cover the filling. Lightly spray the pie with vegetable oil spray.

Bake for 30 to 35 minutes, or until the filling is warm and the phyllo is golden brown. Cut into 6 wedges.

cornish game hens with plum glaze

serves 4; ½ hen and 2 tablespoons sauce per serving

You can cut the hens in half before roasting for ease in serving or roast the hens whole to save a few minutes of preparation time. Either way, the soy- and ginger-perfumed rub adds great flavor, and the plum-sauce glaze adds a sweet touch to the tender hens. Cornish game hens are a little high in cholesterol, so eat them only occasionally.

Vegetable oil spray

½ cup fat-free, low-sodium chicken broth

½ cup water

1 tablespoon low-salt soy sauce

1 tablespoon dry sherry or white wine vinegar

1 teaspoon minced peeled gingerroot

1 teaspoon toasted sesame oil

1 medium garlic clove, minced, or ½ teaspoon bottled minced garlic

2 Cornish game hens (about 14 ounces each), tails and giblets removed

2 teaspoons cornstarch

2 teaspoons water

2 tablespoons plum sauce

Preheat the oven to 350° F. Lightly spray a 13 × 9 × 2-inch baking pan with vegetable oil spray.

In a measuring cup, combine the chicken broth and ½ cup water. Set aside.

In a small bowl, stir together the soy sauce, sherry, gingerroot, sesame oil, and garlic.

If cutting the hens, using poultry shears or sturdy kitchen scissors, start on the back of a hen and cut down both sides of the backbone from one end to the other. Discard the backbone or use it to make stock. Carefully snip between the breasts, separating the hen into halves. Repeat with the other hen.

Gently loosen the skin from the meat on the breast and legs by breaking the membrane that holds the skin to the meat and sliding your fingers between the two halves. Try to not tear the skin. Carefully remove all visible

Calories 173	Cholesterol 109 mg
Total Fat 5.0 g	Sodium 220 mg
Saturated 1.0 g	Carbohydrate 5 g
Polyunsaturated 1.5 g	Fiber 0 g
Monounsaturated 1.5 g	Protein 25 g

fat. Spoon the soy mixture under the skin. Place the hen halves with the skin side up or place the whole hens with the breast side up in the prepared pan.

Bake halves for 50 to 60 minutes, whole hens for 60 to 70 minutes, basting every 10 to 15 minutes with the chicken broth mixture. Hens are done when a meat thermometer inserted between the thigh and breast registers 180°F or when the juice runs clear when the skin of a thigh is cut and the thickest part of the meat near the bone is no longer pink.

Transfer the hens to a platter and cover with aluminum foil to keep warm. Pour the pan juices into a measuring cup. Add water if necessary to measure ½ cup. Pour into a small saucepan. Skim off any fat on top with a spoon or gravy skimmer. Place over medium heat.

Put the cornstarch in a small bowl. Add the water, stirring to dissolve. Add the mixture and plum sauce to the pan juices. Bring to a simmer. Reducing the heat if necessary, simmer for 1 to 2 minutes, or until thickened, whisking occasionally.

Remove the skin from the hens. Place half a hen on each plate. Pour 2 tablespoons glaze over each serving.

COOK'S TIP ON MAKING BROTH

Create a "stock pile" by saving items that can be used for making broth or stock. Keep an airtight plastic bag in the freezer and fill it with chicken or beef bones and aromatic vegetable pieces, such as onion trimmings, carrot peels, and celery tops. When you're ready to make broth or stock, you have a head start.

COOK'S TIP ON PLUM SAUCE

Plum sauce is a sweet, jamlike sauce of plums, apricots, vinegar, and, sometimes, chile peppers. Find it in the Asian section of the grocery or in Asian markets. Try it as a dipping sauce with Crispy Baked Chicken Strips (page 115).

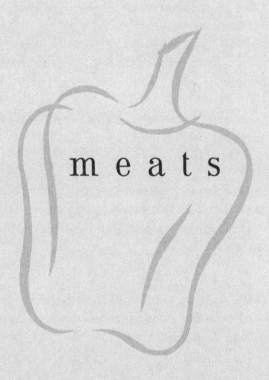

meats

Asian-Inspired Grilled
    Flank Steak

Beef and Broccoli Stir-Fry

Slow-Cooker Beef
    in Tarragon-Tomato Sauce

Beef and Mushroom Stir-Fry

Hungarian Goulash with
    Dumplings

Beef Stroganoff

Tex-Mex Beef Stew

Sirloin Cubes with Onion
    and Bell Pepper

Grilled Sirloin
    with Chimichurri Sauce

Sichuan Fillet
    with Colorful Vegetables

Royal Pot Roast with Gravy

Jaffle with Roast Beef
    and Spinach

Meat Loaf with Spaghetti Sauce

Pineapple Meatballs

Almost Tamales

Upside-Down Shepherd's Pie

Ground Beef, Shiitake Mushroom,
    and Barley Skillet Dinner

Moussaka

Italian Cabbage Rolls

Pork Kebabs with Orange Sauce

Pork Chops Stuffed with Fruit

Jerked Pork with Cranberry
    Apples

Sweet-and-Sour Pork Fried Rice

Ginger Pork and Crisp Shredded
    Vegetables

Spicy Pork and Onion Wraps

Ham-and-Swiss Stuffed
    Mushrooms

Tomatoes Farci

Buffaloaf

Veal Madeira

asian-inspired grilled flank steak

serves 4; 3 ounces steak per serving (plus 8 ounces reserved)

A zesty marinade of pineapple juice and fresh ginger imparts flavor to lean flank steak. Save and refrigerate about eight ounces of the cooked steak to use in Beef and Broccoli Stir-Fry (page 155) for a really easy entrée later in the week.

marinade

½ cup pineapple juice

¼ cup sliced green onions (green and white parts)

2 teaspoons minced peeled gingerroot

2 teaspoons low-salt soy sauce

2 medium garlic cloves, minced, or 1 teaspoon bottled minced garlic

¼ teaspoon pepper

❖ ❖ ❖

1½ to 1¾ pounds flank steak, all visible fat removed

Vegetable oil spray

In an airtight plastic bag or glass baking dish, combine the marinade ingredients. Add the meat and turn to coat. Seal and refrigerate for 1 to 12 hours, turning occasionally.

If using an outdoor grill, preheat on medium-high. If using a ridged stovetop grill pan, lightly spray with vegetable oil spray.

Remove the meat from the marinade; pat dry with paper towels. Discard the marinade.

Cook the steak indoors or outdoors over medium-high heat for 7 to 8 minutes on each side for medium-rare, or until the desired doneness. Let stand for 5 minutes on a cutting board before thinly slicing across the grain.

COOK'S TIP ON PINEAPPLE JUICE

Pineapple contains an enzyme called bromelain, which digests protein and is a natural tenderizer, especially for leaner cuts of meat. When a marinade recipe calls for an acid, such as lemon juice, substitute the same amount of pineapple juice for the same effect but a different taste.

Calories 153	Cholesterol 71 mg
Total Fat 4.0 g	Sodium 91 mg
Saturated 1.5 g	Carbohydrate 0 g
Polyunsaturated 0 g	Fiber 0 g
Monounsaturated 1.5 g	Protein 27 g

beef and broccoli stir-fry

Preparing this entrée is a snap using cooked flank steak left over from a previous meal—Asian-Inspired Grilled Flank Steak (page 154) is perfect. Serve this easy stir-fry over rice, broad rice noodles, or orzo.

8 ounces grilled flank steak, all visible fat removed

½ cup fat-free, no-salt-added beef broth

2 tablespoons dry sherry

2 tablespoons reduced-sodium teriyaki sauce

1 teaspoon minced peeled gingerroot

1 large garlic clove, minced, or ¾ teaspoon bottled minced garlic

¼ teaspoon pepper

2 teaspoons cornstarch

¼ cup cold water

1 tablespoon acceptable vegetable oil

8 ounces broccoli florets, cut into bite-size pieces

¼ cup sliced green onions (green and white parts)

8-ounce can whole or sliced water chestnuts, rinsed and drained

Thinly slice the steak on the diagonal; cut into bite-size pieces.

In a small bowl, combine the broth, sherry, teriyaki sauce, gingerroot, garlic, and pepper. Set aside.

Put the cornstarch in another small bowl. Add the water, stirring to dissolve.

Heat a wok or large nonstick skillet over medium heat. Pour the oil into the skillet and swirl to coat the bottom. Cook the broccoli and green onions for 3 minutes, or until the broccoli is crisp-tender, stirring frequently. Stir in the broth mixture, steak, and water chestnuts. Cook for 3 minutes, stirring occasionally.

Stir the cornstarch mixture; pour it into the wok. Cook for 1 minute, or until thickened, stirring frequently.

COOK'S TIP ON BROCCOLI FLORETS

Broccoli florets cook quickly and evenly, and there is no waste. Look for them loose or in packages in the produce department, or buy them from the supermarket's salad bar.

Calories 130	Cholesterol 28 mg
Total Fat 4.5 g	Sodium 172 mg
Saturated 1.0 g	Carbohydrate 9 g
Polyunsaturated 1.0 g	Fiber 2 g
Monounsaturated 2.5 g	Protein 13 g

slow-cooker beef in tarragon-tomato sauce

This simply scrumptious stew goes well with almost any cooked grain.

- **2 medium sweet onions (Vidalia preferred), chopped**
- **2 pounds top round steak or top round roast, all visible fat removed, cut into 1-inch pieces**
- **2 bay leaves**
- **½ teaspoon dried tarragon or herbes de Provence, crumbled**
- **½ teaspoon salt**
- **¼ teaspoon pepper**
- **1 cup fat-free, no-salt-added beef broth**
- **8-ounce can no-salt-added tomato sauce**
- **8 ounces fresh small mushrooms**
- **2 tablespoons cornstarch**
- **¼ cup cold water**

Put the onions in a slow cooker. Add the meat, bay leaves, tarragon, salt, and pepper. Stir in the broth and tomato sauce. Cook on low for 5 hours or on high for 2 hours.

Stir in the mushrooms. Cook on low for 3 hours or on high for 2½ to 3 hours, or until the meat is tender. Remove the bay leaves. Turn the slow cooker setting to high.

Put the cornstarch in a small bowl. Add the water, stirring to dissolve. Stir into the beef mixture. Cook, covered, for 15 to 20 minutes, or until the liquid is slightly thickened.

Calories 182	Cholesterol 65 mg
Total Fat 4.0 g	Sodium 221 mg
Saturated 1.5 g	Carbohydrate 8 g
Polyunsaturated 0 g	Fiber 1 g
Monounsaturated 1.5 g	Protein 28 g

beef and mushroom stir-fry

serves 4; 1½ cups per serving

The flavor of this simple stir-fry will hit your palate from all sides.

3.75-ounce package dried cellophane noodles (mung bean noodles)

2 teaspoons acceptable vegetable oil (peanut oil preferred)

⅛ to ¼ teaspoon crushed red pepper flakes, or to taste

2 tablespoons minced peeled gingerroot

1 pound boneless lean beef, such as round, sirloin, or flank steak, all visible fat removed, cut crosswise into thin strips

1 pound fresh mushrooms (wild preferred), stems discarded, thickly sliced

1½ cups fat-free, no-salt-added beef broth

1 tablespoon light tamari or low-salt soy sauce

2 cups fresh or frozen sugar snap peas (thawed if frozen) or fresh snow peas, trimmed

1 medium red bell pepper, cut into thin strips

2 medium green onions, sliced or chopped (green and white parts)

Put the noodles in a large bowl. Pour in enough hot water to cover. Let stand for 10 minutes; drain well. Cut into 2-inch pieces. Set aside.

Heat a wok or large nonstick skillet over medium-high heat. Pour the oil into the skillet and swirl to coat the bottom. Cook the pepper flakes and gingerroot for 1 minute. Add the beef and mushrooms. Cook for 3 minutes, or until the beef is browned all over and the mushrooms release their juices, stirring frequently.

Add the noodles, broth, and tamari sauce, stirring to coat. Stir in the peas and bell peppers. Reduce the heat to medium-low. Cook, covered, for 3 to 5 minutes, or until the beef is cooked through and the vegetables are crisptender. Remove from the heat. Stir in the green onions.

Calories 329	Cholesterol 65 mg
Total Fat 6.5 g	Sodium 251 mg
Saturated 2.0 g	Carbohydrate 35 g
Polyunsaturated 1.0 g	Fiber 4 g
Monounsaturated 2.5 g	Protein 32 g

hungarian goulash with dumplings

According to tradition, there is a certain etiquette to follow when making Hungarian goulash. One should not thicken the mixture with flour, caraway is the only spice to be used, using wine would "Frenchify" it, and a brown sauce might appeal to a German but not to a Hungarian, so no brown sauce. Tomatoes, green bell peppers, and hot peppers may be used at the cook's discretion.

> 1 teaspoon acceptable vegetable oil
>
> 2 pounds boneless round steak, all visible fat removed, cubed
>
> 1 medium onion
>
> 1 medium garlic clove or ½ teaspoon bottled minced garlic
>
> 6 cups water
>
> 1 cup fat-free, no-salt-added beef broth
>
> 2 tablespoons no-salt-added tomato paste
>
> 1 tablespoon paprika (Hungarian preferred)
>
> ½ teaspoon caraway seeds, crushed using a mortar and pestle
>
> 4 medium potatoes
>
> 1 medium green bell pepper

dumplings

> ½ cup all-purpose flour (plus more for rolling out dough)
>
> Egg substitute equivalent to 1 egg, or 1 large egg
>
> ⅛ teaspoon salt

Heat a Dutch oven over medium heat. Pour the oil into the pot and swirl to coat the bottom. Cook the meat for 8 to 10 minutes, or until browned, stirring occasionally.

Meanwhile, chop the onion and mince the garlic. When the meat has browned, add the onion and garlic to the pot; cook for 3 to 4 minutes, or until the onion is translucent, stirring occasionally. Stir in the water, broth, tomato paste, paprika, and caraway seeds. Increase the heat to high; bring the mix-

Calories 250	Cholesterol 65 mg
Total Fat 4.5 g	Sodium 130 mg
Saturated 1.5 g	Carbohydrate 23 g
Polyunsaturated 0.5 g	Fiber 3 g
Monounsaturated 2.0 g	Protein 31 g

ture to a boil. Reduce the heat and simmer, covered, for 1 hour. Shortly before the end of simmering time, peel and chop the potatoes and chop the bell pepper. Stir into the meat mixture; simmer, covered, for 30 minutes, or until the meat is very tender and the vegetables are tender.

Meanwhile, in a small bowl, stir together all the dumpling ingredients with a fork. Lightly flour a flat surface. Turn the dough onto the surface; knead for 1 minute. Cover the dough with a damp towel; let the dough rest for 10 minutes. Pinch off ½-inch pieces of dough and carefully drop them into the simmering stew. Cook over medium heat for 2 to 3 minutes, or until the dumplings are cooked through. They should be tender to the bite and uniformly colored if cut in half (the center should not have chalky-looking streaks).

beef stroganoff

This traditional favorite abounds with succulent mushrooms in a rich, creamy sauce.

1 pound boneless sirloin steak, all visible fat removed

1 teaspoon acceptable vegetable oil

8 ounces fresh mushrooms, sliced

1 medium onion, chopped

1 medium garlic clove, minced, or ½ teaspoon bottled minced garlic

3 ounces dried yolk-free noodles

2 tablespoons all-purpose flour

1¼ cups fat-free, no-salt-added beef broth

1 tablespoon no-salt-added tomato paste

¼ teaspoon salt

⅛ teaspoon pepper

⅛ teaspoon ground mace or nutmeg

¼ cup nonfat or light sour cream

2 tablespoons dry white wine (regular or nonalcoholic)

Thinly slice the beef against the grain. Heat a large skillet over medium-high heat. Pour the oil into the skillet and swirl to coat the bottom. Brown the beef for 6 to 8 minutes, stirring occasionally. Add the mushrooms, onion, and garlic. Reduce the heat to medium; cook for 3 minutes, or until the vegetables are tender, stirring occasionally.

Prepare the noodles using the package directions, omitting the salt and margarine.

Meanwhile, stir the flour into the beef mixture. Stir in the broth, tomato paste, salt, pepper, and mace. Increase the heat to medium-high. Bring the mixture to a simmer; simmer until thickened, 3 to 4 minutes, stirring occasionally. Reduce the heat to medium-low; cook for 5 minutes, stirring occasionally.

Stir some of the beef mixture into the sour cream (to prevent curdling); stir the sour cream mixture into the skillet. Reduce the heat to low. Stir in the wine. Cook for 2 minutes, stirring occasionally. Don't let the mixture boil.

To serve, spoon about ½ cup noodles onto each plate. Top each serving with about 1 cup beef mixture.

Calories 308	Cholesterol 69 mg
Total Fat 6.5 g	Sodium 265 mg
Saturated 2.0 g	Carbohydrate 28 g
Polyunsaturated 0.5 g	Fiber 2 g
Monounsaturated 2.5 g	Protein 32 g

tex-mex beef stew

Slow cookers are ideal for busy days, especially those cold, wintry ones.

1 pound top sirloin steak, all visible fat removed, cut into 1-inch pieces

12 ounces red potatoes, cut into 1-inch pieces

1 large green bell pepper, cut into 1-inch pieces

2 medium onions, quartered

⅓ cup water

1½ tablespoons steak sauce

2 teaspoons very low sodium beef bouillon granules

2 teaspoons chili powder

½ teaspoon sugar

¼ teaspoon ground cumin

½ teaspoon salt

¼ teaspoon ground cumin

2 tablespoons low-sodium ketchup

In a slow cooker, combine the steak, potatoes, bell peppers, onions, water, steak sauce, bouillon granules, chili powder, sugar, ¼ teaspoon cumin, and salt. Cook on high for 4 hours or on low for 8 hours.

Just before serving, stir in the remaining cumin and ketchup.

Calories 270	Cholesterol 69 mg
Total Fat 5.5 g	Sodium 411 mg
Saturated 2.0 g	Carbohydrate 30 g
Polyunsaturated 0.5 g	Fiber 5 g
Monounsaturated 2.0 g	Protein 28 g

sirloin cubes with onion and bell pepper

When you have a craving for beef, this sizzling skillet dish is the answer. Try it with corn on the cob and fresh fruit.

> 1 pound boneless top sirloin steak, all visible fat removed, cut into 1-inch cubes
>
> 2 teaspoons chili powder
>
> Vegetable oil spray
>
> 1 large onion, cut into eighths, layers separated
>
> 1 large green bell pepper, cut into 1-inch squares
>
> ¼ teaspoon salt

Put the meat in a large, shallow bowl or baking dish. Sprinkle with the chili powder; stir well. Let stand for 15 minutes.

Heat a large nonstick skillet over high heat until very hot. Remove the skillet from the heat; lightly spray with vegetable oil spray (being careful not to spray near a gas flame). Cook the meat for 2 minutes, or until browned, stirring constantly. Transfer to a medium bowl.

Reduce the heat to medium. Lightly spray the skillet again with vegetable oil spray. Cook the onion and bell pepper for 10 minutes, or until they are tender-crisp and the edges of the onion are richly browned, stirring frequently. Stir in the salt and the meat with any accumulated juices. Cook for 1 minute, or until the mixture is heated thoroughly and the meat is slightly pink in the center, stirring constantly.

COOK'S TIP

Using two utensils for stirring allows the ingredients to cook faster and more evenly.

Calories 181	Cholesterol 69 mg
Total Fat 5.5 g	Sodium 226 mg
Saturated 2.0 g	Carbohydrate 8 g
Polyunsaturated 0.5 g	Fiber 2 g
Monounsaturated 2.0 g	Protein 25 g

grilled sirloin with chimichurri sauce

serves 4; 3 ounces steak and ¼ cup sauce per serving

Chimichurri (*chimi* rhymes with "Jimmy"; *churri* rhymes with "hurry"), a tangy fresh herb sauce popular in Argentina, adds a refreshing taste to grilled meats, such as this sirloin. If you have any extra sauce, try it on toasted bread or puree it to use as salad dressing.

1 pound boneless top sirloin, all visible fat removed

1 tablespoon fresh lemon juice

½ teaspoon pepper

chimichurri sauce

½ cup finely chopped or snipped fresh parsley

½ cup finely chopped red onion

⅓ cup fat-free, low-sodium chicken broth

2 to 3 tablespoons red wine vinegar

2 tablespoons chopped fresh oregano

1 tablespoon olive oil

2 medium garlic cloves, minced, or 1 teaspoon bottled minced garlic

❖ ❖ ❖

½ medium red bell pepper, cut crosswise into ¼-inch slices

Cut the steak into four equal pieces. Put the steak, lemon juice, and pepper in an airtight plastic bag or glass baking dish and turn to coat. Seal and refrigerate while preparing the sauce or for up to 12 hours, turning occasionally.

Preheat the grill on medium-high.

In a medium bowl, stir together all the sauce ingredients except the bell pepper.

Remove the steak from the marinade. Discard the marinade. Grill the steak for 16 to 20 minutes for medium-rare to medium, or until the desired doneness, turning once.

To serve, spoon the sauce over the steak. Top each serving with the bell peppers.

Calories 213	Cholesterol 75 mg
Total Fat 9.5 g	Sodium 66 mg
Saturated 3.0 g	Carbohydrate 5 g
Polyunsaturated 0.5 g	Fiber 1 g
Monounsaturated 5.0 g	Protein 26 g

sichuan fillet with colorful vegetables

serves 4; 3 ounces beef and ¾ cup vegetables per serving

Sichuan, or Szechwan, pepper lends fragrance and a mildly spicy flavor to the marinade in this colorful dish, pictured on the cover. Serve with wedges of crisp Asian pears on the side.

marinade

- 1 tablespoon hoisin sauce
- 2 teaspoons low-salt soy sauce
- 1 teaspoon toasted sesame oil
- ½ teaspoon ground Sichuan pepper or ½ teaspoon crushed red pepper flakes

- 1 pound beef tenderloin, all visible fat removed
- 1 teaspoon acceptable vegetable oil
- 3.3-ounce package fresh shiitake mushrooms, stems removed and caps sliced
- 2 medium garlic cloves, minced, or 1 teaspoon bottled minced garlic
- 1 cup shredded red cabbage
- 1 cup shredded carrot
- 1 cup fresh or frozen no-salt-added sugar snap peas (thawed if frozen)
- ½ medium yellow bell pepper, thinly sliced
- 2 tablespoons fat-free, low-sodium chicken broth
- Vegetable oil spray

In an airtight plastic bag or glass baking dish, combine the marinade ingredients.

Slice the beef crosswise into four pieces. Add the meat to the marinade and turn to coat. Seal and refrigerate while preparing the vegetable mixture or for up to 12 hours, turning occasionally.

Heat a wok or large nonstick skillet over medium-high heat. Pour the oil into the pan and swirl to coat the bottom. Cook the mushrooms and garlic for

Calories 237	Cholesterol 71 mg
Total Fat 9.5 g	Sodium 157 mg
Saturated 3.0 g	Carbohydrate 10 g
Polyunsaturated 0.5 g	Fiber 3 g
Monounsaturated 4.0 g	Protein 26 g

1 to 2 minutes, or until the mushrooms are tender, stirring occasionally. Add the remaining ingredients except the vegetable oil spray; cook for 2 to 3 minutes, or until the vegetables are tender-crisp, stirring occasionally. Reduce the heat to low and keep the vegetables warm (no need to cover).

Lightly spray the grill rack or the broiler pan and rack with vegetable oil spray. Preheat the grill on medium-high or preheat the broiler.

Drain the meat. Discard the marinade. Grill or broil 5 to 6 inches from the heat for 10 to 15 minutes, or until desired doneness, turning once. Watch the steaks carefully; the sugar from the hoisin sauce may cause the outside to burn if the temperature is too high and the steaks are cooked too long.

To serve, mound ¾ cup vegetables on each plate. Top each mound with steak.

royal pot roast
with gravy

serves 12; 3 ounces meat plus about ¼ cup gravy per serving

Don't wait for a special occasion to serve this mouthwatering pot roast. The preparation is simple, the taste is succulent, and the leftovers (if there are any) are superb. If you're not a big fan of anchovies, you *can* leave them out. However, the flavor they impart to this dish is tremendous—and not "fishy"—so why not give them a try?

Vegetable oil spray
1 tablespoon acceptable vegetable oil
3-pound rump roast, all visible fat removed
½ cup chopped onion
3 flat anchovy fillets, rinsed, or ½ teaspoon anchovy paste (optional)
2 cups fat-free, no-salt-added beef broth
12 ounces beer (regular or nonalcoholic)
2 tablespoons vinegar
1 teaspoon juniper berries, crushed
1 bay leaf
⅛ teaspoon pepper
1 tablespoon cornstarch
3 tablespoons water

Preheat the oven to 325° F.

Heat a Dutch oven over medium heat. Remove from the heat and lightly spray with vegetable oil spray (being careful not to spray near a gas flame). Pour the oil into the pot and swirl to coat the bottom. Cook the roast for 5 minutes on each side, or until brown. Remove from the pot. Set aside.

Lightly spray the pot with vegetable oil spray. Cook the onion for 3 to 4 minutes, or until translucent, stirring occasionally.

Rinse the anchovies and pat dry with paper towels. Add the anchovies to the onion. Stir in the broth, beer, vinegar, juniper berries, bay leaf, and pepper. Return the roast to the pot.

Calories 184	Cholesterol 71 mg
Total Fat 5.5 g	Sodium 102 mg
Saturated 1.5 g	Carbohydrate 2 g
Polyunsaturated 0.5 g	Fiber 0 g
Monounsaturated 2.5 g	Protein 28 g

Bake, covered, for about 3 hours, or until the roast is tender. Check the roast once every hour, adding water as needed, ½ cup at a time, to keep 1 to 1¼ cups liquid in the pot.

Place the roast on a warm plate, covering the roast loosely with aluminum foil. Measure the remaining liquid, adding water if needed for 1¼ cups. Return the liquid to the pot; bring to a simmer over medium-high heat. Remove the bay leaf.

Put the cornstarch in a small bowl. Add 3 tablespoons water, stirring to dissolve. Stir into the meat liquid. Increase the heat to medium-high; cook for 2 to 3 minutes, or until the mixture comes to a boil and thickens, stirring occasionally.

Slice the roast and serve with the gravy on top or on the side.

COOK'S TIP ON CORNSTARCH

To prevent clumping (and lumpy gravy), be sure the cornstarch is completely dissolved before adding it to a hot liquid.

jaffle with roast beef and spinach

serves 4; 1 sandwich per serving

Jaffles, grilled sandwiches from Australia, are traditionally made with a jaffle iron, which looks like a waffle iron with two handles. If you don't happen to have a jaffle iron, no worries, mate! For our heart-healthy jaffle, we use a nonstick griddle, dinner plates, and light weights to get the traditional compact, pressed texture. You can also use an electric sandwich maker.

1 tablespoon plus 1 teaspoon light tub or stick margarine

8 slices light honey whole-wheat bread

2 ounces goat cheese, softened

1 tablespoon plus 1 teaspoon snipped fresh chives or finely chopped green onions (green part only)

8 yellow or red teardrop or cherry tomatoes, thinly sliced

4 slices Royal Pot Roast (about 4 ounces) (page 166) or 4 ounces home-roasted low-fat, low-sodium beef or turkey

1 cup baby spinach leaves

Vegetable oil spray

Spread ½ teaspoon margarine on each slice of bread. Place 4 slices of bread with the spread side down on a cutting board.

Spread 1 tablespoon goat cheese on each of those 4 slices of bread. Top each slice with chives, tomato, beef, and spinach leaves. Top with the remaining bread with the spread side up.

Preheat a nonstick griddle over medium heat. Lightly spray the bottoms of four medium-size, heatproof plates with vegetable oil spray.

Place the sandwiches on the griddle; cook for 1 to 2 minutes, or until browned. Turn the sandwiches over. Put a plate with the bottom side down on each sandwich. Put a weight (a can of soup works well) on each plate; cook for 1 to 2 minutes, or until the bread is browned. Serve warm, or cover and refrigerate until needed and serve chilled.

Calories 208	Cholesterol 35 mg
Total Fat 8.0 g	Sodium 385 mg
Saturated 3.5 g	Carbohydrate 20 g
Polyunsaturated 0.5 g	Fiber 8 g
Monounsaturated 2.5 g	Protein 17 g

meat loaf with spaghetti sauce

serves 5; 2 slices per serving

Spaghetti sauce keeps this meat loaf moist, inside and out.

Vegetable oil spray
1 pound lean ground beef
1 cup fat-free meatless spaghetti sauce
½ to ¾ **cup finely chopped green bell pepper**
½ **cup finely chopped onion**
½ **cup snipped fresh parsley (Italian, or flat-leaf, preferred)**
½ **cup uncooked rolled oats**
Whites of 2 large eggs
2 tablespoons dried basil or 1 tablespoon dried basil and 1 tablespoon dried oregano, crumbled
2 medium garlic cloves, minced, or 1 teaspoon bottled minced garlic
¼ **teaspoon salt**
¼ **teaspoon crushed red pepper flakes, or to taste**
½ **cup fat-free meatless spaghetti sauce**

Preheat the oven to 350°F. Lightly spray a broiler pan and rack or a roasting pan and baking rack with vegetable oil spray.

In a baking dish, combine all the ingredients except ½ cup spaghetti sauce. Shape into a 7 × 5 × 2-inch oval loaf. Carefully slide the meat loaf onto the rack in the pan. Spread the remaining spaghetti sauce over the top and sides of the meat loaf.

Bake for 1 hour, or until the meat loaf is no longer pink in the center. For easier handling, let stand for 5 minutes before slicing.

Calories 242	Cholesterol 52 mg
Total Fat 10.0 g	Sodium 443 mg
Saturated 3.5 g	Carbohydrate 15 g
Polyunsaturated 0.5 g	Fiber 3 g
Monounsaturated 3.5 g	Protein 22 g

pineapple meatballs

To be prepared for a hectic day, cook a double batch of these sweet-and-sour meatballs and freeze half. All you'll have to do is heat the extras and make the fast sauce.

sauce

8-ounce can pineapple tidbits in their own juice

3 tablespoons low-salt soy sauce

2 tablespoons sugar

2 tablespoons cider vinegar

2 teaspoons cornstarch

meatballs

1 pound lean ground beef

¾ cup finely chopped green bell pepper

½ cup uncooked rolled oats or quick-cooking oatmeal

Whites of 2 large eggs

1 tablespoon low-sodium Worcestershire sauce

¾ teaspoon crushed red pepper flakes

½ teaspoon ground nutmeg

¼ teaspoon salt

Vegetable oil spray

In a small bowl, combine all the sauce ingredients, stirring until the cornstarch has completely dissolved. Set aside.

In a medium bowl, combine meatball ingredients. Shape into 40 balls.

Heat a large nonstick skillet over medium-high heat until very hot. Remove from the heat and lightly spray with vegetable oil spray (being careful not to spray near a gas flame). Cook the meatballs for 10 minutes, or until lightly browned on all sides, turning constantly. (Using two spoons works well.) Drain well on paper towels. Wipe the skillet with paper towels. Return the meatballs to the skillet.

Stir the sauce. Spoon over the meatballs. Increase the heat to high; cook for 3 minutes, or until thickened, stirring constantly with a rubber scraper.

Calories 263	Cholesterol 52 mg
Total Fat 10.0 g	Sodium 447 mg
Saturated 3.5 g	Carbohydrate 21 g
Polyunsaturated 0.5 g	Fiber 2 g
Monounsaturated 3.5 g	Protein 21 g

almost tamales

Making tamales is a cherished, but time-consuming, tradition in Mexico. This tamale-inspired dish, however, is quick to fix.

- 1 pound lean ground beef
- 15-ounce can no-salt-added whole-kernel corn, drained
- 1 cup water
- 8-ounce can no-salt-added tomato sauce
- ¼ cup diced canned green chiles, rinsed and drained
- 1 teaspoon chili powder
- 1 teaspoon ground cumin
- ½ teaspoon onion powder
- ½ teaspoon garlic powder
- ¼ teaspoon salt
- 2 ounces dried vermicelli, broken into 2-inch pieces
- 2 tablespoons masa harina (optional)
- ½ cup shredded fat-free or reduced-fat Cheddar or Monterey Jack cheese, or a combination
- ¼ cup nonfat or light sour cream
- 8 cherry tomatoes, halved (optional)

In a large nonstick skillet, cook the beef over medium-high heat for 7 to 8 minutes, or until browned, stirring occasionally. Pour the beef into a colander and rinse under hot water to remove excess fat. Drain well. Wipe the skillet with paper towels. Return the beef to the skillet.

Stir in the corn, water, tomato sauce, chiles, chili powder, cumin, onion powder, garlic powder, and salt. Bring to a simmer. Stir in the vermicelli and masa harina; cook for 8 minutes, or until the pasta is tender, stirring occasionally.

To serve, spoon about 1 cup mixture onto each plate. Top each serving with cheese, sour cream, and cherry tomato halves.

COOK'S TIP ON MASA HARINA

Look for masa harina, flour made from corn kernels cooked in lime water, near the flour and cornmeal at the supermarket. In this dish, it helps thicken the mixture and gives a touch of tamale taste.

Calories 328	Cholesterol 53 mg
Total Fat 5.0 g	Sodium 407 mg
Saturated 1.5 g	Carbohydrate 40 g
Polyunsaturated 0.5 g	Fiber 4 g
Monounsaturated 2.0 g	Protein 31 g

upside-down
shepherd's pie

serves 4; 1½ cups per serving

You won't need the oven or the broiler for this "cheeseburger pie."

1½ pounds baking potatoes, such as russet, cut into ½-inch cubes
   Vegetable oil spray
1 pound lean ground beef
1 cup chopped onion
½ cup water
2 teaspoons very low sodium beef bouillon granules
1 tablespoon chili powder
¼ teaspoon cayenne (optional)
½ cup fat-free evaporated milk
¼ teaspoon garlic powder
¼ teaspoon salt
¾ cup shredded reduced-fat sharp Cheddar cheese

Set a steamer basket in a small amount of simmering water in a medium saucepan. Put the potatoes in the basket. Cook, covered, for about 10 minutes, or until tender. Drain well. Return the potatoes to the empty pan.

Meanwhile, heat a large nonstick skillet over high heat. Remove from the heat and lightly spray with vegetable oil spray (being careful not to spray near a gas flame). Cook the beef for 3 minutes, or until no longer pink, stirring constantly. Pour into a colander and rinse under hot water to remove excess fat. Drain well. Wipe the skillet with paper towels.

Reduce the heat to medium. Cook the onion for 3 to 4 minutes, or until translucent, stirring occasionally. Increase the heat to medium-high. Add the water, bouillon granules, chili powder, cayenne, and ground beef. Cook for 2 to 5 minutes, or until most of the liquid has evaporated.

Using an electric mixer, beat the potatoes on low for 1 minute. Add the milk, garlic powder, and salt. Beat until smooth. Spread in a 12 × 8 × 2-inch baking dish. Spoon the meat mixture over the potatoes; top with the cheese. Cover with aluminum foil; let stand for 3 minutes to let cheese melt slightly.

Calories 351	Cholesterol 65 mg
Total Fat 8.0 g	Sodium 389 mg
Saturated 4.0 g	Carbohydrate 40 g
Polyunsaturated 0.5 g	Fiber 5 g
Monounsaturated 2.5 g	Protein 34 g

ground beef, shiitake mushroom, and barley skillet dinner

serves 4; 1½ cups per serving

Dried shiitake mushrooms add a touch of the exotic to this all-in-one meal.

- ½ ounce dried shiitake mushrooms
- 1¼ cups warm water
- 1 teaspoon acceptable vegetable oil
- 1 small onion, chopped
- 2 medium garlic cloves, minced, or 1 teaspoon bottled minced garlic
- 8 ounces lean ground beef
- 8 ounces button mushrooms, thickly sliced
- 1¼ cups uncooked medium pearl (pearled) barley
- 2 cups low-sodium mixed-vegetable juice
- 14.5-ounce can no-salt-added stewed tomatoes, undrained
- 1 teaspoon dried oregano, crumbled
- 1 teaspoon dried basil, crumbled

Put the mushrooms in a small bowl. Add the water; let soak for 20 to 30 minutes, or until softened. Drain, retaining the soaking liquid. Coarsely chop the mushrooms. Strain the soaking liquid through a coffee filter into a small bowl.

Heat a large nonstick skillet over medium heat. Pour the oil into the skillet and swirl to coat the bottom. Cook the onion and garlic for 3 to 4 minutes, or until the onion is translucent, stirring occasionally.

Add the beef, breaking it into small pieces with a spoon. Cook for 3 to 4 minutes, or until it browns, stirring frequently. Pour into a colander and rinse under hot water to remove excess fat. Drain well. Return the beef to the skillet.

Stir in the mushrooms; cook for 1 minute. Stir in the barley; cook for 2 minutes, stirring frequently. Stir in the reserved mushroom liquid, vegetable juice, undrained tomatoes, oregano, and basil. Bring to a boil over high heat. Reduce the heat to low; cook, covered, for 45 to 50 minutes, or until the barley is tender (no stirring needed).

Calories 391	Cholesterol 26 mg
Total Fat 4.0 g	Sodium 115 mg
Saturated 1.0 g	Carbohydrate 68 g
Polyunsaturated 1.0 g	Fiber 14 g
Monounsaturated 1.5 g	Protein 21 g

moussaka

Bring a hint of Greece to your table with this layered eggplant casserole. It provides a good balance of vegetable, meat, and dairy products, plus a lot of flavor.

Vegetable oil spray

2 medium eggplants, peeled and cut crosswise into ½-inch slices (about 3 pounds)

1 pound lean ground beef

1 medium onion, chopped

¼ cup snipped fresh parsley

¼ cup dry red wine (regular or nonalcoholic)

1 tablespoon no-salt-added tomato paste

1 teaspoon dried oregano, crumbled

¼ to ½ teaspoon crushed red pepper flakes

¼ teaspoon ground cinnamon

⅛ teaspoon black pepper

1 tablespoon acceptable vegetable oil

2 tablespoons all-purpose flour

2 cups fat-free milk

1 cup fat-free or low-fat cottage cheese

Egg substitute equivalent to 2 eggs, or 2 large eggs

¾ cup plain dry bread crumbs

¼ cup shredded or grated Parmesan cheese

Heat a large nonstick skillet over medium heat. Remove the skillet from the heat and lightly spray with vegetable oil spray (being careful not to spray near a gas flame). Cook the eggplants for 4 to 6 minutes, or until lightly browned on both sides, turning once. (You may have to do this in batches.) Remove from the heat. Set aside.

Increase the heat to medium-high. In the same skillet, cook the beef and onion for 5 to 6 minutes, or until the meat is no longer pink, stirring occasionally. Pour into a colander and rinse under hot water to remove excess fat. Drain well. Wipe the skillet clean with paper towels. Return the beef mixture to the skillet.

Calories 245	Cholesterol 32 mg
Total Fat 5.5 g	Sodium 332 mg
Saturated 1.5 g	Carbohydrate 25 g
Polyunsaturated 1.0 g	Fiber 5 g
Monounsaturated 2.5 g	Protein 22 g

Add the parsley, wine, tomato paste, oregano, red pepper flakes, cinnamon, and black pepper to the beef mixture. Reduce the heat to medium-low; cook for 5 minutes. Set aside.

Heat a medium saucepan over low heat. Pour the oil into the saucepan and swirl to coat the bottom. Whisk in the flour; cook for 30 seconds. Whisk in the milk. Increase the heat to medium-high; cook for 5 to 8 minutes, or until the mixture thickens, whisking occasionally. Let cool for 5 minutes.

Meanwhile, preheat the oven to 375°F. Lightly spray a 13 × 9 × 2-inch baking pan with vegetable oil spray.

Stir the cottage cheese and egg substitute into the meat mixture.

To assemble, lightly sprinkle the bottom of the baking pan with bread crumbs. Place one-third of the eggplant slices in a layer on the bread crumbs. Spread half the meat mixture over the eggplant. Sprinkle half the bread crumbs and half the cheese over the meat. Repeat the layers, ending with a layer of eggplant. Pour the milk mixture over all.

Bake for 1 hour, or until the casserole is set (doesn't jiggle when gently shaken) and a knife inserted in the center comes out clean. Let cool for 15 to 20 minutes before cutting into squares.

COOK'S TIP ON TOMATO PASTE

What do you do when you need only a small amount of tomato paste and don't want to waste what remains in the can? Freeze the rest in tablespoon-size mounds on wax paper or in the compartments of an ice tray. Store the cubes in an airtight plastic bag for up to four months. Whenever you need another tablespoon or two, just reach into your freezer.

When buying tomato paste, check the ingredients. Some tomato paste has no salt added, even though the label doesn't tout that benefit.

italian cabbage rolls

Tuck well-seasoned ground beef and rice into softened cabbage leaves, then top with spaghetti sauce for an Italian twist.

12 cups water
8 large cabbage leaves
Vegetable oil spray
8 ounces lean ground beef
1 cup finely chopped green bell peppers
½ cup finely chopped onion (yellow preferred)
1½ tablespoons dried basil, crumbled
1 teaspoon salt-free Italian seasoning
2 medium garlic cloves, minced, or 1 teaspoon bottled minced garlic
¼ teaspoon crushed red pepper flakes (optional)
½ cup uncooked white rice
1 cup fat-free meatless spaghetti sauce
¾ cup water
½ tablespoon dried basil, crumbled
½ tablespoon red wine vinegar
½ teaspoon sugar

Pour 12 cups water into a Dutch oven or stockpot. Bring to a boil, covered, over high heat. Cook the cabbage for 1 minute, or until limp. Drain well and pat dry with paper towels.

Meanwhile, heat a large nonstick skillet over high heat. Remove from the heat and lightly spray with vegetable oil spray (being careful not to spray near a gas flame). Cook the beef for 2 to 3 minutes, or until no longer pink, stirring constantly and breaking the beef into small pieces. Pour into a colander and rinse under hot water to remove excess fat. Drain well. Wipe the skillet with paper towels.

Reheat the skillet over medium-high heat. Remove from the heat and lightly spray with vegetable oil spray (being careful not to spray near a gas flame). Cook the bell peppers, onion, 1½ tablespoons basil, Italian seasoning, garlic,

Calories 211	Cholesterol 26 mg
Total Fat 2.5 g	Sodium 233 mg
Saturated 1.0 g	Carbohydrate 33 g
Polyunsaturated 0.5 g	Fiber 4 g
Monounsaturated 1.0 g	Protein 15 g

and red pepper flakes for 5 minutes, or until the onion is translucent, stirring frequently. Remove from the heat; stir in the rice and beef.

Spoon ⅓ cup meat mixture down the center of each cabbage leaf. Roll up each leaf lengthwise, tucking in the sides while rolling. Place the cabbage rolls with the seam side down in the skillet.

In a small bowl, stir together the remaining ingredients. Pour over the cabbage rolls. Bring to a boil over high heat. Reduce the heat and simmer, covered, for 25 to 30 minutes, or until the rice is tender (no stirring needed). Before serving the cabbage rolls, spoon the sauce from the skillet over them.

pork kebabs
with orange sauce

serves 4; 1 skewer per serving

A sweet orange glaze and a hint of curry provide a break from the barbecue routine.

Vegetable oil spray
12 ounces pork tenderloin, cut into 16 cubes
½ medium red bell pepper, cut into 16 pieces
1 medium onion, cut into eighths and layers separated (32 pieces)
½ cup all-fruit orange marmalade
2 tablespoons cider vinegar
1½ tablespoons low-salt soy sauce
1 teaspoon curry powder
¼ teaspoon crushed red pepper flakes

Lightly spray four 12-inch metal or bamboo skewers with vegetable oil spray. (If using bamboo skewers, first soak them for at least 10 minutes in cold water to keep them from charring.) Preheat the broiler. Lightly spray a broiler pan and rack with vegetable oil spray.

Alternating 1 cube of pork, 1 piece of bell pepper, and 2 pieces of onion, thread the pork and vegetables on the skewers. Place on the broiler rack.

In a small saucepan, whisk together the remaining ingredients. Bring to a boil over high heat; boil for 3 minutes, or until the sauce has reduced to ½ cup. Transfer half the sauce to a cup or small bowl.

Meanwhile, broil the kebabs 4 to 6 inches from the heat for 5 minutes. Turn the kebabs over; brush with the sauce remaining in the saucepan. Broil for 3 minutes, or until the pork is no longer pink in the center.

To serve, spoon the reserved sauce over the kebabs.

COOK'S TIP

Why divide the sauce in half? To protect against harmful bacteria. You don't want to dip your basting brush into the sauce, wipe it across partially cooked pork, then dip it back into the sauce.

Calories 210	Cholesterol 55 mg
Total Fat 3.0 g	Sodium 191 mg
Saturated 1.0 g	Carbohydrate 26 g
Polyunsaturated 0.5 g	Fiber 3 g
Monounsaturated 1.5 g	Protein 19 g

pork chops stuffed with fruit

Pork combined with prunes, apples, and onions adds flair to your weekly meals and also elicits enthusiastic compliments from guests.

1 medium Granny Smith apple, peeled, cored, and chopped

½ cup coarsely chopped pitted prunes

6 lean, boneless pork loin chops (about 4 ounces each), ¾ inch thick, all visible fat removed

1 teaspoon acceptable vegetable oil

Vegetable oil spray (optional)

1 medium onion, finely chopped

1 cup cold water

¼ cup unsweetened apple juice or Sauterne

¼ teaspoon salt

⅛ teaspoon pepper

In a small bowl, combine the apple and prunes. Set aside.

With a sharp knife, make a horizontal cut into the side of each pork chop to form a pocket for stuffing. Stuff with the apple mixture; secure each opening with a wooden toothpick.

Heat a large nonstick skillet over medium-high heat. Pour the oil into the skillet and swirl to coat the bottom. Cook the pork chops for 3 minutes; remove the skillet from the heat and lightly spray the top of the pork chops with the vegetable oil spray. Turn and cook for 3 minutes, or until browned. Stir in the onion; cook for 1 minute, stirring occasionally. Stir in the remaining ingredients. Reduce the heat to low; cook, covered, for 40 minutes, or until the pork chops are no longer pink in the center. Transfer the pork chops to a serving platter.

Increase the heat to medium-high; reduce the pan juices for 1 to 2 minutes, or until slightly thickened. Pour over the pork chops.

COOK'S TIP

Spraying the pork chops with vegetable oil spray will help them brown when they are turned over.

Calories 223	Cholesterol 62 mg
Total Fat 7.0 g	Sodium 151 mg
Saturated 2.0 g	Carbohydrate 15 g
Polyunsaturated 1.0 g	Fiber 2 g
Monounsaturated 3.0 g	Protein 25 g

jerked pork
with cranberry apples

serves 4; 3 ounces pork and ½ apple per serving

Bake sweet cranberry apples alongside this simple, spicy pork tenderloin for a winter-holiday feast. It's as easy to prepare two tenderloins as to prepare one, so why not make extra and have Spicy Pork and Onion Wraps (page 186) later this week?

Vegetable oil spray (optional)

jerked pork

½ **teaspoon ground cinnamon**
½ **teaspoon ground allspice**
¼ to ½ **teaspoon cayenne**
¼ **teaspoon ground nutmeg**
1-**pound pork tenderloin, all visible fat removed**

cranberry apples

2 8-**ounce tart baking apples, such as Granny Smith, halved crosswise and cored**
¼ **cup dried cranberries**
1 **tablespoon fresh orange juice**
1 **tablespoon sugar**
1 **teaspoon grated orange zest**
1 **teaspoon vanilla extract**

Preheat the oven to 425° F. Heavily spray a broiler pan with vegetable oil spray or line the pan with aluminum foil and spray heavily.

In a small bowl, stir together the cinnamon, allspice, cayenne, and nutmeg. Rub the mixture evenly over the pork. Let stand for 15 minutes. Put the pork in the broiler pan (without a rack), tucking any thin ends of the pork under so it will cook evenly. Arrange the apple halves with cut side up around the pork.

Calories 220	Cholesterol 74 mg
Total Fat 4.0 g	Sodium 57 mg
Saturated 1.5 g	Carbohydrate 20 g
Polyunsaturated 0.5 g	Fiber 3 g
Monounsaturated 2.0 g	Protein 24 g

In the same small bowl, stir together the remaining ingredients. Spoon onto each apple half, mounding slightly. Lightly spray apples and cranberry mixture with vegetable oil spray.

Bake for 25 minutes, or until the internal temperature of the pork registers 155° F on a meat thermometer. (The meat should have a hint of pink. It will continue to cook for a few minutes after you remove it from the oven.) Transfer the pork to a cutting board and let stand for 5 minutes.

To serve, slice the pork and place it on a serving platter. Arrange the apples around the pork.

sweet-and-sour
pork fried rice

Will dinner be sweet-and-sour pork or pork fried rice tonight? With this dish, you don't have to choose—it's two favorites in one.

1 tablespoon low-salt soy sauce

1 tablespoon dry sherry or plain rice vinegar

1 teaspoon cornstarch

1 pound pork tenderloin, all visible fat removed

½ cup fat-free, low-sodium chicken broth

½ cup apricot all-fruit spread

2 tablespoons white wine vinegar or plain rice vinegar

1 tablespoon low-salt soy sauce

8-ounce can sliced water chestnuts

4 medium green onions

Vegetable oil spray

Egg substitute equivalent to 2 eggs, or 2 large eggs

1 teaspoon acceptable vegetable oil

2 to 3 teaspoons crushed red pepper flakes

½ medium green bell pepper, cut into ¾-inch cubes

1 medium carrot, shredded

2 medium ribs of bok choy (stalks and leaves), sliced

3 cups cooked white or brown rice (chilled preferred)

8-ounce can pineapple chunks in their own juice, drained

In an airtight plastic bag or glass baking dish, combine the soy sauce, sherry, and cornstarch.

Cut the pork into ¾-inch cubes. Add the pork to the marinade and turn to coat. Seal and refrigerate for 10 minutes to 8 hours, turning occasionally.

Meanwhile, in a small bowl, whisk together the broth, all-fruit spread, 2 tablespoons white wine vinegar, and soy sauce. Set aside.

Calories 469	Cholesterol 74 mg
Total Fat 5.5 g	Sodium 356 mg
Saturated 1.5 g	Carbohydrate 69 g
Polyunsaturated 1.0 g	Fiber 5 g
Monounsaturated 2.5 g	Protein 32 g

Rinse and drain the water chestnuts. Slice the green onions (green and white parts).

Heat a wok or large nonstick skillet over medium-high heat. Remove from the heat and lightly spray with vegetable oil spray (being careful not to spray near a gas flame). Add the egg substitute; swirl to distribute evenly over the bottom. Cook until set, 1 to 2 minutes. Using a spoon, break the egg "pancake" into small pieces. Transfer the pieces to a plate. Wipe the skillet with paper towels.

Pour the vegetable oil into the wok and swirl to coat the bottom. Add the red pepper flakes and pork with marinade. Cook for 5 minutes, stirring occasionally.

Stir in the bell pepper and carrot. Cook for 2 to 3 minutes, or until the vegetables are tender-crisp, stirring occasionally. Stir in the bok choy. Cook for 1 minute, or until the stems are just tender-crisp and the greens are slightly wilted, stirring occasionally. Stir in the water chestnuts and green onions; cook for 2 to 3 minutes, or until warmed through.

Stir in the rice, pineapple, reserved broth mixture, and reserved egg pieces. Reduce the heat to medium; cook for 3 to 5 minutes, or until the mixture is warmed through, stirring occasionally.

ginger pork and crisp shredded vegetables

Gingerroot has a spicy-lemony aroma and flavor that enhance these stir-fried pork strips. A favorite in Japan, the strips traditionally are shaved wafer-thin.

4 boneless pork loin chops (about 4 ounces each) or 1 pound pork tenderloin (partially frozen if possible)

marinade

3 tablespoons low-salt soy sauce

3 tablespoons dry sherry or 2 tablespoons white wine vinegar

2 teaspoons sugar

1 teaspoon minced peeled gingerroot

½ cup uncooked rice

1 cup shredded red cabbage and 1 cup shredded carrots, or 2 cups packaged broccoli slaw mix

1 teaspoon acceptable vegetable oil

2 medium green onions (green and white parts), thinly sliced

Trim all visible fat from the pork. Cut the pork into strips about 2 inches long. Cut into lengthwise strips as thin as possible (easier if pork is partially frozen). Put the pork in an airtight plastic bag or glass baking dish. Add the marinade ingredients. Seal the bag and turn to coat. Refrigerate for 15 minutes to 8 hours, turning occasionally.

Prepare the rice using the package directions, omitting the salt and margarine.

Meanwhile, place the red cabbage and carrots side by side on each dinner plate.

Heat a nonstick wok or large nonstick skillet over medium-high heat. Pour the oil into the wok and swirl to coat the bottom. Cook the pork and marinade

Calories 296	Cholesterol 62 mg
Total Fat 7.5 g	Sodium 358 mg
Saturated 2.0 g	Carbohydrate 26 g
Polyunsaturated 1.0 g	Fiber 2 g
Monounsaturated 3.5 g	Protein 28 g

for 2 to 3 minutes, or until the pork is browned on the outside, stirring constantly. Cook for 5 to 6 minutes, or until most of the liquid has evaporated and forms a glaze on the pork slices, stirring occasionally. Remove from the heat.

To serve, spoon the pork over the vegetables on each plate. Garnish with the green onions. Arrange the rice on the plates.

spicy pork
and onion wraps

Sweetly caramelized onions and dried apricots complement the spicy heat of the pork tenderloin in these quick-to-fix wraps.

2 teaspoons olive oil

2 medium onions, thinly sliced and separated into rings

12 ounces cooked low-fat, low-sodium spicy pork, such as Jerked Pork (page 180) or Ginger Pork (page 184)

12 dried apricot halves

4 fat-free 8-inch flour tortillas

1 tablespoon light or dark brown sugar

1 tablespoon balsamic vinegar or orange juice

2 cups baby spinach leaves, stems removed and larger leaves torn

Preheat the oven to 350° F.

Heat a large nonstick skillet over medium-low heat. Pour the oil into the skillet and swirl to coat the bottom. Cook the onions, covered, for 14 minutes, or until very tender and limp, stirring once.

Meanwhile, thinly slice the pork and cut the apricots into slivers.

Wrap the tortillas tightly in aluminum foil. When the onions are ready, heat the tortillas in the oven until warm, about 5 minutes.

Stir the brown sugar into the onions. Increase the heat to medium; cook, uncovered, until the onions brown, about 3 minutes, stirring occasionally. Stir in the pork, apricots, and vinegar. Cook until the pork is heated through, about 2 minutes, stirring occasionally.

For each wrap, spread about ½ cup spinach leaves and about ¾ cup pork mixture down the center of a warm tortilla. Fold the bottom edge of the tortilla up over the meat. Fold in the sides of the tortilla, overlapping on top of the filling. Fasten with a wooden toothpick. Serve immediately.

Calories 352	Cholesterol 73 mg
Total Fat 7.0 g	Sodium 414 mg
Saturated 1.5 g	Carbohydrate 43 g
Polyunsaturated 0.5 g	Fiber 5 g
Monounsaturated 3.5 g	Protein 30 g

ham-and-swiss
stuffed mushrooms

Ham and Swiss, together again, only this time the delectable duo fills baked mushrooms for a yummy main dish.

Olive oil spray

16 large fresh mushrooms, stems discarded (about 24 ounces)

filling

2 cups cooked long-grain and wild rice mix (cooked without seasoning packet or margarine)

½ cup lower-sodium, low-fat chopped ham

1 ounce shredded Swiss cheese

Egg substitute equivalent to 1 egg, or 1 large egg

2 medium green onions, sliced (green and white parts)

½ teaspoon garlic powder

½ teaspoon dried dillweed, crumbled

2 tablespoons sliced almonds

Preheat the oven to 375° F.

Lightly spray the tops of the mushrooms with olive oil spray. Place with the stem side up on a nonstick baking sheet.

In a large bowl, stir together all the filling ingredients except the almonds. Spoon the filling into the mushrooms. Sprinkle with the almonds.

Bake, uncovered, for 20 to 25 minutes, or until the filling is cooked through and the mushrooms are tender.

Calories 97	Cholesterol 6 mg
Total Fat 2.0 g	Sodium 87 mg
Saturated 1.0 g	Carbohydrate 14 g
Polyunsaturated 0.5 g	Fiber 1 g
Monounsaturated 1.0 g	Protein 6 g

tomatoes farci

This recipe takes its name from France and its flavors from the Middle East. In French, *farci* means "stuffed," like these juicy tomatoes. The lamb, mint, lemon, and parsley represent the tart, tangy flavors from the Middle Eastern desert.

stuffed tomatoes

8 firm tomatoes, about 2½ inches in diameter

1 teaspoon sugar

12 ounces extra-lean ground lamb

1 medium garlic clove, minced, or ½ teaspoon bottled minced garlic
Vegetable oil spray

½ cup firmly packed snipped fresh parsley

½ cup fat-free or reduced-fat feta cheese, rinsed, drained, and crumbled (about 2 ounces)

Juice of 1 medium lemon

2 tablespoons fresh mint, chopped

2 tablespoons fresh oregano, chopped, or 2 teaspoons dried, crumbled

¼ teaspoon pepper

1 tablespoon pine nuts

❖ ❖ ❖

6 ounces fresh baby spinach

Juice of ½ medium lemon

1 tablespoon olive oil

Core each tomato, leaving the flesh and being sure not to pierce the bottom. With your fingers, remove any remaining seeds. Sprinkle a pinch of the sugar into each tomato; invert to drain.

Heat a large nonstick skillet over medium-high heat. Cook the lamb and garlic for 2 minutes, stirring constantly. Remove from the heat. Pour into a colander and rinse under hot water to remove excess fat. Drain well.

Preheat the oven to 425°F. Lightly spray a 12-cup muffin pan with vegetable oil spray.

Calories 241	Cholesterol 55 mg
Total Fat 7.0 g	Sodium 326 mg
Saturated 1.0 g	Carbohydrate 21 g
Polyunsaturated 1.0 g	Fiber 4 g
Monounsaturated 3.5 g	Protein 25 g

In a medium bowl, stir together the remaining stuffed tomato ingredients except the pine nuts. Stuff the tomatoes, firmly pressing the filling. Put the tomatoes in the muffin pan. (The muffin pan helps keep the tomatoes upright and holds their shape.) Sprinkle the pine nuts over each tomato.

Bake for 12 minutes, or until the tomato skins are slightly shriveled and the stuffing is heated through.

Meanwhile, in a medium bowl, toss the remaining ingredients. Arrange on plates; top each serving with 2 tomatoes.

COOK'S TIP

If you can't find extra-lean ground lamb, have the butcher grind a lean cut of lamb for you. Another substitute is combining 6 ounces of ground lamb with 6 ounces of lean ground turkey breast, skin removed before grinding.

buffaloaf

Buffalo meat, which is very low in fat, saturated fat, and calories, makes a light and luscious meat loaf.

Vegetable oil spray

1½ pounds ground buffalo or bison

1¼ cups plain dry bread crumbs

1 large onion, chopped

Whites of 3 large eggs

⅔ cup low-sodium mixed-vegetable juice

½ tablespoon fresh lime juice

2 medium garlic cloves, minced, or 1 teaspoon bottled minced garlic

¾ teaspoon salt

¾ to 1 teaspoon dried basil, crumbled

¾ to 1 teaspoon dried oregano, crumbled

¾ to 1 teaspoon ground allspice

¼ to ½ teaspoon cayenne

Preheat the oven to 300° F. Lightly spray a 9 × 5 × 3-inch loaf pan with vegetable oil spray.

In a large bowl, thoroughly combine the remaining ingredients. (Your hands work best for this.) Put the mixture in the prepared loaf pan; gently press the mixture into the pan, smoothing the top.

Bake for 1 hour 30 minutes, or until nicely browned and no longer pink in the center. Remove the buffaloaf from the oven and pour off any excess liquid. Let stand for 10 minutes before slicing.

COOK'S TIP

To remove excess liquid from the loaf pan, use a baster, or carefully tilt the pan to drain off the fat.

Calories 184	Cholesterol 53 mg
Total Fat 2.5 g	Sodium 443 mg
Saturated 1.0 g	Carbohydrate 16 g
Polyunsaturated 0.5 g	Fiber 1 g
Monounsaturated 1.0 g	Protein 22 g

veal madeira

This popular restaurant item is elegant enough to serve to guests for a special meal, yet easy enough to serve to your family after a full day on the job or on the go.

3 tablespoons all-purpose flour

½ tablespoon snipped fresh parsley

¼ teaspoon salt

¼ teaspoon pepper

12 ounces veal scaloppine, all visible fat removed

1 tablespoon olive oil

¼ cup dry Madeira or dry red wine (regular or nonalcoholic)

¼ cup fat-free, no-salt-added beef broth

1 tablespoon fresh orange juice

1 tablespoon snipped fresh parsley

In a shallow dish or pie pan, combine the flour, parsley, salt, and pepper. Lightly dust both sides of the veal, shaking off the excess flour.

Heat a large nonstick skillet over medium-high heat. Pour the oil into the skillet and swirl to coat the bottom. Cook the veal for 3 to 4 minutes, or until lightly browned and cooked through, turning once. Transfer the veal to a plate; cover with aluminum foil to keep warm.

Stir in the remaining ingredients except the parsley. Bring to a boil; cook for 1 minute, or until the sauce is reduced slightly, using a wooden spoon to scrape up any browned bits on the bottom of the pan. Stir in the parsley.

To serve, spoon the sauce over the veal.

Calories 168	Cholesterol 66 mg
Total Fat 5.0 g	Sodium 207 mg
Saturated 1.0 g	Carbohydrate 7 g
Polyunsaturated 0.5 g	Fiber 0 g
Monounsaturated 3.0 g	Protein 19 g

vegetarian

entrées

Mexican Pizza

Corn Tortilla Stackups

10-Minute Fettuccine in Tomato Broth

Tortellini Skillet Toss

Macaroni and Cheese with Spinach
   ❖ Southwestern Macaroni and Cheese

Shells Stuffed with Spinach and Tofu

Smoky Corn Risotto with Peas and Parmesan

Moroccan Lentil Stew

Pinto and Corn "Tamale Pie"

Tuscan White Bean Stew

Mozzarella Portobellos

Couscous with Chick-Peas and Feta Cheese

Spinach and Mushroom Phyllo Purses

Gnocchi with Spaghetti Sauce
   ❖ Baked Gnocchi with Spaghetti Sauce

Quinoa and Lentils à la Grecque

Barley and Edamame with Oranges

Grilled Vegetable Muffuletta

Vegetarian Jambalaya

mexican pizza

serves 4; 1 pizza per serving

Quick to fix, this pizza is the perfect dish to serve to teenagers—though it will also be popular with any other age!

¾ cup canned no-salt-added black beans, rinsed if desired, drained

¼ teaspoon ground cumin

4 6-inch corn tortillas

⅔ cup shredded reduced-fat Monterey Jack, mozzarella, or sharp Cheddar cheese

2 medium Italian plum tomatoes, seeded and chopped (about ½ cup)

1 medium poblano or Anaheim pepper or ½ large green bell pepper, chopped

2 tablespoons snipped fresh cilantro

Preheat the oven to 475° F.

In a small bowl, stir together the beans and cumin.

To assemble, put the tortillas on a baking sheet. Top each tortilla with cheese, tomatoes, chile peppers, and bean mixture.

Bake for 5 minutes, or until the cheese has melted. Remove from the oven.

Sprinkle with the cilantro.

COOK'S TIP

It's easy to turn your pizza into a tostada. Before topping the tortillas, put them on a baking sheet and lightly spray them with vegetable oil spray. Bake at 475° F for 6 minutes, or until crisp. Proceed as directed above.

Calories 142	Cholesterol 10 mg
Total Fat 4.0 g	Sodium 146 mg
Saturated 2.0 g	Carbohydrate 17 g
Polyunsaturated 0.5 g	Fiber 3 g
Monounsaturated 1.0 g	Protein 10 g

corn tortilla stackups

For a fun Tex-Mex meal, start with these stackups. Instead of sprinkling cheese on top of the finished dish, you put it on corn tortillas before lightly baking them.

salsa

4 to 6 ounces tomatoes, Italian plum or regular, seeded and chopped

4- or 4.5-ounce can chopped green chiles, rinsed and well drained

2.25-ounce can sliced black olives, well drained

¼ cup finely chopped red onion

2 tablespoons fresh lime juice

❖ ❖ ❖

4 6-inch corn tortillas

1 cup shredded reduced-fat sharp Cheddar cheese

2 cups shredded lettuce (romaine preferred)

½ cup nonfat or light sour cream

2 to 3 tablespoons snipped fresh cilantro

Preheat the oven to 350°F.

In a medium bowl, stir together all the salsa ingredients.

Put the tortillas in a single layer on a nonstick baking sheet. Sprinkle with the cheese.

Bake for 5 minutes, or until the cheese is bubbly.

Meanwhile, drain the salsa well.

To assemble, place a tortilla on each plate. Top each tortilla with lettuce, salsa, sour cream, and cilantro. Roll jelly-roll style, if desired. Serve immediately.

Calories 187	Cholesterol 15 mg
Total Fat 7.5 g	Sodium 475 mg
Saturated 4.0 g	Carbohydrate 19 g
Polyunsaturated 0.5 g	Fiber 3 g
Monounsaturated 2.5 g	Protein 12 g

10-minute fettuccine in tomato broth

Cooking the pasta in the mixture that becomes its sauce gives you the shortcut you need to get dinner on the table in a hurry. As the pasta cooks, it releases starch, which thickens the broth. Instead of serving this easy dish as an entrée, you may sometimes want to serve half-cup portions as a side dish with seafood, meat, or poultry.

14.5-ounce can no-salt-added diced tomatoes, undrained

2 cups fat-free, low-sodium chicken broth

**2 pepperoncini (Tuscan peppers), stemmed, seeded, and minced, or
1 tablespoon white wine vinegar (peppers preferred)**

2 medium garlic cloves, minced, or 1 teaspoon bottled minced garlic

1 teaspoon sugar

¼ teaspoon salt

⅛ teaspoon pepper (optional)

8 to 9 ounces fresh fettuccine

6 to 8 ounces sliced or coarsely chopped fresh mushrooms (optional)

2 large zucchini, grated

3 tablespoons chopped fresh basil or 1 tablespoon dried, crumbled

**1 tablespoon plus 1 teaspoon shredded or grated Parmesan
or Romano cheese**

Heat a large, deep skillet over high heat. Put the undrained tomatoes, broth, pepperoncini, garlic, sugar, salt, and pepper in the skillet; stir. Bring to a simmer. Gently stir in the pasta, mushrooms, and zucchini; cook for 2 minutes, stirring occasionally. Reduce the heat to medium-high. Stir gently; cook for 2 minutes, or until tender. (The pasta will become gummy if overcooked.) Stir in the basil.

To serve, spoon the pasta and sauce into bowls; sprinkle with cheese.

COOK'S TIP ON PEPPERONCINI, OR TUSCAN PEPPERS

Check the condiment section of your grocery store for jars of pepperoncini. These long chiles range from medium to medium-hot.

Calories 217	Cholesterol 1 mg
Total Fat 2.0 g	Sodium 430 mg
Saturated 0.5 g	Carbohydrate 43 g
Polyunsaturated 0.5 g	Fiber 4 g
Monounsaturated 0.5 g	Protein 10 g

tortellini skillet toss

Team with your family or friends to get dinner on the table in a hurry. While you make the entrée, enlist some help with preparing a salad and setting the table. Everyone will enjoy the fruits of the combined labor, not to mention the tantalizing aromas in the kitchen.

9-ounce package cheese tortellini or spinach-cheese tortellini

1 teaspoon salt-free garlic and herb seasoning or salt-free Italian seasoning, crumbled

1 teaspoon olive oil

2 small yellow summer squash, thinly sliced

2 small zucchini, thinly sliced

2 medium garlic cloves, minced, or 1 teaspoon bottled minced garlic

14.5-ounce can no-salt-added diced tomatoes, undrained

9-ounce package frozen no-salt-added artichoke hearts, thawed and quartered

2 tablespoons dry red or white wine (regular or nonalcoholic) (optional)

2 teaspoons fresh lemon juice

½ teaspoon sugar

½ teaspoon salt

⅛ teaspoon pepper

1 cup frozen no-salt-added green beans, thawed

2 tablespoons chopped fresh basil or 2 teaspoons dried, crumbled

¼ cup shredded or grated Parmesan cheese

Cook the tortellini using the package directions, omitting the salt and oil and adding the garlic and herb seasoning. Drain well. Set aside.

Meanwhile, heat a Dutch oven or large nonstick skillet over medium heat. Pour the oil into the pot and swirl to coat the bottom. Cook the yellow squash, zucchini, and garlic for 3 minutes, or until tender, stirring occasionally.

Stir in the tomatoes, artichoke hearts, wine, lemon juice, sugar, salt, and pepper. Bring to a simmer over medium-high heat; cook for 5 to 10 minutes, or until the artichokes are warmed through and the flavors have blended, stirring occasionally. Add the green beans, basil, and tortellini. Cook for 4 to 5 minutes, or until the green beans are warmed through. Sprinkle with the Parmesan.

Calories 157	Cholesterol 9 mg
Total Fat 4.0 g	Sodium 413 mg
Saturated 1.5 g	Carbohydrate 25 g
Polyunsaturated —	Fiber 5 g
Monounsaturated —	Protein 9 g

macaroni and cheese with spinach

All the satisfaction you remember from this favorite comfort food is here, but with very little fat. A colorful layer of spinach adds vitamins A and C and folic acid.

> **Vegetable oil spray**
>
> 1½ **cups dried elbow macaroni (tricolor preferred)**
>
> 2 **tablespoons all-purpose flour**
>
> 1¼ **cups fat-free milk or fat-free evaporated milk, divided use**
>
> ¾ **cup grated reduced-fat Cheddar cheese**
>
> ¾ **cup fat-free or low-fat buttermilk**
>
> ¼ **teaspoon dry mustard**
>
> ⅛ **teaspoon ground nutmeg**
>
> ⅛ **teaspoon cayenne**
>
> 8 **cups fresh spinach, stems removed, leaves torn if large, or 2 10-ounce packages frozen chopped spinach, thawed and squeezed dry**
>
> 2 **tablespoons soft light whole-wheat bread crumbs or coarse plain dry bread crumbs**
>
> 1 **tablespoon shredded or grated Parmesan cheese**

Preheat the oven to 350°F. Lightly spray a 2-quart casserole dish with vegetable oil spray. Set aside.

In a stockpot, cook the macaroni until slightly firm using the package directions, omitting the salt and oil. Drain well. Set aside.

Meanwhile, in a small bowl, whisk together the flour and ¼ cup milk. In a large saucepan, heat the remaining 1 cup milk over medium heat until tiny bubbles begin to form around the side, about 2 minutes.

Whisk the flour mixture into the hot milk; cook for 2 minutes, or until the mixture bubbles and thickens, whisking frequently. Remove from the heat. Add the cheese, buttermilk, mustard, nutmeg, and cayenne, whisking constantly until the cheese melts. Stir in the macaroni.

macaroni and cheese with spinach

Calories 197	Cholesterol 10 mg
Total Fat 4.0 g	Sodium 214 mg
Saturated 2.5 g	Carbohydrate 28 g
Polyunsaturated 0.5 g	Fiber 2 g
Monounsaturated 1.0 g	Protein 12 g

In a large skillet, cook the spinach over medium heat for 1 minute, or until wilted, stirring constantly. Drain well.

Pour half the macaroni mixture into the prepared dish, spread the spinach over the mixture, and cover with the remaining macaroni. Sprinkle with the bread crumbs and Parmesan.

Bake, uncovered, for 20 minutes, or until bubbly.

southwestern macaroni and cheese

Vegetable oil spray

1½ cups dried elbow macaroni (tricolor preferred)

2 tablespoons all-purpose flour

1¼ cups fat-free milk or fat-free evaporated milk, divided use

¾ cup grated reduced-fat jalapeño Cheddar or Monterey Jack cheese

¾ cup fat-free or low-fat buttermilk

1 to 2 tablespoons finely snipped fresh cilantro

⅛ teaspoon cayenne

1½ cups frozen no-salt-added white corn

1½ cups salsa

2 tablespoons soft light whole-wheat bread crumbs or coarse plain dry bread crumbs

Prepare as above through combining the cooked macaroni with the cheese mixture, substituting the jalapeño Cheddar for the regular Cheddar and the cilantro for the dry mustard and nutmeg.

Pour half the macaroni mixture into the prepared dish. Scatter the corn over the macaroni layer and spread the salsa over the corn. Cover with the remaining macaroni mixture.

Brown the bread crumbs as directed, sprinkle over the macaroni, and bake as directed. Serves 6; 1 cup per serving.

southwestern macaroni and cheese

Calories 231	Cholesterol 10 mg
Total Fat 3.5 g	Sodium 433 mg
Saturated 2.0 g	Carbohydrate 37 g
Polyunsaturated 0.5 g	Fiber 2 g
Monounsaturated 0.5 g	Protein 12 g

shells stuffed
with spinach and tofu

Unless you tell, no one will ever guess that tofu provides the creaminess in this dish, a delicious blend of typical Italian flavors.

18 dried jumbo pasta shells
  Vegetable oil spray
8 ounces frozen chopped spinach, thawed and squeezed dry
2 tablespoons finely chopped green onions (green and white parts)
2 medium garlic cloves, minced, or 1 teaspoon bottled minced garlic
14 ounces soft or silken reduced-fat tofu, drained if necessary
1 cup loosely packed fresh basil, stems removed, leaves minced
  **Whites of 2 large eggs, egg substitute equivalent to 1 egg,
  or 1 large egg**
2 tablespoons shredded or grated Parmesan cheese
⅛ teaspoon ground nutmeg
  Pepper to taste
1½ cups fat-free tomato-based meatless pasta sauce
12 ounces no-salt-added tomato sauce
2 tablespoons shredded or grated Parmesan cheese

Cook the shells using the package directions, omitting the salt and oil. Carefully rinse in cool water. Drain well.

Meanwhile, heat a large skillet over medium heat. Remove the skillet from the heat and lightly spray with vegetable oil spray (being careful not to spray near a gas flame). Cook the spinach, green onions, and garlic until any liquid has evaporated and the spinach is warmed through, 3 to 4 minutes, stirring constantly. Transfer the spinach to a large bowl.

Crumble the tofu into the spinach mixture. Mash the tofu with a fork, breaking it into very small pieces, about the same size as the spinach pieces. Stir in the basil.

Calories 194	Cholesterol 2 mg
Total Fat 2.0 g	Sodium 374 mg
Saturated 1.0 g	Carbohydrate 31 g
Polyunsaturated 0.5 g	Fiber 4 g
Monounsaturated 0.5 g	Protein 12 g

In a small bowl, lightly whisk the egg whites. Add 2 tablespoons Parmesan, nutmeg, and pepper; whisk together. Stir into the spinach mixture.

In a medium bowl, stir together the pasta sauce and tomato sauce. Pour half the sauce into a 13 × 9 × 2-inch baking dish.

Fill the shells with the spinach mixture. Arrange the shells in a single layer in the baking dish. Top with the remaining sauce and 2 tablespoons Parmesan.

Bake for 30 minutes, or until the sauce is bubbling.

COOK'S TIP ON DECREASING THE SODIUM IN SPAGHETTI OR PASTA SAUCE

Starting from scratch is the best way to have a low-sodium spaghetti or pasta sauce. When you want the convenience of a prepared sauce, however, be sure to read the nutrition label and choose the sauce with the least amount of sodium. You can dilute the sodium by mixing 2 parts sauce with 1 part no-salt-added tomato sauce.

COOK'S TIP ON TOFU

If you have leftover tofu, you can puree it and use it in place of sour cream, cream cheese, ricotta cheese, or mayonnaise. Since it has virtually no flavor, tofu is also good for adding creaminess to a variety of food from smoothies to scrambled eggs. You can freeze tofu, but the texture changes. Crumble thawed tofu and add it to sauces, casseroles, and stews for extra protein.

smoky corn risotto with peas and parmesan

A mild smokiness creates the perfect backdrop for the sweet white corn and baby peas in this rich-tasting dish. Use it as an entrée, or serve half portions with grilled chicken or seafood.

2 tablespoons low-sodium vegetable or fat-free, low-sodium chicken broth

1 cup uncooked arborio rice

2 teaspoons dried oregano, crumbled

1 to 2 teaspoons liquid smoke

3¾ cups plus 2 tablespoons low-sodium vegetable or fat-free, low-sodium chicken broth, divided use

1 cup fresh or frozen no-salt-added baby white corn (thawed if frozen)

⅓ cup fresh or frozen baby green peas (thawed if frozen)

2 tablespoons shredded or grated Parmesan cheese

In a medium saucepan, heat 2 tablespoons broth over medium-high heat. Cook the rice for 1 minute, or until translucent, stirring constantly. Add the oregano and liquid smoke, stirring to coat the rice.

Stir in ½ cup broth. Reduce the heat and simmer until the liquid is absorbed, stirring frequently (constantly is even better). Repeat with the remaining broth, ½ cup at a time, except the final addition of ¼ cup plus 2 tablespoons, letting the mixture simmer until the liquid is absorbed after each addition. (The risotto will take about 20 minutes from the time the first broth is added.)

Stir in the remaining ingredients. Serve immediately so the peas don't get mushy and the risotto doesn't lose its creaminess.

COOK'S TIP ON RISOTTO

Arborio, the rice used in risotto, is a short-grain rice with a higher starch content than medium- and long-grain rice. As the risotto cooks, the starch from the rice absorbs liquid while creating a rich, creamy sauce. For the best results, stir the risotto frequently (if not constantly) during cooking to keep it from clumping and sticking to the pan.

Calories 376	Cholesterol 2 mg
Total Fat 1.5 g	Sodium 134 mg
Saturated 0.5 g	Carbohydrate 75 g
Polyunsaturated 0.5 g	Fiber 4 g
Monounsaturated 0.5 g	Protein 12 g

moroccan lentil stew

Perfect for cold winter nights, this hearty stew simmers in a mild curry-tomato sauce.

2 teaspoons olive oil

1 cup chopped Spanish or other mild onion

2 teaspoons ground cumin

2 teaspoons curry powder

⅛ teaspoon cayenne (optional)

28-ounce can no-salt-added crushed tomatoes, undrained

8 ounces red potatoes, cut into 1-inch chunks

1 cup low-sodium vegetable or fat-free, low-sodium chicken broth

½ cup lentils, sorted for stones or shriveled lentils and rinsed

1 medium carrot, chopped

Low-sodium vegetable or fat-free, low-sodium chicken broth or water (as needed)

½ cup frozen green peas, thawed

¼ cup fresh parsley, snipped or chopped

Heat a large saucepan over medium heat. Pour the oil into the pan and swirl to coat the bottom. Cook the onion for 3 to 4 minutes, or until translucent, stirring frequently.

Increase the heat to medium-high. Stir in the cumin, curry powder, and cayenne; cook for 30 seconds to release flavor. Stir in the tomatoes, potatoes, broth, lentils, and carrots. Bring to a boil. Reduce the heat and simmer, covered, for 30 to 40 minutes, or until the lentils are tender, stirring occasionally and adding more broth or water if needed to keep from sticking. Stir in the peas; simmer for 1 minute. Remove from the heat. Stir in the parsley.

COOK'S TIP ON LENTILS

If the lentils have been stored for an extended time, they may take up to 1 hour of cooking time to become tender.

Calories 254	Cholesterol 0 mg
Total Fat 3.0 g	Sodium 79 mg
Saturated 0.5 g	Carbohydrate 46 g
Polyunsaturated 0.5 g	Fiber 14 g
Monounsaturated 2.0 g	Protein 14 g

pinto and corn "tamale pie"

serves 4; 1¼ cups per serving

Packed with tamale flavors, this skillet dish will be a hit each time you serve it.

14.5-ounce can no-salt-added pinto beans

¾ cup frozen no-salt-added whole-kernel corn

4- or 4.5-ounce can diced green chiles

Vegetable oil spray

1 small onion (yellow preferred), finely chopped

14.5-ounce can no-salt-added diced tomatoes, undrained

½ cup water

½ tablespoon chili powder

¾ teaspoon sugar

½ teaspoon ground cumin

4 6-inch corn tortillas, cut into ¼-inch strips

½ teaspoon ground cumin

⅛ teaspoon salt

½ cup shredded reduced-fat sharp Cheddar cheese

In a colander, rinse the beans, corn, and green chiles until the water runs clear. Drain well.

Heat a large nonstick skillet over medium-high heat. Remove the skillet from the heat and lightly spray with vegetable oil spray (being careful not to spray near a gas flame). Cook the onion for 2 minutes, or until the edges are lightly browned, stirring occasionally. Add the tomatoes with their liquid, water, chili powder, sugar, ½ teaspoon cumin, and reserved bean mixture; increase the heat to high and bring to a boil. Reduce the heat and simmer, covered, for 15 minutes.

Remove from the heat and stir in the remaining ingredients except the cheese. Sprinkle with the cheese. Let stand, covered, for 4 minutes, or until the cheese has melted.

Calories 229	Cholesterol 8 mg
Total Fat 3.5 g	Sodium 310 mg
Saturated 2.0 g	Carbohydrate 38 g
Polyunsaturated 0.5 g	Fiber 8 g
Monounsaturated 0.5 g	Protein 13 g

tuscan white bean stew

Serve this filling soup with a hearty bread, such as pumpernickel or rye.

Olive oil spray

2 to 3 medium **carrots, diced**

3 medium ribs of **celery, sliced**

2 medium **onions, chopped**

5 medium **garlic cloves, minced,** or 2½ teaspoons **bottled minced garlic**

4 cups **low-sodium mixed-vegetable juice**

2 15-ounce cans no-salt-added **Great Northern beans,** rinsed if desired, drained

2 teaspoons **dried oregano, crumbled**

4 cups chopped **Swiss chard**

1 cup **fat-free** or **low-fat plain yogurt**

6 medium **green onions, chopped (green parts only)**

Heat a small stockpot or large saucepan over medium-high heat. Remove from the heat and lightly spray with olive oil spray (being careful not to spray near a gas flame). Cook the carrots, celery, onion, and garlic, covered, for 10 to 15 minutes, or until the carrots are tender, stirring occasionally. If the vegetables begin to stick, gradually add part of the vegetable juice, ¼ cup at a time. When the vegetables are tender, add the remaining vegetable juice, beans, and oregano. Simmer, covered, for 5 minutes. Stir in the Swiss chard; simmer, covered, for 3 to 5 minutes, or until tender.

To serve, ladle 1½ cups stew into each of four bowls. Top each serving with yogurt and green onions.

Calories 346	Cholesterol 1 mg
Total Fat 0.5 g	Sodium 318 mg
Saturated 0 g	Carbohydrate 65 g
Polyunsaturated 0 g	Fiber 15 g
Monounsaturated 0 g	Protein 20 g

mozzarella portobellos

serves 4; 1 mushroom plus ½ cup vegetables and
1 ounce cheese per serving

Popular portobello mushrooms serve as edible plates on which you stack mouthwatering vegetables and gooey mozzarella cheese.

Vegetable oil spray

4 fresh portobello mushrooms (3 to 4 ounces each), stems removed

1 medium zucchini, thinly sliced

1 medium green bell pepper, chopped

1 medium onion (yellow preferred), chopped

2 teaspoons dried basil, crumbled

8-ounce can no-salt-added tomato sauce

½ teaspoon sugar

¼ teaspoon salt

⅛ teaspoon crushed red pepper flakes

⅔ cup shredded part-skim mozzarella cheese

2 teaspoons shredded or grated Parmesan cheese

Preheat the oven to 400°F. Lightly spray a nonstick baking sheet with vegetable oil spray. Lightly spray both sides of the mushrooms with vegetable oil spray; place with the stem side up on the baking sheet.

Bake for 12 minutes, or until fork tender. Set aside.

Meanwhile, heat a large nonstick skillet over medium-high heat. Remove from the heat and lightly spray with vegetable oil spray (being careful not to spray near a gas flame). Cook the zucchini, bell peppers, onion, and basil for 5 minutes, or until the zucchini is tender. Stir in the tomato sauce, sugar, salt, and red pepper flakes; cook for 4 minutes, or until thickened, stirring frequently.

Spoon ½ cup zucchini mixture over each mushroom; top with the mozzarella cheese.

Bake for 5 minutes, or until the mozzarella has melted. Remove from the oven. Sprinkle with the Parmesan.

Calories 118	Cholesterol 12 mg
Total Fat 3.5 g	Sodium 272 mg
Saturated 2.0 g	Carbohydrate 15 g
Polyunsaturated 0.5 g	Fiber 3 g
Monounsaturated 1.0 g	Protein 8 g

couscous with chick-peas and feta cheese

Try a mixture of red, yellow, and orange bell peppers for a burst of color in this tasty dish.

⅔ cup uncooked couscous (whole-wheat preferred)

1⅓ cups boiling water

Juice of 1 medium lemon

15-ounce can no-salt-added chick-peas, rinsed if desired, drained

1 large red bell pepper or a combination of red, yellow, and orange bell peppers, cut into ¼-inch pieces

½ cup finely chopped fresh basil, stems removed

½ cup chopped fresh parsley

2 medium garlic cloves, minced, or 1 teaspoon bottled minced garlic

1 tablespoon plus 1 teaspoon olive oil

¼ cup fat-free or reduced-fat feta cheese, rinsed, drained, and crumbled

Fresh parsley sprigs (optional)

Put the couscous in a large, heatproof bowl. Pour the water and lemon juice over the couscous. Let the mixture sit for 15 minutes; fluff with a fork.

In a large bowl, stir together the couscous and chick-peas. Stir in the bell peppers, basil, parsley, and garlic. Drizzle with olive oil and sprinkle with feta; stir.

Serve at room temperature or cover and refrigerate for 2 to 12 hours.

To serve, garnish with parsley sprigs.

COOK'S TIP ON COUSCOUS

When preparing couscous for this or other recipes, try using low-sodium vegetable broth instead of water for more flavor. If you want a slightly sweet side dish, instead of plain couscous substitute unsweetened apple juice for water, and add some cinnamon and raisins.

Calories 298	Cholesterol 6 mg
Total Fat 8.5 g	Sodium 84 mg
Saturated 1.5 g	Carbohydrate 45 g
Polyunsaturated 1.5 g	Fiber 11 g
Monounsaturated 5.0 g	Protein 12 g

spinach and mushroom phyllo purses

serves 4; 1 purse per serving

First-time and seasoned phyllo cooks alike will delight in the ease of preparing this artistic dish. Shaping the phyllo like a drawstring purse is simple and quick. When you slice into your purse, you'll reveal a tender spinach, mushroom, and ricotta mixture.

Olive oil spray

1 teaspoon olive oil

½ medium onion, sliced

8 ounces fresh mushrooms, sliced

10 ounces frozen chopped spinach, thawed and squeezed dry

¼ cup roasted red bell pepper, rinsed and drained if bottled, chopped

½ teaspoon dried oregano, crumbled

1 medium garlic clove, minced, or ½ teaspoon bottled minced garlic

½ cup fat-free or low-fat ricotta cheese

2 ounces fat-free or reduced-fat feta cheese, rinsed, drained, and crumbled

6 sheets frozen phyllo dough, thawed

Preheat the oven to 375° F. Lightly spray a baking sheet with olive oil spray.

Heat a large nonstick skillet over medium heat. Pour the olive oil into the skillet and swirl to coat the bottom. Cook the onions for 3 to 4 minutes, or until translucent, stirring occasionally. Stir in the mushrooms. Cook for 3 to 4 minutes, or until tender, stirring occasionally. Stir in the spinach, bell pepper, oregano, and garlic. Cook for 1 to 2 minutes, or until the mixture is warmed through, stirring occasionally. Remove from the heat. Stir in the ricotta and feta. Let cool while working with the phyllo.

Stack the phyllo sheets on a cutting board. Cut in half crosswise (you will have 12 rectangles, each about 12 × 8 inches). Lay 1 piece of phyllo dough on a separate cutting board, covering the remaining pieces with a damp cloth to

Calories 174	Cholesterol 3 mg
Total Fat 3.5 g	Sodium 487 mg
Saturated 0.5 g	Carbohydrate 25 g
Polyunsaturated 0.5 g	Fiber 4 g
Monounsaturated 1.5 g	Protein 13 g

keep them from drying out. Lightly spray the phyllo piece with olive oil spray. Working quickly, repeat until you have 4 stacks, each with 3 layers of phyllo.

To assemble, spoon a scant ¾ cup spinach mixture onto the center of each phyllo stack. Continuing to work quickly, gather the edges of a phyllo rectangle toward the center, covering the filling mixture. You now have a phyllo purse. Tie the purse with kitchen string or gently twist the ends of the phyllo like the ends of a candy wrapper and pinch to seal. Repeat with the remaining rectangles.

Place the purses with the flat side down on the prepared baking sheet. Lightly spray the purses with olive oil spray.

Bake for 25 to 30 minutes, or until the phyllo is golden brown and the filling is warmed through. Cut and remove the strings before serving the purses.

COOK'S TIP ON FROZEN SPINACH

Having spinach in your freezer is helpful when you need a vegetable boost for your meals. Thaw a 10-ounce package of spinach in the microwave on 50 percent power (medium), or cook using the package directions. Let the spinach cool, then drain it well in a colander. Either use your hands to squeeze the liquid from the spinach or put the spinach in the middle of a clean dish towel, gather the edges of the towel, and squeeze the spinach to remove the liquid.

gnocchi with spaghetti sauce

serves 4; 24 gnocchi and ½ cup sauce per serving

Take a walk on your treadmill while the potatoes cook, then involve your family and friends in the fun of preparing the gnocchi. Make several batches and freeze some for another time.

> **2 medium Yukon gold or russet potatoes (about 12 ounces)**
>
> **2 cups all-purpose flour**
>
> **Egg substitute equivalent to 2 eggs, or 2 large eggs, lightly beaten**
>
> **2 teaspoons salt-free Italian seasoning**
>
> **½ teaspoon salt**
>
> **¼ teaspoon pepper**
>
> **Flour for rolling gnocchi**

spaghetti sauce

> **2 8-ounce cans no-salt-added tomato sauce**
>
> **2 teaspoons salt-free Italian seasoning**
>
> **1 teaspoon sugar**
>
> **½ teaspoon garlic powder**
>
> **⅛ to ¼ teaspoon crushed red pepper flakes**
>
> **⅛ teaspoon pepper**
>
> ❖ ❖ ❖
>
> **3 tablespoons shredded or grated Parmesan cheese**

Put the potatoes in a medium saucepan; fill the pan with water to cover by 1 inch. Bring to a boil over high heat. Reduce the heat; simmer for 30 to 40 minutes, or until the potatoes are tender when pierced in the center with a sharp knife, adding hot water if needed. Drain the potatoes well; let cool on a plate for about 10 minutes, or until cool enough to handle but still slightly warm. Peel the potatoes.

Mash the potatoes in a medium bowl with a potato masher or push through a potato ricer.

Fill a stockpot with water. Bring to a simmer over medium-high heat.

Calories 375	Cholesterol 3 mg
Total Fat 2.0 g	Sodium 464 mg
Saturated 1.0 g	Carbohydrate 74 g
Polyunsaturated 0.5 g	Fiber 4 g
Monounsaturated 0.5 g	Protein 13 g

Meanwhile, add the 2 cups flour, egg substitute, Italian seasoning, salt, and pepper to the potatoes. Stir just until the dough forms a ball; don't overmix or the dough may be gummy. Divide the dough into 4 pieces.

Lightly flour a flat surface. Using your hands, lightly roll each piece into a 12-inch rope on the floured surface. Cut each rope into twenty-four ½-inch pieces. Lightly press a fork on top of each piece, making slight indentations (like the indentations on peanut butter cookies).

Put one half of the gnocchi in the simmering water. After they float to the top (about 1 minute), cook them for 3 to 4 minutes (6 to 8 minutes if frozen), or until tender to the bite and cooked through the center (no chalky look from uncooked flour when cut in half), stirring occasionally. Using a slotted spoon, transfer the cooked gnocchi to a plate and cover with aluminum foil to keep warm. Repeat with the remaining gnocchi.

Meanwhile, in a medium saucepan, combine all the sauce ingredients. Heat over medium heat for 5 to 8 minutes, or until warmed through, stirring occasionally.

To serve, spoon ½ cup sauce into each of four bowls. Place 24 gnocchi in each bowl. Sprinkle each serving with 1 tablespoon Parmesan.

baked gnocchi
with spaghetti sauce

Follow the directions above through shaping the gnocchi. Preheat the oven to 350° F. Lightly spray a 13 × 9 × 2-inch baking dish with vegetable oil spray. Put the gnocchi in the dish and top with the spaghetti sauce. Sprinkle with the Parmesan. Bake, covered, for 30 to 35 minutes (40 to 50 minutes if the gnocchi are frozen), or until the gnocchi are cooked through.

COOK'S TIP ON FORMING GNOCCHI

There are several ways to form gnocchi, but the style is not so important as having fun! If you don't want to use the method mentioned in the recipe above, roll each piece into a ball and, if you wish, slightly flatten the balls with your thumb, forming dented disks. The dents and grooves help catch the sauce. Uncooked gnocchi can be refrigerated in a single layer in an airtight container for up to 12 hours.

COOK'S TIP ON POTATO RICERS

One part of this handheld metal gadget pushes cooked potatoes, carrots, and other root vegetables through tiny holes in the other part. The result looks a bit like grains of rice. A ricer makes easy work of mashing potatoes and provides an interesting twist for serving cooked root vegetables. If you press carefully, you can even use a ricer to remove excess water from cooked spinach.

quinoa and lentils
à la grecque

In cool weather, serve this hearty main dish at room temperature. In the summer, try two medium cucumbers, diced, in place of the zucchini and serve it chilled.

3½ cups water (plus more as needed)

1 cup uncooked quinoa

½ cup dried lentils, sorted for stones or shriveled lentils and rinsed

2 teaspoons crushed red pepper flakes, or to taste

2 teaspoons salt-free garlic and herb seasoning

¼ teaspoon salt

2 medium tomatoes or 14.5-ounce can no-salt-added diced tomatoes, drained

16 kalamata or black olives

½ cup loosely packed fresh Italian, or flat-leaf, parsley

4 small zucchini

Vegetable oil spray

In a medium saucepan, bring the water to a boil over high heat. Stir in the quinoa, lentils, red pepper flakes, garlic and herb seasoning, and salt. Reduce the heat and simmer, covered, for 20 to 25 minutes, or until the water has evaporated and the lentils are tender. If needed, add water, ¼ cup at a time, to keep the lentils from burning.

Meanwhile, dice the tomatoes, finely chop the olives, and snip the parsley. Cut the zucchini in half lengthwise; lightly spray with vegetable oil spray.

Lightly spray the broiler pan and rack or the grill rack with vegetable oil spray. Preheat the broiler or preheat the grill on high.

Broil the zucchini 2 to 3 inches from the heat or grill for about 10 minutes, or until browned on both sides, turning once.

When cool enough to handle, cut the zucchini into ½-inch pieces. Add to the quinoa mixture with the tomatoes, olives, and parsley, stirring gently. Serve at room temperature.

Calories 322	Cholesterol 0 mg
Total Fat 7.0 g	Sodium 424 mg
Saturated 1.0 g	Carbohydrate 53 g
Polyunsaturated 2.0 g	Fiber 13 g
Monounsaturated 4.0 g	Protein 15 g

barley and edamame with oranges

Hearty barley teams with green soybeans and fresh oranges, making a fabulous taste sensation in this meatless entrée.

- 1¼ cups frozen shelled green soybeans (edamame)
- 1 cup water
- ¾ cup chopped onions
- ½ cup chopped red bell pepper
- 2 medium garlic cloves, minced, or 1 teaspoon bottled minced garlic
- ½ teaspoon ground ginger
- 1¼ cups uncooked quick-cooking barley
- 1¼ cups fresh orange juice
- 1 tablespoon low-salt soy sauce
- 2 small carrots, shredded
- ⅓ cup snipped dried apricots
- 2 tablespoons toasted wheat germ
- 2 medium oranges, peeled and sectioned

In a medium saucepan, bring the soybeans, water, onions, bell pepper, garlic, and ginger to a boil over high heat. Reduce the heat and simmer, covered, for 5 minutes. Stir in the barley, orange juice, and soy sauce. Increase the heat to medium and return to a boil. Reduce the heat and simmer, covered, for 10 to 12 minutes, or until the liquid is absorbed and the barley is tender. Remove from the heat.

Stir in the remaining ingredients except the oranges.

To serve, arrange the orange sections on each plate. Spoon the barley mixture over the oranges. You can also make a circle with the oranges and spoon the mixture into the center.

Calories 500	Cholesterol 0 mg
Total Fat 6.5 g	Sodium 163 mg
Saturated 1.5 g	Carbohydrate 99 g
Polyunsaturated 3.0 g	Fiber 20 g
Monounsaturated 1.0 g	Protein 20 g

grilled vegetable muffuletta

For something different for a tailgate party, picnic, or buffet, or for a hungry crowd after an athletic event, try this delectable layered sandwich, cut into wedges. Leftovers brighten up brown-bag lunches.

vinaigrette

¼ cup olive oil

2 tablespoons balsamic vinegar

1 medium garlic clove, cut into several small pieces, or ½ teaspoon bottled minced garlic

¼ teaspoon salt

⅛ teaspoon cayenne

❖ ❖ ❖

8- to 9-inch round Italian, pumpernickel, or rye bread

½ medium eggplant or 2 thin Asian eggplants, grilled, skin removed, and cut into ½-inch-thick slices

2 to 3 medium red bell peppers, grilled, peeled, seeded, and cut into matchstick-size strips

1 medium sweet onion (Vidalia preferred), thinly sliced, grilled

2 tablespoons fat-free or reduced-fat feta cheese, rinsed, drained, and crumbled

6 to 8 very large fresh mushrooms, grilled and sliced

8 fresh basil leaves

1 to 2 medium tomatoes, thinly sliced

1 medium yellow or orange bell pepper, roasted, peeled, seeded, and cut into matchstick-size strips

⅛ to ¼ teaspoon pepper

Calories 166	Cholesterol 0 mg
Total Fat 6.5 g	Sodium 270 mg
Saturated 1.0 g	Carbohydrate 23 g
Polyunsaturated 1.0 g	Fiber 3 g
Monounsaturated 4.0 g	Protein 5 g

In a food processor or blender, process all the vinaigrette ingredients until the garlic is barely visible.

Cut a "lid" off the bread. Remove the bread inside the crust, leaving ½ inch or less of the bread attached to the crust. (Keep the remaining bread for another use, such as making bread crumbs or croutons, or discard.)

To assemble, brush the inside of the bread and the cut side of the lid with the vinaigrette. Fill the loaf in the following order: eggplant, red bell peppers, onion, feta, mushrooms, 1 tablespoon vinaigrette, basil leaves, tomato slices, and yellow bell pepper. (The bread will be brimming.) Sprinkle with the pepper. Drizzle with the remaining vinaigrette. Place the lid on the bread; press down to join the lid with the bowl of the bread.

Cover the entire bread bowl with plastic wrap, then with aluminum foil. Refrigerate for 18 to 24 hours before serving.

COOK'S TIP

Add some spices or fresh herbs to the vinaigrette. Caraway seeds and parsley would make an interesting flavor change. You can use these in addition to or in place of the salt and cayenne.

COOK'S TIP ON GRILLING VEGETABLES

Lightly spray the grill rack with vegetable oil spray. Preheat the grill to medium-high. Grill the eggplant, bell peppers, and mushrooms, covered if possible, until cooked to desired doneness, turning to blacken on all sides. It will take about 30 minutes for the eggplant and bell peppers, 15 to 30 minutes for the mushrooms. The eggplant should be tender, peppers should be blackened, and mushrooms should be softened. Set aside until cool enough to handle.

Peel the eggplant and bell peppers, removing and discarding the seeds and stems. Slice the eggplant into bite-size pieces. Cut the peppers into matchstick-size strips. Grill the thinly sliced onions in a stovetop grill pan or cook them in a skillet over medium heat for 8 to 10 minutes, or until golden brown.

vegetarian jambalaya

This zesty one-dish meal gets a nutrition boost from collard greens. Follow it with peaches or other fresh fruit for dessert.

- **1 teaspoon acceptable vegetable oil**
- **½ cup chopped onion**
- **½ cup chopped red bell pepper**
- **½ cup chopped celery**
- **2 medium garlic cloves, minced, or 1 teaspoon bottled minced garlic**
- **4 cups collard greens or kale, cut into 1-inch pieces**
- **1 cup uncooked rice (long-grain preferred)**
- **1½ cups low-sodium vegetable or fat-free, low-sodium chicken broth**
- **8-ounce can no-salt-added tomato sauce**
- **1 tablespoon very low sodium or low-sodium Worcestershire sauce**
- **2 teaspoons salt-free Cajun/Creole seasoning (page 147)**
- **2 teaspoons liquid smoke**
- **12-ounce package cooked soy protein (meat substitute), crumbled, or 10-ounce package vegetarian burgers (made with soy protein), cubed**

Heat a nonstick Dutch oven over medium heat. Pour the oil into the pot and swirl to coat the bottom. Cook the onion, bell pepper, celery, and garlic over medium heat for 3 to 4 minutes, or until the vegetables are tender-crisp, stirring occasionally. Stir in the greens; cook for 2 minutes, stirring occasionally.

Rinse and drain the rice if using long-grain. Stir the rice into the vegetable mixture; cook for 1 to 2 minutes, stirring occasionally (this helps the rice absorb flavor before the liquid is added). Increase the heat to high.

Stir in the remaining ingredients except the soy protein. Bring to a boil; reduce heat to low and cook, covered, for 20 to 25 minutes, or until the rice is tender (no stirring needed). Stir in the soy protein; cook, covered, for 3 to 5 minutes, or until the mixture is warmed through. Don't overcook; the soy protein could become tough.

Calories 360	Cholesterol 0 mg
Total Fat 4.5 g	Sodium 369 mg
Saturated 0.5 g	Carbohydrate 55 g
Polyunsaturated 2.0 g	Fiber 8 g
Monounsaturated 1.5 g	Protein 24 g

COOK'S TIP ON RINSING RICE

Rinsing long-grain rice before cooking helps remove excess starch, which can cause a gummy and sticky consistency when cooked. Other rice varieties that should be rinsed include imported rice, rice from bulk bins, short- or medium-grain rice that is not enriched, and brown rice that is not enriched. Rice varieties that should *not* be rinsed before cooking are converted rice, enriched rice, and arborio rice (starch from arborio rice is vital to the creamy texture of the popular Italian rice dish called risotto). The no-rinse varieties, along with many packaged rice mixes and boiling bag rice packages, have nutrients added to them, and rinsing could remove some of these nutrients.

vegetables and

side dishes

Dill Mustard Asparagus

Wild Mushroom and Barley Pilaf

Mediterranean Green Beans

Tarragon Balsamic Green Beans

Broccoli with Blue Cheese Sauce
    and Walnuts

Beets Anna

Scalloped Brussels Sprouts

Baked Red Cabbage

Roasted Carrots and Onions
    with Balsamic Vinegar

Cauliflower and Carrots
    with Cumin

Baked Chayote
    with Cilantro-Chili Topping

Sesame-Dusted Collard Greens
    ❖ Sesame-Dusted Spinach

Corn Pudding

Orange-Flavored Couscous
    with Golden Raisins
    and Toasted Almonds

Braised Kasha

Mushrooms Stuffed
    with Rice and Vegetables

Pasta with Roasted Tomato
    and Chipotle Sauce

Wild Mushroom and Tomato
    Penne Pasta

Potato and Mushroom Napoleon

Brown Rice and Walnuts
    ❖ Brown Rice and Pine Nuts

Snow Pea Rice

Coriander Spinach

Yellow Squash Skillet Casserole

Squash "Blossoms"

Skinny Sweet Potato Fries

Tomato and Goat Cheese
    Bread Pudding

Broiled Tomatoes with
    Blue Cheese Bread Crumbs
    ❖ Broiled Zucchini with Feta Bread
    Crumbs

Skillet-Grilled Zucchini
    and Red Bell Peppers

dill mustard asparagus

Dijon mustard and dillweed top fresh asparagus to create this sophisticated-tasting side dish.

> 2 cups water
> 1 pound asparagus spears, trimmed
> 1 tablespoon light tub margarine
> 2 teaspoons Dijon mustard
> 1 tablespoon snipped fresh dillweed or 1 teaspoon dried, crumbled
> ⅛ teaspoon salt

In a large nonstick skillet, bring the water to a boil over high heat. Add the asparagus. Reduce the heat; simmer, covered, for 2 minutes, or until just tender-crisp.

Meanwhile, in a small bowl, stir together the remaining ingredients.

Drain the asparagus well on paper towels; place on a serving platter. Spoon the margarine mixture on top and spread evenly or toss gently to coat.

Calories 29	Cholesterol 0 mg
Total Fat 1.0 g	Sodium 106 mg
Saturated 0 g	Carbohydrate 3 g
Polyunsaturated 0 g	Fiber 2 g
Monounsaturated 0.5 g	Protein 2 g

wild mushroom and barley pilaf

Here's a delicious way to use healthful barley. This recipe features portobellos, but feel free to substitute another variety of wild or cultivated mushroom.

1 tablespoon acceptable vegetable oil

8 ounces portobello mushrooms, tough ends removed, caps and stems coarsely chopped

1 small onion, chopped

2 medium garlic cloves, minced, or 1 teaspoon bottled minced garlic

1¼ cups uncooked medium pearl (pearled) barley

3 cups fat-free, low-sodium chicken broth

¼ teaspoon salt

¼ teaspoon pepper

2 tablespoons snipped fresh dillweed or 2 teaspoons dried, crumbled

Heat a medium nonstick saucepan over medium heat. Pour the oil into the pan and swirl to coat the bottom. Cook the mushrooms, onion, and garlic for 5 minutes, or until the mushrooms have released some of their juices and the onions are translucent, stirring occasionally.

Stir in the barley; cook for 1 minute. Stir in the broth, salt, and pepper. Bring to a boil over high heat. Reduce the heat to low; cook, covered, for 45 to 50 minutes, or until the barley is tender. Remove from the heat. Stir in the dillweed.

COOK'S TIP ON BARLEY

A very versatile grain, barley is good in soups, salads, main dishes, and even desserts. Try substituting it in some of your favorite brown or white rice recipes, allowing additional cooking time. With its mildly nutlike flavor, pearl, or pearled, barley—available coarse, medium, or fine—is the most common.

Calories 95	Cholesterol 0 mg
Total Fat 1.5 g	Sodium 67 mg
Saturated 0 g	Carbohydrate 18 g
Polyunsaturated 0.5 g	Fiber 4 g
Monounsaturated 0.5 g	Protein 3 g

mediterranean green beans

Green beans team with roasted garlic cloves, sun-dried tomatoes, and toasted pine nuts for a side dish that goes with grilled turkey cutlets, red snapper, or Citrus-Poached Fish Fillets (page 77). You may find that you like the mellow taste of roasted garlic so well that you use more than eight cloves the next time you prepare this dish.

8 medium garlic cloves, unpeeled

1 tablespoon pine nuts

½ cup boiling water

4 dry-packed sun-dried tomato halves

1 teaspoon olive oil

9-ounce package frozen no-salt-added cut green beans, thawed

1 tablespoon snipped fresh dillweed or 1 teaspoon dried, crumbled

⅛ teaspoon pepper

2 tablespoons shredded or grated Parmesan cheese

Preheat the oven to 350°F.

Put the garlic cloves on an ungreased nonstick baking sheet. Roast for 15 minutes, or until tender to the touch. Add the pine nuts; roast for 5 minutes. Put the baking sheet on a cooling rack.

Meanwhile, in a small bowl, combine the water and tomatoes. Let stand for 10 to 15 minutes, or until soft. Drain well, discarding the water. Squeeze any excess liquid from the tomatoes. Cut the tomatoes into thin slices.

When the garlic has cooled to the touch, squeeze it out of the skins into a small bowl.

Heat a large nonstick skillet over medium heat. Pour the oil into the skillet and swirl to coat the bottom. Cook the garlic for 15 to 20 seconds, stirring constantly. Stir in the green beans; cook for 3 to 5 minutes, or until warmed through, stirring occasionally. Stir in the tomatoes, dillweed, and pepper.

Calories 72	Cholesterol 2 mg
Total Fat 3.0 g	Sodium 46 mg
Saturated 1.0 g	Carbohydrate 9 g
Polyunsaturated 0.5 g	Fiber 2 g
Monounsaturated 1.5 g	Protein 3 g

Cook for 1 minute, or until the mixture is warmed through, stirring occasionally. Transfer the mixture to a serving bowl.

To serve, sprinkle with the Parmesan and pine nuts.

COOK'S TIP ON SUN-DRIED TOMATOES

Sweet, rich-tasting sun-dried tomatoes add a concentrated tomato flavor. Look for them in the produce section, near the canned tomato products, or in the Italian section of your grocery store. Try cutting 6 dry-packed sun-dried tomatoes into small pieces and adding them to 1 quart of a simmering broth-based soup, such as chicken noodle or French onion. Simmer for 10 to 15 minutes to soften the tomatoes.

COOK'S TIP ON THAWING VEGETABLES

Forget to set the frozen vegetables out to thaw? No problem. Put them in a colander, let cold water run over them until they thaw, then drain thoroughly.

tarragon balsamic green beans

The sweetness of tarragon mellows the tanginess of balsamic vinegar in this ultrasimple dish.

1 pound fresh green beans, trimmed

1 tablespoon light tub margarine

2 teaspoons balsamic vinegar

1 tablespoon finely chopped fresh tarragon or 1 teaspoon dried, crumbled

¼ teaspoon salt

Put a steamer basket in a small amount of simmering water in a medium saucepan. Put the green beans in the basket. Cook, covered, for about 6 minutes, or until tender.

Meanwhile, in a small bowl, stir together the remaining ingredients.

Drain the beans well. Return the beans to the empty pan; stir in the margarine mixture.

Calories 32	Cholesterol 0 mg
Total Fat 1.0 g	Sodium 115 mg
Saturated 0 g	Carbohydrate 5 g
Polyunsaturated 0 g	Fiber 3 g
Monounsaturated 0.5 g	Protein 1 g

broccoli with blue cheese sauce and walnuts

serves 4; ½ cup broccoli, ¼ cup sauce, and
½ teaspoon walnuts per serving

When you need to dress up a simple entrée, this combination of rich green broccoli and contrasting creamy white sauce is the perfect fit. The small amount of blue cheese adds zip to the sauce without overpowering the dish.

2 cups broccoli florets and stems

½ cup water

2 teaspoons chopped walnuts

1 cup fat-free milk

2 tablespoons all-purpose flour

¼ teaspoon salt

⅛ teaspoon pepper

2½ tablespoons crumbled blue cheese

Put the broccoli in a microwave-safe container. Add the water. Cook, covered, on 100 percent power (high) for 5 to 7 minutes, or until tender. Keep covered to keep warm. To steam instead, put a steamer basket in a small amount of simmering water in a medium saucepan. Put the broccoli in the basket. Cook, covered, for 3 to 4 minutes for tender-crisp broccoli, 5 to 6 minutes for tender broccoli.

Heat a medium saucepan over medium heat. Dry-roast the walnuts for 3 to 7 minutes, or until fragrant and light, stirring occasionally. Remove the pan from the heat, set the walnuts aside, and wipe the pan with paper towels.

In the same pan, combine the remaining ingredients except the blue cheese; bring to a simmer over medium-high heat. Reducing the heat if necessary, simmer for 4 to 5 minutes, or until the mixture is thickened, stirring occasionally. Remove from the heat. Stir in the blue cheese. Spoon ¼ cup sauce onto each plate. Drain the broccoli well; arrange on each plate. Sprinkle with walnuts.

Calories 78	Cholesterol 5 mg
Total Fat 2.5 g	Sodium 267 mg
Saturated 1.0 g	Carbohydrate 9 g
Polyunsaturated 0.5 g	Fiber 2 g
Monounsaturated 0.5 g	Protein 6 g

beets anna

In this twist on the classic French dish Potatoes Anna, beets and apples are layered and baked, making a vibrant addition to a holiday buffet.

Vegetable oil spray (butter flavored preferred)
1 medium or large Golden Delicious apple, peeled and thinly sliced
½ teaspoon grated peeled gingerroot
2 15-ounce cans sliced beets, drained
1 small or medium leek, thinly sliced (white part only)
1 tablespoon finely snipped fresh Italian, or flat-leaf, parsley

Preheat the oven to 350°F. Lightly spray a 10-inch ceramic or glass pie or tart pan with vegetable oil spray.

In a medium bowl, stir together the apple and gingerroot.

To assemble, arrange about half the beet slices in a single layer in the pan so they cover the bottom without overlapping. Arrange the apple mixture on the beets. Sprinkle with the leeks. Cover with the remaining beets.

Place a sheet of aluminum foil over the pan; place another pie or tart pan, bottom side down, on the beets to keep the top layer from drying out and curling.

Bake for 1 hour, or until a sharp knife can be easily inserted through all the layers. Allow to cool slightly, about 15 minutes, on a cooling rack with the top pie pan in place.

To serve, sprinkle with the parsley and cut in wedges.

Calories 40	Cholesterol 0 mg
Total Fat 0 g	Sodium 154 mg
Saturated 0 g	Carbohydrate 10 g
Polyunsaturated 0 g	Fiber 2 g
Monounsaturated 0 g	Protein 1 g

scalloped brussels sprouts

Sour cream, cheese, and sesame seeds embellish the often-maligned brussels sprout, making it gourmet fare. Serve with roasted chicken or turkey for a special dinner.

1 pound fresh or frozen no-salt-added brussels sprouts

1 cup nonfat or light sour cream

2 tablespoons fresh lemon juice

3 tablespoons shredded or grated Parmesan cheese, divided use

2 teaspoons sesame seeds

Steam the fresh brussels sprouts or cook the frozen brussels sprouts using the package directions, omitting the salt and margarine. Drain.

Preheat the broiler.

In a small bowl, stir together the sour cream, lemon juice, and 1½ tablespoons Parmesan. Stir into the brussels sprouts. Pour into a broilerproof 1½-quart glass baking dish. Sprinkle with the remaining Parmesan and sesame seeds.

Broil about 3 inches from the heat for 3 to 5 minutes, or until the cheese is melted and the sesame seeds are browned.

Calories 89

Total Fat 1.5 g

Saturated 0.5 g

Polyunsaturated 0.5 g

Monounsaturated 0.5 g

Cholesterol 9 mg

Sodium 104 mg

Carbohydrate 13 g

Fiber 3 g

Protein 5 g

baked red cabbage

This vibrantly colored dish goes especially well with Royal Pot Roast with Gravy (page 166). They bake at the same temperature, so you can pop the cabbage into the oven during the last hour of cooking the roast. The cabbage reheats beautifully and tastes even better the second day.

⅓ cup cider vinegar

3 tablespoons light brown sugar

1 tablespoon light tub margarine

1 teaspoon grated lemon zest

2 tablespoons fresh lemon juice

⅛ teaspoon salt

⅛ teaspoon pepper

½ large head red cabbage, very thinly sliced (about 1½ pounds)

2 medium Granny Smith apples, peeled and chopped

¼ cup cranberry juice

Preheat the oven to 325°F.

In a Dutch oven, stir together the vinegar, brown sugar, margarine, lemon zest, lemon juice, salt, and pepper. Bring to a boil over high heat. Reduce the heat to medium; cook for 1 minute. Remove from the heat.

Stir the cabbage and apples into the Dutch oven. Bring to a simmer over medium-high heat. Reduce the heat to medium-low; cook, covered, for 40 to 45 minutes, or until the cabbage is tender, stirring occasionally. Add water if needed to keep the mixture from drying out.

Stir in the apple cranberry juice. Cook for 5 to 10 minutes, or until the desired consistency, stirring occasionally.

Calories 98	Cholesterol 0 mg
Total Fat 1.0 g	Sodium 79 mg
Saturated 0 g	Carbohydrate 23 g
Polyunsaturated 0.5 g	Fiber 3 g
Monounsaturated 0.5 g	Protein 2 g

roasted carrots and onions with balsamic vinegar

A touch of balsamic vinegar adds zing to roasted vegetables.

Vegetable oil spray

3 tablespoons dark brown sugar

2 teaspoons balsamic vinegar

12 ounces carrots, peeled and cut into matchstick-size strips (about 3 cups)

2 medium onions, quartered

Preheat the oven to 425°F.

Lightly spray a rimmed baking sheet with vegetable oil spray. Put the brown sugar and vinegar in the pan; stir (the sugar doesn't need to dissolve). Add the carrots and onions; stir to coat completely. Spread in a single layer.

Roast for 20 minutes, or until the vegetables begin to caramelize or brown richly, stirring after 10 minutes. If the onions seem to be browning too quickly, stir the mixture more frequently.

Calories 72	Cholesterol 0 mg
Total Fat 0 g	Sodium 25 mg
Saturated 0 g	Carbohydrate 18 g
Polyunsaturated 0 g	Fiber 3 g
Monounsaturated 0 g	Protein 1 g

cauliflower and carrots with cumin

serves 4; ½ cup per serving

Cumin is the secret ingredient in this mellow, buttery-tasting vegetable medley.

1½ cups small cauliflower florets
2 medium carrots, thinly sliced
⅛ to ¼ teaspoon ground cumin
¼ teaspoon salt
Nonfat pump margarine spray

Put a steamer basket in a small amount of simmering water in a medium saucepan. Put the cauliflower and carrots in the basket. Cook, covered, for 6 minutes, or until tender-crisp.

Place the vegetables on a serving platter. Sprinkle with the cumin and salt. Spray with 20 pumps of margarine spray.

Calories 20	Cholesterol 0 mg
Total Fat 0 g	Sodium 164 mg
Saturated 0 g	Carbohydrate 4 g
Polyunsaturated 0 g	Fiber 2 g
Monounsaturated 0 g	Protein 1 g

baked chayote with cilantro-chili topping

serves 4; ½ squash per serving

Fill the hollow of baked chayote halves with fresh cilantro, lemon juice, and chili powder for a terrific accompaniment to Mexican food.

2 medium chayote (about 8 ounces each)

Vegetable oil spray

1 tablespoon light tub margarine

½ tablespoon snipped fresh cilantro

½ tablespoon fresh lemon juice

½ teaspoon chili powder

Preheat the oven to 400°F.

Cut each squash in half lengthwise; remove the pits. Using a fork, pierce the skin of the squash in several places. Lightly spray the cut side of the squash halves with vegetable oil spray. Place the squash with the cut side down on a nonstick baking sheet.

Bake for 40 minutes, or until tender when pierced with a fork, a skewer, or the point of a knife with a thin blade.

Meanwhile, in a small mixing bowl, combine the remaining ingredients.

Place the squash with the cut side up on a serving platter. Spoon about 1 teaspoon margarine mixture in the center of each squash half.

COOK'S TIP ON CHAYOTE

Known in the South as mirliton, chayote (*chy-O-tay*) is about the size and shape of a large pear but is similar in flavor to a mild yellow summer squash. Ripe chayote ranges from white to dark green, has a large, soft seed in the center, and is a good source of potassium. If cutting raw chayote, peel it first under running water so the liquid it exudes won't irritate your hands. Unless the squash is very young, the skin is too tough to eat.

Calories 31	Cholesterol 0 mg
Total Fat 1.5 g	Sodium 28 mg
Saturated 0 g	Carbohydrate 5 g
Polyunsaturated 0.5 g	Fiber 2 g
Monounsaturated 0.5 g	Protein 1 g

sesame-dusted collard greens

Steeped in the Asian flavors of ginger, citrus, and soy sauce, these collard greens are finished with a dusting of lightly toasted sesame seeds. This dish is perfect with fish, such as Broiled Tuna Steak with Lemongrass-Chamomile Glaze (page 90), or poultry.

1 large bunch collard greens (about 1 pound)

1 tablespoon sesame seeds

1 cup water

¼ cup sake or semisweet white wine (regular or nonalcoholic), such as Riesling or Gewürztraminer, or 2 tablespoons plain rice vinegar plus 2 tablespoons water

1 to 1½ teaspoons minced peeled gingerroot

1 teaspoon finely grated lemon zest

1 teaspoon toasted sesame oil

½ teaspoon low-salt soy sauce

Remove the thick part of the collard green stems; cut the leaves crosswise into 1-inch strips (makes about 5 cups). Spread the strips on a baking sheet; put in the freezer for 30 minutes to 1 hour, or until chilled but not too stiff to bend.

When the collard greens are ready, heat a large nonstick skillet over medium-high heat. Dry-roast the sesame seeds for 1 minute, stirring constantly. Remove from the skillet. Set aside.

In a small bowl, stir together the remaining ingredients. Pour into the hot skillet; bring to a boil over high heat. Add the collard greens; cook, uncovered, for 1 minute, stirring constantly. Cook, covered, for 15 minutes, stirring every 2 to 3 minutes. Don't let the mixture dry out; add water, ¼ cup at a time, as necessary. After 15 minutes, uncover and cook just until most of the liquid has evaporated. The collard greens should still look wet. Remove the skillet from the heat.

sesame-dusted collard greens

Calories 79	Cholesterol 0 mg
Total Fat 3.0 g	Sodium 42 mg
Saturated 0.5 g	Carbohydrate 8 g
Polyunsaturated 1.5 g	Fiber 4 g
Monounsaturated 1.0 g	Protein 4 g

To serve, transfer the greens to a serving plate; sprinkle with the sesame seeds.

sesame-dusted spinach

Dry-roast the sesame seeds as directed above. In a small bowl, stir together the sake, ginger-root, lemon zest, sesame oil, and soy sauce (omit water). Heat a large nonstick skillet over high heat. Pour the mixture into the skillet; bring to a boil. Boil until the mixture is reduced by half, 1 to 2 minutes. Replace the collard greens with 12 ounces baby spinach (about 8 cups); cook until wilted, 1 to 1½ minutes, stirring constantly. Remove from the heat immediately. Transfer to a serving plate; sprinkle with the sesame seeds. Serves 4; ½ cup per serving.

COOK'S TIP ON COLLARD GREENS

Partially freezing collard greens softens them and reduces their cooking time, minimizing vitamin loss from heat exposure.

sesame-dusted spinach

Calories 63	Cholesterol 0 mg
Total Fat 2.5 g	Sodium 85 mg
Saturated 0.5 g	Carbohydrate 4 g
Polyunsaturated 1.0 g	Fiber 3 g
Monounsaturated 1.0 g	Protein 3 g

corn pudding

Comfort food at its best, this delicious corn pudding gets a hint of tanginess from buttermilk.

> Vegetable oil spray
> 2 cups frozen no-salt-added whole-kernel corn, thawed
> 1¼ cups fat-free or low-fat buttermilk
> Egg substitute equivalent to 2 eggs, or 2 large eggs
> 1 tablespoon light tub margarine, melted
> 1 teaspoon sugar
> ¼ teaspoon salt
> ¼ teaspoon pepper (white preferred)

Preheat the oven to 350° F. Lightly spray a 6½-inch square baking pan with vegetable oil spray.

In a medium bowl, combine all the ingredients. Pour into the baking pan.

Bake for 45 to 50 minutes, or until a knife inserted in the center comes out clean. Let set for 5 minutes before serving.

Calories 133	Cholesterol 3 mg
Total Fat 2.5 g	Sodium 313 mg
Saturated 0.5 g	Carbohydrate 22 g
Polyunsaturated 0.5 g	Fiber 2 g
Monounsaturated 1.0 g	Protein 8 g

orange-flavored couscous with golden raisins and toasted almonds

serves 8; ½ cup per serving

One of the fastest and easiest grains to prepare, couscous is a great accompaniment to meat or poultry. This dish goes especially well with lean lamb or ham, or serve it as part of a vegetarian dinner. Leftovers are equally good at room temperature or reheated.

- 2 tablespoons slivered almonds
- 2 teaspoons grated orange zest
- 1½ cups fresh orange juice
- ¼ cup raisins (golden preferred)
- ½ teaspoon ground cinnamon
- ¼ teaspoon ground mace or nutmeg
- 1 cup uncooked couscous

In a large nonstick skillet, dry-roast the almonds over medium-low heat for 1 to 1½ minutes, or until beginning to lightly brown, stirring occasionally. Transfer to a paper towel to cool.

In the same skillet, stir together the remaining ingredients except the couscous. Bring to a boil over high heat. Stir in the couscous. Remove the pan from the heat. Cover and let stand for 5 minutes. Fluff with a fork.

To serve, transfer the couscous mixture to a large serving bowl and sprinkle with the almonds.

COOK'S TIP ON MACE

The flavor of mace is similar to that of nutmeg but is a bit more intense. Mace is derived from grinding the vivid red membrane that covers the nutmeg seed. The red color turns to yellow-orange when the membrane is dried.

Calories 132	Cholesterol 0 mg
Total Fat 1.5 g	Sodium 4 mg
Saturated 0 g	Carbohydrate 26 g
Polyunsaturated 0.5 g	Fiber 2 g
Monounsaturated 0.5 g	Protein 4 g

braised kasha

Hulled, crushed buckwheat kernels are known as buckwheat groats, or kasha. Available in most health food stores and many supermarkets, this native Russian herb has a slightly nutty taste. Kasha is a hearty side dish that is very easy to prepare.

1 cup coarse kasha

Egg substitute equivalent to 1 egg, or 1 large egg

2½ cups fat-free, low-sodium chicken broth, heated

1 medium onion, chopped

1 tablespoon light tub margarine

¼ teaspoon salt

In a large nonstick skillet, stir together the kasha and egg substitute. Cook over medium-low heat for 2 to 3 minutes, or until the kasha is lightly toasted and the egg substitute is absorbed, stirring occasionally.

Stir in the remaining ingredients. Increase the heat to high; bring the mixture to a boil. Reduce the heat to low; cook, covered, for 5 to 10 minutes, or until the kasha is tender and the mixture has thickened.

Calories 72	Cholesterol 0 mg
Total Fat 1.5 g	Sodium 239 mg
Saturated 0 g	Carbohydrate 11 g
Polyunsaturated 0.5 g	Fiber 1 g
Monounsaturated 0.5 g	Protein 5 g

mushrooms stuffed with rice and vegetables

serves 8; 2 mushrooms per serving

Since you can stuff these plump mushrooms ahead of time, they make great dinner party food, whether as appetizers or a side dish.

Olive oil spray

16 large fresh mushrooms, stems discarded or reserved for stock (about 24 ounces)

filling

1 teaspoon olive oil

½ medium carrot, shredded

½ medium red bell pepper, chopped

2 cups cooked long-grain and wild rice mix (cooked without seasoning packet or margarine)

¼ cup shredded or grated Parmesan cheese

Egg substitute equivalent to 1 egg, or 1 large egg

2 medium green onions, sliced (green and white parts)

½ teaspoon dried thyme, crumbled

½ teaspoon garlic powder

2 tablespoons sliced almonds

Preheat the oven to 375°F.

Lightly spray the tops of the mushrooms with olive oil spray. Place with the stem side up on a nonstick baking sheet.

Heat a large nonstick skillet over medium heat. Pour the olive oil into the skillet and swirl to coat the bottom. Cook the carrot and bell pepper for 2 to 3 minutes, or until tender-crisp, stirring occasionally. Remove the skillet from the heat.

Stir in the remaining ingredients except the almonds. Spoon about 3 tablespoons mixture into each mushroom, pressing slightly. Sprinkle with the almonds. If desired, cover and refrigerate for up to 8 hours at this point.

Bake, uncovered, for 20 to 25 minutes, or until the filling is cooked through and the mushrooms are tender.

Calories 96	Cholesterol 2 mg
Total Fat 2.5 g	Sodium 63 mg
Saturated 0.5 g	Carbohydrate 15 g
Polyunsaturated 0.5 g	Fiber 1 g
Monounsaturated 1.0 g	Protein 5 g

pasta with roasted tomato and chipotle sauce

Two terrific cooking traditions—Italian and Mexican—collaborate to produce this taste-tempting side dish.

Vegetable oil spray (olive oil spray preferred)

5 medium tomatoes, cored and halved crosswise (about 1½ pounds)

1 canned chipotle pepper packed in adobo sauce (see Cook's Tip on Chipotle Peppers, page 131)

2 medium onions, finely chopped

1 medium garlic clove, minced, or ½ teaspoon bottled minced garlic

½ tablespoon very low sodium chicken bouillon granules

½ teaspoon sugar

¼ teaspoon ground cumin

¼ teaspoon salt

2 tablespoons no-salt-added tomato paste

2 teaspoons olive oil

8 ounces dried penne pasta

Preheat the broiler.

Line a baking sheet with aluminum foil; lightly spray the foil with vegetable oil spray. Put the tomatoes with the cut side down on the foil; lightly spray the tomatoes with vegetable oil spray.

Broil the tomatoes 3 to 4 inches from the heat for 5 minutes, or until blackened. Put the tomatoes in a medium bowl and cover. Let stand for 20 minutes.

Meanwhile, put the chipotle pepper on a nonporous surface, such as a plate; mash the pepper with a fork to a paste consistency.

Heat a medium saucepan over medium heat. Remove the pan from the heat and lightly spray with vegetable oil spray (being careful not to spray near a gas

Calories 151	Cholesterol 0 mg
Total Fat 2.0 g	Sodium 103 mg
Saturated 0.5 g	Carbohydrate 29 g
Polyunsaturated 0.5 g	Fiber 2 g
Monounsaturated 1.0 g	Protein 5 g

flame). Cook the onions for 3 to 4 minutes, or until translucent, stirring frequently. Add the garlic; cook for 15 seconds. Remove from the heat.

Peel the cooled tomatoes. Put the tomatoes and any accumulated liquid in the saucepan; add the bouillon granules and mashed chipotle. Break up large pieces of tomato with a fork or spatula. Bring to a boil over high heat. Reduce the heat; simmer for 15 minutes, stirring occasionally. Stir in the remaining ingredients except the pasta. Remove from the heat; let stand, covered, for 10 minutes to allow the flavors to blend.

Meanwhile, cook the pasta according to the package directions, omitting the salt and oil.

To serve, spoon the sauce over the pasta.

COOK'S TIP ON COOKING PASTA

Use at least 4 quarts boiling water per pound of pasta. Keep the water boiling and stir the pasta occasionally to prevent sticking. As soon as the pasta has cooked to your liking, drain it and rinse in cold water to keep it from overcooking.

wild mushroom and tomato penne pasta

serves 8; ½ cup per serving

A sprinkling of Parmesan tops this light, mushroom-laced pasta.

½ ounce dried wild mushrooms (any variety or combination)

8 ounces dried penne pasta

1 teaspoon light tub margarine

1 medium sweet onion (Vidalia preferred), chopped

2 large garlic cloves, minced, or ½ tablespoon bottled minced garlic

1 teaspoon olive oil

2 medium tomatoes or 2 cups canned no-salt-added tomatoes, cut into bite-size pieces

2 tablespoons finely chopped fresh basil or 2 teaspoons dried, crumbled

¾ cup fat-free, low-sodium chicken broth or white wine (regular or nonalcoholic)

¼ teaspoon salt

⅛ to ¼ teaspoon pepper

3 tablespoons chopped fresh Italian, or flat-leaf, parsley

½ cup shredded or grated Parmesan cheese

In a small bowl, cover the mushrooms with hot water; soak for 20 to 30 minutes.

Meanwhile, cook the pasta using the package directions, omitting the salt and oil. Drain well.

Drain the reconstituted mushrooms; coarsely chop. Put the margarine and mushrooms in a large skillet. Cook over medium heat until the mushrooms are partially cooked and heated through, 5 to 6 minutes, stirring occasionally. Stir in the onion, garlic, and olive oil. Cook for 3 to 4 minutes, or until the onions are translucent, stirring frequently. Reduce the heat to low. Stir in the tomatoes and basil. Cook for 2 minutes, stirring occasionally. Increase the heat to medium. Add the broth and bring to a boil. Reduce the heat; simmer for 5 minutes. Stir in the salt, pepper, and pasta.

Spoon the pasta onto plates. Garnish with parsley and cheese.

Calories 155	Cholesterol 4 mg
Total Fat 2.5 g	Sodium 173 mg
Saturated 1.0 g	Carbohydrate 26 g
Polyunsaturated 0.5 g	Fiber 2 g
Monounsaturated 1.0 g	Protein 7 g

potato and mushroom napoleon

A frosting of sour cream tops layers of crispy herbed potatoes and savory marsala mushrooms.

2 large russet potatoes (8 to 10 ounces each)

2 teaspoons olive oil

2 teaspoons finely chopped fresh rosemary or ½ teaspoon dried, crushed

2 teaspoons finely chopped fresh sage or ½ teaspoon dried

¼ teaspoon sour salt (citric acid) or 1 tablespoon lemon juice

¼ teaspoon pepper

6 ounces fresh mushrooms, sliced

¼ cup marsala or mixture of 1 tablespoon sugar, 2 tablespoons balsamic vinegar, and 2 tablespoons water

½ teaspoon pepper, or to taste

¼ cup plus 2 tablespoons nonfat or light sour cream, at room temperature

2 tablespoons chopped green onions (green part only)

Preheat the oven to 450°F. Line a baking sheet with parchment paper.

Trim each potato to form a rectangle 3 to 3½ inches long, 1¾ to 2 inches wide, and 1¾ to 2 inches high. Cut each potato widthwise into six equal slices.

In a small bowl, stir together the olive oil, rosemary, sage, sour salt, and pepper. Brush on both sides of potatoes. Place the potatoes on the baking sheet.

Bake until golden brown and crisp, about 20 minutes (no turning necessary).

Meanwhile, heat a large skillet over medium-high heat. Cook the mushrooms, marsala, and pepper for 1 minute, stirring constantly. Reduce the heat to low; cook, covered, for 15 minutes, stirring occasionally. If any liquid remains, uncover the mixture and increase the heat to medium-high. Cook until the liquid has evaporated, stirring frequently.

To assemble, place a potato slice on each plate. Spread mushrooms over each potato slice. Spread about 1 tablespoon sour cream on each of the remaining potato slices, and place them on the mushroom-topped slices. Sprinkle with the green onions.

Calories 104	Cholesterol 1 mg
Total Fat 1.5 g	Sodium 19 mg
Saturated 0 g	Carbohydrate 17 g
Polyunsaturated 0 g	Fiber 2 g
Monounsaturated 1.0 g	Protein 3 g

brown rice and walnuts

serves 4; ½ cup per serving

The nutty flavor of the brown rice combined with the skillet-toasted walnuts gives this side dish a warmth and earthiness that's particularly complementary to autumn and winter entrées.

½ cup uncooked brown rice

2 tablespoons walnut pieces

½ cup finely chopped red bell peppers

¼ cup frozen green peas, thawed

¼ teaspoon salt

Cook the rice using the package directions, omitting the salt and margarine.

Meanwhile, heat a small skillet over medium-high heat. Dry-roast the walnuts for 4 minutes, or until beginning to lightly brown, stirring constantly. Transfer the walnuts to a sheet of aluminum foil or a plate to prevent overcooking.

When the rice is tender, stir in the walnuts and the remaining ingredients.

brown rice and pine nuts

Substitute dry-roasted pine nuts for walnuts and chopped dates for peas.

brown rice and walnuts

Calories 122	Cholesterol 0 mg
Total Fat 3.0 g	Sodium 158 mg
Saturated 0.5 g	Carbohydrate 21 g
Polyunsaturated 2.0 g	Fiber 2 g
Monounsaturated 0.5 g	Protein 3 g

brown rice and pine nuts

Calories 145	Cholesterol 0 mg
Total Fat 3.0 g	Sodium 148 mg
Saturated 0.5 g	Carbohydrate 28 g
Polyunsaturated 1.0 g	Fiber 2 g
Monounsaturated 1.0 g	Protein 3 g

snow pea rice

You can dress up the simplest pork or chicken entrée with minimal effort by serving this colorful side dish.

1 cup water

⅓ cup uncooked brown rice

2 ounces fresh or frozen snow peas (thawed if frozen)

4 ounces canned water chestnuts, rinsed and drained, cut into matchstick-size strips

1½ tablespoons low-salt soy sauce

1 teaspoon sugar

In a small saucepan, bring the water to a boil over high heat. Add the rice and return to a boil. Reduce the heat; simmer, covered, for 20 minutes, or until almost all the liquid is absorbed. Stir in the peas and water chestnuts. Cook, covered, for 5 minutes, or until the peas are just tender-crisp. Remove from the heat.

Stir in the soy sauce and sugar.

Calories 80	Cholesterol 0 mg
Total Fat 0.5 g	Sodium 152 mg
Saturated 0 g	Carbohydrate 17 g
Polyunsaturated 0 g	Fiber 2 g
Monounsaturated 0 g	Protein 2 g

coriander spinach

If you haven't used dried coriander before, this will be a great introduction. Its subtly sweet taste enhances spinach, much as nutmeg does. Serve this easy side dish with grilled or roasted poultry, pork, or fish.

>   **Vegetable oil spray**
>   **2 tablespoons minced onion**
>   **16 ounces frozen chopped spinach**
>   **2 tablespoons water (plus more as needed)**
> **2 to 3 large garlic cloves, minced, or 1½ to 2¼ teaspoons bottled minced garlic**
>   **½ teaspoon ground coriander (see Cook's Tip on Coriander, page 247)**
>   **¼ teaspoon salt**
>   **Pepper to taste**

Heat a large skillet over medium heat. Remove the skillet from the heat and lightly spray with vegetable oil spray (being careful not to spray near a gas flame). Cook the onion for 3 to 4 minutes, or until translucent, stirring occasionally.

Stir in the spinach, water, and garlic. Cook, covered, for 6 minutes, stirring frequently. If the spinach starts to stick to the skillet, add more water, about 1 tablespoon at a time.

Stir in the remaining ingredients. Cook, covered, for 2 to 3 minutes, or until the spinach is wilted, stirring occasionally.

Calories 22	Cholesterol 0 mg
Total Fat 0.5 g	Sodium 153 mg
Saturated 0 g	Carbohydrate 4 g
Polyunsaturated 0 g	Fiber 2 g
Monounsaturated 0 g	Protein 2 g

yellow squash skillet casserole

Vegetable casseroles can be time-consuming, but not this one. It only looks and tastes as if it were.

Vegetable oil spray

12 ounces yellow summer squash, thinly sliced

½ cup shredded carrots

½ cup finely chopped green bell pepper

½ teaspoon dried oregano, crumbled

⅛ teaspoon pepper

⅛ teaspoon salt

2 tablespoons snipped fresh parsley

¼ cup shredded reduced-fat sharp Cheddar cheese

2 tablespoons plain dry bread crumbs

Preheat the broiler.

Heat a large nonstick or ovenproof skillet over medium-high heat. Remove skillet from the heat and lightly spray with vegetable oil spray (being careful not to spray near a gas flame). Cook the squash, carrots, bell pepper, oregano, and pepper for 6 minutes, or until the squash is tender-crisp, stirring frequently. Remove from the heat. Sprinkle with the salt, parsley, and cheese. Top with the bread crumbs.

If using a nonstick skillet, cover the handle with aluminum foil to prevent discoloration. Broil 3 to 4 inches from the heat for 30 to 45 seconds, or until the bread crumbs begin to lightly brown.

Calories 63	Cholesterol 4 mg
Total Fat 1.5 g	Sodium 155 mg
Saturated 1.0 g	Carbohydrate 9 g
Polyunsaturated 0 g	Fiber 3 g
Monounsaturated 0.5 g	Protein 4 g

squash "blossoms"

Two kinds of squash, simply arranged, turn into a lovely "blossom." A splash of exotic fig balsamic vinegar enhances the dish, though regular balsamic vinegar works well, too.

Vegetable oil spray

6 green or yellow pattypan squash (preferably about 3 inches in diameter)

2 small tomatoes, peeled, seeded, and diced

1 medium yellow chile, such as Hungarian wax pepper or banana pepper, stemmed and seeded, minced

1 medium shallot, minced

1 teaspoon olive oil

¼ teaspoon pepper

1 small zucchini, very thinly sliced

2 tablespoons shredded or grated Parmesan cheese

2 tablespoons fig balsamic vinegar or balsamic vinegar

Preheat the oven to 350°F. Lightly spray a rimmed baking sheet with vegetable oil spray.

Slice just enough off the stem end of each pattypan squash so that it will stand up without tipping over. This is the bottom of the "blossom." Make a well 1½ to 2 inches across and about ¾ inch deep in the center of the top of each squash. Be careful to leave the bottoms and walls intact. A melon baller works well for this.

In a small bowl, stir together the tomatoes, yellow pepper, shallot, olive oil, and pepper.

To assemble, line the well in each pattypan squash with the zucchini slices. These "petals" should extend slightly over the edge of the well. Mound the tomato mixture on the zucchini slices. Sprinkle with Parmesan. Place the assembled squash on the prepared baking sheet and cover with a sheet of aluminum foil.

Bake for 15 minutes; remove the foil. Bake until the pattypan squash are tender and the edges of the zucchini petals are slightly browned, about 15 minutes.

Before serving, drizzle the vinegar over the tomato mixture.

Calories 48	Cholesterol 1 mg
Total Fat 1.5 g	Sodium 35 mg
Saturated 0.5 g	Carbohydrate 8 g
Polyunsaturated 0 g	Fiber 2 g
Monounsaturated 0.5 g	Protein 2 g

skinny sweet potato fries

serves 6; ½ cup per serving

Fill a basket with these spicy delights and serve them at your next barbecue. They're terrific with grilled chicken or fish.

> **Vegetable oil spray (olive oil spray preferred)**
> **2 pounds sweet potatoes (about 2 large)**
> **1 teaspoon olive oil**
> **½ teaspoon ground cumin**
> **¼ teaspoon chili powder**
> **¼ teaspoon ground coriander**
> **⅛ teaspoon cayenne (optional)**

Preheat the oven to 500° F. Heavily spray a rimmed baking sheet with vegetable oil spray.

Peel the potatoes. Cut in half crosswise, then cut lengthwise into 1-inch slices. Put the potatoes in a large bowl. Add the oil, stirring to coat each piece. Arrange in a single layer on the baking sheet. Lightly spray with vegetable oil spray.

In a small bowl, combine the remaining ingredients. Sprinkle half over the potato slices.

Bake for 5 minutes. Turn the potatoes over; sprinkle with the remaining spice mix. Bake for 5 to 10 minutes, or until the potatoes are browned on the outside and soft on the inside when pierced with a fork.

COOK'S TIP ON CORIANDER

Coriander, the tiny seeds of the cilantro plant, has a flavor very different from that of the pungent leaves. With its hint of lemon, sage, and caraway, coriander often is used to flavor Asian, Middle Eastern, and Indian dishes.

Calories 103	Cholesterol 0 mg
Total Fat 1.0 g	Sodium 11 mg
Saturated 0 g	Carbohydrate 23 g
Polyunsaturated 0 g	Fiber 3 g
Monounsaturated 0.5 g	Protein 2 g

tomato and goat cheese bread pudding

serves 6; ⅔ cup per serving

Making your own goat cheese is the easy trick to this creamy, tangy, guilt-free bread pudding. Just remember to start draining the yogurt at least a day before you need it.

8 ounces goat's milk yogurt

Vegetable oil spray

14.5-ounce can no-salt-added diced peeled tomatoes, undrained

3 tablespoons fresh basil, coarsely chopped (about 9 large leaves), or 1 tablespoon dried, crumbled

½ 13- to 15-ounce French bread (baguette style), cut into 18 slices, ⅓ inch thick

2 medium green onions, chopped (green and white parts)

Egg substitute equivalent to 3 eggs

½ cup fat-free milk

½ teaspoon salt-free Italian seasoning, crumbled

¼ teaspoon pepper

12 cherry tomatoes

One to three days before making the bread pudding, make goat yogurt cheese. Line a rustproof colander or large strainer with two layers of cheesecloth or an unused paper coffee filter. Put the colander into a deep glass or stainless steel bowl. The colander must not touch the bottom of the bowl. Pour the yogurt into the colander; cover the bowl. Let drain at room temperature for 1 hour. Discard the liquid. Put the colander back into the bowl; cover the bowl loosely. Refrigerate for 24 to 72 hours, or until most of the liquid has drained off and the yogurt has thickened. Discard the liquid. Carefully scrape the goat cheese back into the bowl.

Lightly spray a 9-inch square glass baking dish with vegetable oil spray.

To assemble, drain the tomatoes, reserving the liquid. Spread the tomatoes in the baking dish. Sprinkle with the basil. Spread the goat cheese on

Calories 150	Cholesterol 4 mg
Total Fat 2.0 g	Sodium 298 mg
Saturated 1.0 g	Carbohydrate 25 g
Polyunsaturated 0.5 g	Fiber 2 g
Monounsaturated 0.5 g	Protein 9 g

each slice of bread. Arrange the bread slices on the tomatoes in three even rows, with each slice slightly overlapping the next. Sprinkle with the green onions.

Preheat the oven to 425°F.

In a medium bowl, whisk together the egg substitute, milk, Italian seasoning, and pepper. Whisk in the reserved tomato juice. Drizzle half the liquid evenly over the casserole. Let stand for 5 minutes so the bread absorbs the liquid.

Meanwhile, pierce each cherry tomato with a knife. Arrange with the pierced side down on the casserole. After the 5-minute waiting period, drizzle the casserole with the remaining liquid mixture. Let stand for 5 minutes.

Bake for about 20 minutes, or until the liquid is absorbed and the top has puffed up and is slightly browned.

COOK'S TIP

You can make the goat yogurt cheese up to three days in advance. The longer you allow the cheese to drain, the firmer and more flavorful it will become. For the bread pudding, 24 hours of draining will do; but if you have time, the extra day or two will make the end result even better. Look for goat's milk yogurt at health food stores.

COOK'S TIP ON NO-SALT-ADDED CANNED TOMATOES

If you can't find no-salt-added canned tomatoes, substitute an 8-ounce can of no-salt-added tomato sauce plus 3 fresh Italian plum tomatoes, peeled, seeded if desired, and diced, sliced, or chopped.

broiled tomatoes with blue cheese bread crumbs

serves 4; ½ tomato per serving

Dijon mustard and blue cheese give these tomatoes lots of tangy taste.

2 large tomatoes (about 8 ounces each), halved crosswise
1 tablespoon plus 1 teaspoon Dijon mustard
2½ tablespoons crumbled blue cheese
¼ cup plain dry bread crumbs
2 tablespoons finely chopped green onions (green and white parts)

Preheat the broiler.

Put the tomatoes with the cut side up on a baking sheet. Spread 1 teaspoon mustard on each half. Broil about 5 inches from the heat for 4 minutes.

Meanwhile, put the remaining ingredients in a small bowl. Using a fork, gently stir together.

Remove the tomatoes from the broiler, but leave the broiler on. Place about 2 tablespoons of the mixture on each tomato half.

Turn off the broiler. Return the tomatoes to the oven and let stand for 4 minutes, or until just fork-tender.

broiled zucchini with feta bread crumbs

Substitute 2 medium zucchini, halved lengthwise, for the tomatoes, and feta cheese, rinsed, drained, and crumbled, for the blue cheese, with tomato and basil.

broiled tomatoes
with blue cheese bread crumbs

Calories 71	Cholesterol 4 mg
Total Fat 2.0 g	Sodium 260 mg
Saturated 1.0 g	Carbohydrate 10 g
Polyunsaturated 0 g	Fiber 1 g
Monounsaturated 0.5 g	Protein 3 g

broiled zucchini
with feta bread crumbs

Calories 67	Cholesterol 5 mg
Total Fat 2.0 g	Sodium 237 mg
Saturated 1.0 g	Carbohydrate 8 g
Polyunsaturated 0 g	Fiber 2 g
Monounsaturated 0 g	Protein 3 g

skillet-grilled zucchini and red bell peppers

serves 4; ½ cup vegetables and 2 tablespoons sauce per serving

Cooking these vegetables over high heat pulls out and lightly caramelizes their natural sugars.

horseradish-mustard sauce

½ cup nonfat or light sour cream

2 teaspoons prepared mustard

1½ to 2 teaspoons prepared horseradish

¼ teaspoon salt

2 teaspoons olive oil (extra-virgin preferred)

1 large zucchini

½ large red bell pepper

Vegetable oil spray

In a small bowl, stir together all the sauce ingredients except the olive oil. Gently stir in the oil. Set aside.

Cut the zucchini lengthwise into eighths, then cut crosswise into 2-inch pieces. Cut the bell pepper into thin strips.

Heat a large nonstick skillet over high heat. Remove the skillet from the heat and lightly spray with vegetable oil spray (being careful not to spray near a gas flame). Cook the zucchini and bell peppers for 4 minutes, or until the zucchini is just tender-crisp, stirring occasionally.

Serve the sauce on the side, or spoon it over the vegetables.

cayenne-lime sauce

Substitute ⅛ teaspoon cayenne for the horseradish and 1 tablespoon lime juice for the mustard.

with horseradish-mustard sauce		with cayenne-lime sauce	
Calories 70	Cholesterol 3 mg	Calories 69	Cholesterol 3 mg
Total Fat 2.5 g	Sodium 208 mg	Total Fat 2.5 g	Sodium 172 mg
Saturated 0.5 g	Carbohydrate 9 g	Saturated 0.5 g	Carbohydrate 9 g
Polyunsaturated 0.5 g	Fiber 1 g	Polyunsaturated 0 g	Fiber 1 g
Monounsaturated 1.5 g	Protein 3 g	Monounsaturated 1.5 g	Protein 3 g

breads and

breakfast

dishes

Cumin-Pepper Batter Bread

Tex-Mex Cornbread

Zucchini Raisin Breakfast Bread

Orange-Scented Poppy Seed Muffins

Breakfast Parfait

Whole-Wheat and Oat Bran Waffles
    with Fruit Salsa

Overnight French Toast with Peaches

Fruit and Cinnamon Oatmeal

Toasted Granola with Dried Fruit

Vegetable Scramble in Toast Cups

Puffy Tex-Mex Omelet

cumin-pepper batter bread

Earthy cumin seeds and pungent black pepper make this batter bread a perfect accompaniment to winter soups and stews.

2 teaspoons cumin seeds

1 cup all-purpose flour

¼-ounce package active dry yeast

½ cup water

½ cup fat-free or low-fat cottage cheese

1 tablespoon sugar

1 tablespoon acceptable vegetable oil

1 teaspoon pepper

1 teaspoon dried minced onion or ½ teaspoon onion powder

¼ teaspoon salt

Egg substitute equivalent to 1 egg, or 1 large egg

1 cup all-purpose flour

⅓ cup toasted wheat germ

Vegetable oil spray

1 tablespoon toasted wheat germ

In a small, heavy saucepan, dry-roast the cumin seeds over medium heat until fragrant, about 2 minutes, shaking the pan several times. Remove the seeds from the saucepan. Set aside.

In a large mixing bowl, stir together 1 cup flour and yeast.

In the same small saucepan, stir together the water, cottage cheese, sugar, oil, pepper, onion, and salt. Heat over medium heat until the mixture reaches 120°F to 130°F on an instant-read thermometer, stirring constantly.

Add the cottage cheese mixture to the flour mixture. Add the egg substitute and cumin seeds. Beat with an electric mixer on low until combined, about 30 seconds. Increase the speed to medium and beat for 3 minutes.

Calories 88	Cholesterol 1 mg
Total Fat 1.5 g	Sodium 69 mg
Saturated 0 g	Carbohydrate 15 g
Polyunsaturated 0.5 g	Fiber 1 g
Monounsaturated 0.5 g	Protein 4 g

Using a wooden spoon, stir in the remaining 1 cup flour and ⅓ cup wheat germ. (The dough will be stiff.)

Lightly spray an 8 × 1½-inch round baking pan with vegetable oil spray. Sprinkle with 1 tablespoon wheat germ. Tilt the pan to coat the bottom and side with wheat germ. Pat the bread dough into the pan. Cover with a damp dish towel; let rise in a warm place until doubled in bulk, about 1 hour.

Preheat the oven to 375°F. Bake the bread for 25 to 30 minutes, or until a wooden toothpick inserted in the center comes out clean. Remove the bread from the pan; let cool completely on a wire rack. Cut into wedges to serve.

tex-mex cornbread

This rich cornbread—livened up with the bold flavors of cumin, chili powder, and jalapeño—is an excellent partner for spicy chili, hearty stews, and savory soups. Lightly toasted leftovers make great breakfast treats.

Vegetable oil spray

1 cup yellow cornmeal

1 cup all-purpose flour

2 teaspoons baking powder

2 teaspoons chili powder

1 teaspoon ground cumin

½ teaspoon baking soda

⅛ teaspoon cayenne

1 cup fat-free milk or fat-free or low-fat buttermilk

1 tablespoon plus 1 teaspoon acceptable vegetable oil

2 tablespoons honey

¾ cup frozen no-salt-added whole-kernel corn, thawed

1 jalapeño, seeded and ribs removed if desired, chopped, or 2 tablespoons canned chopped green chiles, rinsed and drained

Preheat the oven to 400° F. Lightly spray an 8-inch square baking pan with vegetable oil spray. Set aside.

In a large bowl, thoroughly combine the cornmeal, flour, baking powder, chili powder, cumin, baking soda, and cayenne, using a fork. Make a well in the center.

In a medium bowl, whisk together the milk, oil, and honey. Pour into the well in the cornmeal mixture, whisking just until blended. Stir in the corn and jalapeño. Pour the batter into the prepared pan.

Bake for 20 to 25 minutes, or until a wooden toothpick inserted in the center comes out clean. Let cool in the pan on a cooling rack for 10 minutes. Cut into squares.

Calories 92	Cholesterol 0 mg
Total Fat 1.5 g	Sodium 112 mg
Saturated 0 g	Carbohydrate 18 g
Polyunsaturated 0.5 g	Fiber 1 g
Monounsaturated 0.5 g	Protein 2 g

zucchini raisin breakfast bread

Expect this bread to be a giant in moistness and flavor, but don't expect it to rise to great heights. It will become only about 2 inches tall.

Vegetable oil spray
1½ cups all-purpose flour
½ tablespoon baking soda
1 teaspoon ground cinnamon
⅛ teaspoon salt
Egg substitute equivalent to 1 egg, or 1 large egg
⅓ cup firmly packed light brown sugar
1½ cups grated zucchini
½ cup unsweetened applesauce
¾ cup nonfat or low-fat plain yogurt
1 teaspoon vanilla extract
⅓ cup regular or golden raisins

Preheat the oven to 350°F. Lightly spray a 9×5×3-inch loaf pan with vegetable oil spray.

In a medium bowl, stir together the flour, baking soda, cinnamon, and salt.

In a large bowl, whisk together the remaining ingredients except the raisins. Add the egg mixture and the raisins to the flour mixture, stirring until just combined. (Don't overmix; the batter should be lumpy.) Spread the batter in the loaf pan.

Bake for 50 to 55 minutes, or until a toothpick inserted in the center comes out clean. Let the bread rest in the pan for 5 minutes. Remove the bread from the pan and let cool completely on a cooling rack.

Calories 75	Cholesterol 0 mg
Total Fat 0 g	Sodium 139 mg
Saturated 0 g	Carbohydrate 16 g
Polyunsaturated 0 g	Fiber 1 g
Monounsaturated 0 g	Protein 2 g

orange-scented
poppy seed muffins

serves 12; 1 muffin per serving

Pop a muffin in a brown bag along with a piece of fruit, and you have a quick to-go breakfast or a wholesome afternoon snack. You will love the moist texture, orange flavor, and delicate crunch of these muffins.

Vegetable oil spray (optional)

1½ cups all-purpose flour

½ cup oat bran

½ cup dried unsweetened cranberries

¼ cup sugar

2½ teaspoons baking powder

2 teaspoons poppy seeds

1 cup fresh orange juice

Egg substitute equivalent to 1 egg, or 1 large egg

¼ cup unsweetened applesauce

2 to 3 teaspoons grated orange zest

1 teaspoon vanilla extract or ½ teaspoon almond extract (optional)

Preheat the oven to 375° F. Lightly spray a 12-cup muffin pan with vegetable oil spray or use paper muffin cups.

In a large bowl, stir together the flour, oat bran, cranberries, sugar, baking powder, and poppy seeds. Make a well in the center.

In a medium bowl, whisk together the remaining ingredients. Pour into the well in the flour mixture, stirring just enough to moisten the flour. Do not over-mix; the batter should be lumpy. Fill the muffin cups about half full.

Bake for 14 to 15 minutes, or until a toothpick inserted in the center of a muffin comes out clean. Remove the muffins from the pan and let them cool on a cooling rack.

Calories 115	Cholesterol 0 mg
Total Fat 0.5 g	Sodium 113 mg
Saturated 0 g	Carbohydrate 26 g
Polyunsaturated 0.5 g	Fiber 2 g
Monounsaturated 0 g	Protein 3 g

breakfast parfait

Eating this peach parfait is like having a dessert for breakfast.

¼ cup fresh orange juice

3 tablespoons sugar

2 teaspoons cornstarch

1-pound bag frozen unsweetened sliced peaches, partially thawed

½ teaspoon vanilla extract

1 cup fat-free or low-fat vanilla yogurt

¼ cup fat-free tub cream cheese

1 cup low-fat granola cereal without raisins

¼ teaspoon ground cinnamon (optional)

In a large nonstick skillet, combine the orange juice, sugar, and cornstarch. Stir until the cornstarch has completely dissolved. Stir in the peaches. Bring to a boil over high heat; cook for 2 minutes, stirring constantly. Remove from the heat; stir in the vanilla. Cover to keep warm and allow the flavors to blend.

In a small bowl, beat the yogurt and cream cheese with an electric mixer on medium until well blended.

To serve, spoon ½ cup peach mixture into each of four bowls. Top each serving with ¼ cup yogurt mixture. Sprinkle each with ¼ cup granola and cinnamon.

COOK'S TIP ON THAWING FRUIT

Pierce a one-pound bag of frozen fruit in several places with a fork. Microwave on 100 percent power (high) for 1 minute, or until just beginning to thaw. For recipes calling for thawed fruit, turn the bag over and microwave for 30 seconds.

Calories 264	Cholesterol 2 mg
Total Fat 2.0 g	Sodium 180 mg
Saturated 0.5 g	Carbohydrate 54 g
Polyunsaturated 1.5 g	Fiber 4 g
Monounsaturated 0.5 g	Protein 8 g

whole-wheat and oat bran waffles with fruit salsa

serves 12; 4½ × 5½-inch waffle and ½ cup fruit salsa per serving

Weekends are perfect times for preparing homemade waffles and making extra to freeze for the week ahead. Whole-wheat flour and oat bran give these waffles a nutritional boost and a fuller flavor. Choose whichever minty fruit salsa appeals to you.

americana salsa

- **1½ cups fresh or frozen blueberries (thawed if frozen)**
- **1½ cups sliced fresh strawberries**
- **1½ cups drained canned pineapple tidbits in their own juice**
- **1½ cups drained canned mandarin oranges in water or light syrup**
- **2 tablespoons chopped fresh mint**
- **2 tablespoons honey**

peachy-plum salsa

- **1½ cups chopped peaches**
- **1½ cups chopped plums (6 small)**
- **1½ cups halved and pitted fresh, frozen, or unsweetened canned cherries (thawed if frozen; drained if canned) (10 ounces fresh, pitted; 15 ounces frozen; or 16 ounces canned)**
- **3 medium green kiwifruit, peeled and chopped**
- **2 tablespoons chopped fresh mint**
- **2 tablespoons fresh lemon juice**
- **2 tablespoons honey**

with americana salsa

Calories 158	Cholesterol 1 mg
Total Fat 2.0 g	Sodium 165 mg
Saturated 0.5 g	Carbohydrate 34 g
Polyunsaturated 0.5 g	Fiber 3 g
Monounsaturated 0.5 g	Protein 5 g

1½ cups fat-free milk

Egg substitute equivalent to 2 eggs, or 2 large eggs, lightly beaten

3 tablespoons light brown sugar

3 tablespoons light stick margarine, melted

¾ cup all-purpose flour

¾ cup whole-wheat flour

½ cup oat bran

2½ teaspoons baking powder

½ teaspoon ground cinnamon

Vegetable oil spray

In a large bowl, combine all the ingredients for the desired salsa, gently stirring with a spoon so the fruit retains its shape.

Preheat a nonstick waffle iron using the manufacturer's directions. Preheat the oven to 200°F. Line a baking sheet with aluminum foil.

In a medium bowl, whisk together the milk, egg substitute, brown sugar, and margarine.

In a large bowl, stir together the remaining ingredients except the vegetable oil spray. Make a well in the center of the mixture. Pour the milk mixture into the well; whisk together until the flour is just moistened but still slightly lumpy. Do not overmix, or the waffles will be tough.

Lightly spray the heated waffle iron with vegetable oil spray. Spoon the batter for the first waffle over the waffle iron. Cook for 4 to 5 minutes, or until the steaming stops and the waffle is golden brown. Cooking times may vary, so watch the first batch closely; adjust the time as necessary. Transfer the waffle to the baking sheet. Repeat with the remaining batter. The waffles can be kept warm, uncovered, in the oven for up to 45 minutes.

To serve, spoon the fruit salsa over the waffles.

COOK'S TIP ON CHERRY PITTERS

Available in most gourmet shops, many grocery stores, and even hardware stores with a section for housewares, cherry pitters are a handy tool. If you don't have time to pit cherries, stock some canned or frozen ones.

with peachy-plum salsa

Calories 155	Cholesterol 1 mg
Total Fat 2.0 g	Sodium 161 mg
Saturated 0.5 g	Carbohydrate 32 g
Polyunsaturated 0.5 g	Fiber 3 g
Monounsaturated 0.5 g	Protein 5 g

overnight french toast with peaches

Hosting a brunch? Put this tasty dish together the night before, then let the flavors meld in the refrigerator.

Vegetable oil spray

3 tablespoons light tub margarine, melted

⅓ cup firmly packed light brown sugar

½ teaspoon ground cinnamon

½ teaspoon ground nutmeg

2 cups chopped fresh peaches; unsweetened frozen peaches, thawed; or peaches canned in light syrup

Egg substitute equivalent to 2 eggs, or 2 large eggs

½ cup fat-free milk

1 teaspoon vanilla extract

9 1-inch-thick slices stale French or Italian bread

Lightly spray a 9-inch square baking pan with vegetable oil spray.

In a small bowl, combine the margarine, brown sugar, cinnamon, and nutmeg. Spread in the pan. Top with the peaches.

In a medium shallow bowl or casserole dish, whisk together the egg substitute, milk, and vanilla. Dip the bread in the mixture, turning the slices to coat. Arrange the bread over the peaches. Cover the pan and refrigerate for 2 to 12 hours.

Preheat the oven to 375°F. Bake for 25 minutes. Turn the bread over; bake for 20 to 25 minutes, or until the top is light golden brown. To serve, spoon onto plates.

Calories 152	Cholesterol 0 mg
Total Fat 2.5 g	Sodium 241 mg
Saturated 0 g	Carbohydrate 28 g
Polyunsaturated 0.5 g	Fiber 2 g
Monounsaturated 1.0 g	Protein 5 g

fruit and cinnamon oatmeal

serves 1; 1¼ cups per serving

Greet the morning with a steaming bowl of this hearty, fruit- and spice-enhanced oatmeal. It's perfect for feeding hungry kids before school, getting charged up for an early-morning power meeting, or enjoying on a peaceful Sunday morning.

1 cup fat-free milk

⅛ cup chopped dried fruit

¼ teaspoon grated orange zest

⅛ teaspoon ground cinnamon

½ cup uncooked quick-cooking oatmeal

½ teaspoon vanilla extract

2 tablespoons fat-free or low-fat plain yogurt

1 teaspoon honey

Dash of ground nutmeg

In a medium saucepan, bring the milk, dried fruit, orange zest, and cinnamon to a simmer over medium-high heat, 2 to 3 minutes. Stir in the oatmeal and vanilla. Reduce the heat to low; cook, covered, for 5 minutes. Remove from the heat; let stand, covered, for 5 minutes.

To serve, top the oatmeal with the yogurt, honey, and nutmeg.

COOK'S TIP

To serve two people or to have breakfast prepared for a second day, increase the milk to 1¾ cups and double the remaining ingredients; prepare as directed. Refrigerate any leftovers in an airtight container for up to two days.

COOK'S TIP ON DRIED FRUIT

Keep a few bags of dried fruit on hand for quick snacks on the go. How do your favorite dried fruits measure up? For ¼ cup (4 tablespoons) dried fruit, use one of the following: 4 whole dried figs, 4 whole pitted dried plums, 4 dried nectarine halves, 80 regular or golden raisins, 80 pieces dried cherry mixture, 72 dried cranberries, 12 slices dried apple. If you want to cut the fruit, kitchen scissors are a super tool. For working with fruit that is sticky, lightly spray the scissors with vegetable oil spray before cutting.

Calories 328	Cholesterol 5 mg
Total Fat 3.5 g	Sodium 155 mg
Saturated 1.0 g	Carbohydrate 58 g
Polyunsaturated 1.0 g	Fiber 5 g
Monounsaturated 1.0 g	Protein 17 g

toasted granola
with dried fruit

The aroma of cinnamon fills the air as this wholesome granola mixture toasts in the oven. Serve it for breakfast, or sprinkle half a portion over fat-free or low-fat yogurt to enjoy as a snack.

Vegetable oil spray

4 cups uncooked quick-cooking oatmeal

⅔ cup firmly packed light brown sugar

½ cup toasted wheat germ

½ cup oat bran

½ tablespoon ground cinnamon

¼ teaspoon ground nutmeg

1 cup water

2 tablespoons honey

1 tablespoon acceptable vegetable oil

2 cups chopped mixed dried fruit (see Cook's Tip on Dried Fruit, page 263)

Preheat the oven to 300° F. Lightly spray a rimmed baking sheet with vegetable oil spray.

In a large bowl, stir together the oatmeal, brown sugar, wheat germ, oat bran, cinnamon, and nutmeg.

In a small bowl, whisk together the water, honey, and oil. Pour into the oatmeal mixture. Using a sturdy spoon, stir until the oatmeal mixture is moistened. Spread on the baking sheet.

Bake for 1 hour, or until the mixture is toasted and lightly golden brown, stirring every 20 minutes. Put the baking sheet on a cooling rack.

Stir in the dried fruit. Let the mixture cool thoroughly on the cooling rack, about 30 minutes.

COOK'S TIP

The granola will keep in an airtight container for up to two weeks.

Calories 205	Cholesterol 0 mg
Total Fat 3.0 g	Sodium 7 mg
Saturated 0.5 g	Carbohydrate 42 g
Polyunsaturated 1.0 g	Fiber 4 g
Monounsaturated 1.0 g	Protein 5 g

vegetable scramble in toast cups

Great for breakfast and ideal as an appetizer, this egg white treat is peppered with minced vegetables. Both kids and adults will love these toast cups.

Vegetable oil spray

6 slices light wheat or white bread

8 ounces egg whites (whites of 8 to 10 large eggs)

2 tablespoons fat-free milk

1 tablespoon finely chopped green onions (green part only)

½ medium red bell pepper, finely chopped

1 medium carrot, finely grated

1 tablespoon light tub or light stick margarine

¼ teaspoon salt

Pepper (optional)

Preheat the oven to 350° F. Lightly spray a 6-cup muffin pan with vegetable oil spray.

With a rolling pin, roll the bread until slightly flattened. Using a 3⅝-inch biscuit cutter, a round cookie cutter, or a drinking glass, cut a circle out of each slice of bread. (Keep the remaining bread for another use, such as making bread crumbs or croutons, or discard.) Starting at the center, cut a slit to the edge of each bread circle. Fit each bread circle into a muffin cup, overlapping the bread to fit.

Bake for 15 minutes, or until lightly brown and crisp. Remove from the oven.

Meanwhile, in a large bowl, whisk together the egg whites and milk until frothy, about 1 minute. Stir in the green onions, bell peppers, and carrots.

In a large nonstick skillet, melt the margarine over medium-low heat. Add the egg white mixture to the skillet; cook for 10 minutes, lifting up the mixture as it cooks and letting the liquid part run underneath the cooked part. Sprinkle with the salt. When the eggs appear dry, remove from the heat.

Spoon about 3 tablespoons egg mixture, mounding it 1 tablespoon at a time, into each bread cup. Sprinkle with the pepper.

Calories 68	Cholesterol 0 mg
Total Fat 1.0 g	Sodium 254 mg
Saturated 0 g	Carbohydrate 10 g
Polyunsaturated 0 g	Fiber 2 g
Monounsaturated 0.5 g	Protein 6 g

puffy tex-mex omelet

serves 6; 1 wedge and 3 tablespoons cherry tomato mixture per serving

The presentation is quite dramatic as you remove this puffy omelet from the oven. Unlike a soufflé, the omelet holds its shape and can even be reheated.

Vegetable oil spray

6 6-inch corn tortillas, diced

1 cup cherry tomatoes, halved

1 tablespoon snipped fresh cilantro

1 teaspoon chopped fresh jalapeño, seeded and ribs removed

Egg substitute equivalent to 4 eggs, or whites of 8 large eggs

2 slices fat-free or low-fat American cheese, diced

3 ounces lean ground beef

½ teaspoon chili powder

½ cup chopped red bell peppers

1 teaspoon light tub or light stick margarine

2 medium green onions, sliced (green and white parts)

Whites of 4 large eggs

Preheat the oven to 350°F. Lightly spray a baking sheet with vegetable oil spray.

Spread the tortilla pieces in an even layer on the baking sheet. Lightly spray with vegetable oil spray.

Bake for 5 minutes, or until toasted and slightly crispy. Put the baking sheet on a cooling rack. Leave the oven on.

Meanwhile, in a small bowl, stir together the tomatoes, cilantro, and jalapeño. Set aside.

In a medium bowl, stir together the egg substitute and cheese. Set aside.

In a large ovenproof nonstick skillet, cook the beef over medium-high heat for 6 to 8 minutes, or until no longer pink in the center, stirring occasionally. Pour the beef into a colander and rinse under hot water to remove excess fat. Drain well. Wipe the skillet with paper towels. Return the beef to the skillet.

Stir in the chili powder. Add bell peppers and margarine; cook for 1 to 2 minutes, or until the peppers are tender-crisp, stirring occasionally. Stir in the

Calories 106	Cholesterol 10 mg
Total Fat 1.5 g	Sodium 251 mg
Saturated 0.5 g	Carbohydrate 11 g
Polyunsaturated 0.5 g	Fiber 2 g
Monounsaturated 0.5 g	Protein 13 g

green onions; cook for 1 to 2 minutes, or until the onions are wilted. Stir in the tortillas; cook for 1 to 2 minutes, or until warmed through. Turn off the heat, leaving the skillet on the stove to keep warm.

In a medium mixing bowl, beat the egg whites with an electric mixer on medium until foamy. Increase the speed to high and beat until stiff peaks form.

With a rubber scraper, fold the egg substitute mixture into the egg whites until just combined (the mixture should be fluffy and foamy; a few streaks of egg white may be visible). Spread over the tortilla mixture in the skillet, stirring gently to slightly incorporate (most of the tortillas will stay on the bottom and act as a crust).

Bake for 14 to 15 minutes, or until the top of the omelet is set (the omelet will puff up like a soufflé) and the tip of a knife or a wooden skewer inserted in the center comes out clean.

To serve, cut into 6 wedges and top each with about 3 tablespoons tomato mixture.

COOK'S TIP

If you do not have an ovenproof skillet, bake the omelet in a 9- or 10-inch round cake pan that has been sprayed with vegetable oil spray.

desserts

Chocolate Angel Food Cake

Carrot Cake

Raspberry and Almond Cake
 ❖ Peach and Walnut Cake

Spice Cupcakes with Apricots

Chocolate Cupcakes with
    Chocolate-Peppermint
    Topping

Apricot-Blueberry Crisp

Lemon Kisses
 ❖ Orange Kisses

Chocolate-Coconut Macaroons

Apple-Oat Bars

Cheesecake Pudding
    with Tropical Fruit
 ❖ Cheesecake Pudding with
    Kiwifruit and Strawberries

Individual Blueberry Bread
    Puddings

Cranberry-Orange Pudding

Layered Baked Apples

Apple Dumplings

Granny Smith Caramel Apple
    Wedges

Grilled Pineapple with Port Glaze

Grenadine and Melon Compote

Crunchy Coated Ice Cream Cones

Petite Baked Alaska

Frozen Strawberry Softee

chocolate
angel food cake

Angel food cake turns devilishly delicious with the addition of cocoa powder. Work some fruit into your menu by adding fresh, luscious raspberries.

16-ounce package angel food cake mix
⅓ cup unsweetened cocoa powder
½ teaspoon ground cinnamon
1 cup frozen fat-free or light whipped topping, thawed (optional)
4 cups fresh raspberries (optional)

In a large mixing bowl, stir together the cake mix, cocoa powder, and cinnamon. Prepare the cake using the package directions.

To serve, top each slice of cake with a dollop of whipped topping and raspberries.

with raspberries

Calories 130	Cholesterol 0 mg
Total Fat 0.5 g	Sodium 171 mg
Saturated 0 g	Carbohydrate 29 g
Polyunsaturated 0 g	Fiber 3 g
Monounsaturated 0 g	Protein 3 g

without raspberries

Calories 108	Cholesterol 0 mg
Total Fat 0 g	Sodium 169 mg
Saturated 0 g	Carbohydrate 24 g
Polyunsaturated 0 g	Fiber 1 g
Monounsaturated 0 g	Protein 3 g

carrot cake

The surprising secret in this cake is jarred baby food carrots. No peeling or chopping! Another bonus is that no icing is needed.

Vegetable oil spray
1½ cups all-purpose flour
½ tablespoon baking soda
½ tablespoon ground cinnamon
½ teaspoon ground nutmeg
½ teaspoon ground cloves
8-ounce can crushed pineapple in its own juice, undrained
2 4-ounce jars pureed baby food carrots
⅔ cup sugar
Egg substitute equivalent to 2 eggs, or 2 large eggs
½ cup unsweetened applesauce
¼ cup fat-free or low-fat buttermilk
1 teaspoon vanilla extract

Preheat the oven to 350° F. Lightly spray an 8-inch square baking pan with vegetable oil spray.

In a medium bowl, stir together the flour, baking soda, cinnamon, nutmeg, and cloves.

In a large bowl, whisk together the remaining ingredients. Stir the flour mixture into the pineapple mixture until just combined. Spread the batter in the pan.

Bake for 40 minutes, or until the top is springy to the touch and a wooden toothpick inserted in the center comes out clean. Let cool in the pan on a cooling rack.

COOK'S TIP ON BUTTERMILK

If you don't want to buy buttermilk, you can easily make your own. Whisk 1 tablespoon vinegar or another acid such as lemon juice into 1 cup fat-free milk. Let stand for 5 minutes, then use it to replace buttermilk. If the recipe is for a dessert, you can use cider vinegar or other fruit-flavored vinegar.

Calories 65	Cholesterol 0 mg
Total Fat 0 g	Sodium 97 mg
Saturated 0 g	Carbohydrate 14 g
Polyunsaturated 0 g	Fiber 1 g
Monounsaturated 0 g	Protein 2 g

raspberry
and almond cake

Pureed pears replace the cooking oil in this moist, very light cake.

Vegetable oil spray

cake

18.25-ounce package reduced-fat white cake mix
¾ cup water
6-ounce jar pureed baby food pears
Whites of 3 large eggs
¼ teaspoon almond extract

topping

2 ounces almond slices
2 12-ounce bags frozen unsweetened raspberries, thawed
½ cup sugar
1 tablespoon plus 1 teaspoon cornstarch
¼ teaspoon almond extract

Preheat the oven to 350°F. Lightly spray a 13 × 9 × 2-inch nonstick baking pan with vegetable oil spray.

In a large mixing bowl, combine all the cake ingredients. Using an electric mixer, beat on low for 2 minutes. Pour the batter into the prepared pan.

Bake for 26 minutes, or until a wooden toothpick inserted in the center comes out clean. Leave the oven on for the next step. Let the cake cool completely in the pan on a cooling rack.

Place the almonds in a single layer on a baking sheet. Dry-roast for 5 minutes, or until golden brown, stirring occasionally. Remove from the oven; let cool on the pan on a cooling rack.

In a medium saucepan, combine the remaining topping ingredients except ¼ teaspoon almond extract, stirring gently until the cornstarch has dissolved. Bring to a boil over high heat. Let boil for 1½ to 2 minutes, or until thickened,

raspberry and almond cake

Calories 211	Cholesterol 0 mg
Total Fat 3.5 g	Sodium 238 mg
Saturated 0.5 g	Carbohydrate 43 g
Polyunsaturated 0.5 g	Fiber 3 g
Monounsaturated 1.5 g	Protein 3 g

stirring frequently. Remove from the heat; let cool completely. Stir in the remaining almond extract. Spread the raspberry mixture over the cake.

At serving time, sprinkle with the almonds.

peach and walnut cake

Vegetable oil spray

cake

18.25-ounce package reduced-fat white cake mix

¾ cup water

6-ounce jar pureed baby food peaches or 6 to 8 ounces fat-free or low-fat peach yogurt

Whites of 3 large eggs

¼ teaspoon vanilla, butter, and nut flavoring or vanilla extract

topping

2 ounces walnuts, chopped

2 12-ounce bags frozen unsweetened peaches, thawed

½ cup dark brown sugar, firmly packed

1 tablespoon plus 1 teaspoon cornstarch

¼ teaspoon vanilla, butter, and nut flavoring or vanilla extract

Prepare the cake as directed, substituting the peaches or peach yogurt for the pears and substituting the vanilla, butter, and nut flavoring for the almond extract.

Heat a small skillet over medium-high heat. Dry-roast the walnuts for 4 minutes, or until beginning to lightly brown, stirring constantly. Transfer the walnuts to a sheet of aluminum foil or a plate to prevent overcooking.

Prepare the topping as directed, substituting the peaches, dark brown sugar, and vanilla, butter, and nut flavoring for the raspberries, sugar, and almond extract. Spread the peach mixture over the cake.

At serving time, sprinkle with the walnuts.

COOK'S TIP

To cool the fruit mixture quickly, pour it into a shallow pan, such as a rimmed baking sheet or large rectangular baking dish. Put the pan on a cooling rack; stir the fruit often.

peach and walnut cake

Calories 208	Cholesterol 0 mg
Total Fat 4.0 g	Sodium 239 mg
Saturated 0.5 g	Carbohydrate 40 g
Polyunsaturated 2.0 g	Fiber 2 g
Monounsaturated 1.0 g	Protein 3 g

spice cupcakes
with apricots

These cupcakes are deliciously messy, so serve them with forks.

 Vegetable oil spray
 18.25-ounce box spice cake mix
 1 cup water
 6-ounce jar pureed baby food sweet potatoes
 Whites of 3 large eggs
 ¼ teaspoon ground nutmeg
 15.25-ounce can apricot halves in light syrup, undrained
 1 tablespoon sugar
 1 tablespoon cornstarch
 1 teaspoon vanilla extract
 ½ teaspoon ground nutmeg (optional)
 8-ounce container frozen fat-free or light whipped topping, thawed

Preheat the oven to 350° F. Lightly spray two 12-cup nonstick muffin pans with vegetable oil spray or line with paper muffin cups.

In a medium mixing bowl, combine the cake mix, water, sweet potatoes, egg whites, and ¼ teaspoon nutmeg. Beat according to the package directions. Spoon equal amounts of the batter into each muffin cup.

Bake for 15 to 18 minutes, or until a wooden toothpick inserted in the center of a muffin comes out clean. Cool on a cooling rack; remove paper muffin cups.

Meanwhile, chop the apricots into ½-inch pieces. In a small saucepan, stir with the syrup, sugar, and cornstarch until the cornstarch completely dissolves. Bring to a boil over high heat, stirring frequently. Boil for 1½ minutes, or until slightly thickened. Let cool completely. Stir in vanilla.

Fold the ½ teaspoon nutmeg into the whipped topping. Top each cooled cupcake with 2 tablespoons whipped topping mixture and 1 tablespoon apricot mixture.

Calories 129	Cholesterol 6 mg
Total Fat 2.5 g	Sodium 179 mg
Saturated 1.0 g	Carbohydrate 24 g
Polyunsaturated 0 g	Fiber 1 g
Monounsaturated 1.0 g	Protein 2 g

chocolate cupcakes with chocolate-peppermint topping

serves 24; 1 cupcake and 2 tablespoons topping per serving

No guilt here—just light, minty, and extremely chocolate decadence.

Vegetable oil spray
18.25-ounce box light devil's food cake mix
1⅓ cups cold strong coffee or water
Whites of 6 large eggs
¼ cup fat-free chocolate syrup
½ teaspoon peppermint extract
8-ounce container frozen fat-free or light whipped topping, thawed

Preheat the oven to 350°F. Lightly spray two 12-cup nonstick muffin pans with vegetable oil spray or line with paper muffin cups.

In a large mixing bowl, combine the cake mix, coffee, and egg whites. Using an electric mixer, beat on low for 1 minute. Increase the speed to medium and beat for 2 minutes, or until smooth, scraping the sides with a rubber scraper. Spoon the batter into the muffin cups to about ⅔ full.

Bake for 15 to 18 minutes, or until a wooden toothpick inserted in the center of a muffin comes out clean. Let cool completely on cooling racks.

Meanwhile, in a small bowl, stir together the chocolate syrup and peppermint extract.

In a medium bowl, gently combine the whipped topping and chocolate syrup mixture, stirring just until it has a swirled effect. Cover and refrigerate until needed.

When the cupcakes have cooled, remove from the muffin pans. Spread 2 tablespoons topping over each cupcake.

COOK'S TIP

To save space in your refrigerator, you can refrigerate just the topping and keep the cupcakes at room temperature in an airtight container. Frost the cupcakes when you're ready to eat them.

Calories 110	Cholesterol 0 mg
Total Fat 1.0 g	Sodium 207 mg
Saturated 0.5 g	Carbohydrate 24 g
Polyunsaturated 0.5 g	Fiber 1 g
Monounsaturated 0.5 g	Protein 2 g

apricot-blueberry crisp

serves 6; ½ cup per serving

Oatmeal and wheat germ add a slightly nutty taste to the streusel topping of this year-round favorite dessert and give a nutritional boost as well. Feel free to substitute your favorite fruits for the apricots, blueberries, or both.

Vegetable oil spray

filling

3 8-ounce cans apricots in extra-light syrup, drained and sliced
1 cup fresh or frozen blueberries (thawed if frozen)
1 teaspoon grated lemon zest
1 tablespoon fresh lemon juice

streusel topping

½ cup uncooked quick-cooking oatmeal
⅓ cup firmly packed light brown sugar
¼ cup all-purpose flour
2 tablespoons toasted wheat germ
1 teaspoon ground cinnamon
2 tablespoons light stick margarine

Preheat the oven to 375°F.

Lightly spray an 8-inch square glass baking dish with vegetable oil spray. Put the filling ingredients in the baking dish, stirring lightly to combine.

In a medium bowl, lightly stir together all the topping ingredients except the margarine. Cut in the margarine with a fork, pastry blender, or two knives until the mixture resembles coarse crumbs. Sprinkle over the filling.

Bake until the top is golden brown, 35 to 40 minutes.

COOK'S TIP

Make several batches of streusel topping at once and freeze them in individual plastic freezer bags for future use. The next time you have some fresh, canned, or frozen fruit on hand and want to make a simple dessert, defrost a bag of topping and quickly whip up another crisp.

Calories 182	Cholesterol 0 mg
Total Fat 2.5 g	Sodium 35 mg
Saturated 0.5 g	Carbohydrate 39 g
Polyunsaturated 1.0 g	Fiber 3 g
Monounsaturated 0.5 g	Protein 3 g

lemon kisses

Thanks to lemon juice and zest, these melt-in-your-mouth meringue cookies are not overly sweet.

Vegetable oil spray
Whites of 2 large eggs, at room temperature
½ **teaspoon fresh lemon juice**
⅛ **teaspoon cream of tartar**
½ **cup sugar**
Zest from 1 small lemon

Preheat the oven to 300°F. Lightly spray two baking sheets with vegetable oil spray.

Pour the egg whites into a large mixing bowl. Add the lemon juice and cream of tartar. With an electric mixer, beat on high until soft peaks form.

While the mixer is still running, gradually add the sugar, about 1 table-spoon at a time. Continue to beat until the egg whites are shiny and stiff peaks form. Gently fold in the lemon zest.

Use a spoon to drop 1½-inch mounds of meringue onto the baking sheets about 2 inches apart.

Bake for 20 minutes, or until the cookies are lightly browned. Transfer the cookies to a cooling rack and let cool completely.

orange kisses

Replace the lemon juice and lemon zest with fresh orange juice and 2 to 3 teaspoons orange zest. All the nutrient analysis numbers are identical.

Calories 18	Cholesterol 0 mg
Total Fat 0 g	Sodium 5 mg
Saturated 0 g	Carbohydrate 4 g
Polyunsaturated 0 g	Fiber 0 g
Monounsaturated 0 g	Protein 0 g

chocolate-coconut macaroons

Laced with almonds and coconut, these chocolate cookies are even better when paired with halved strawberries or sliced peaches. Like many other homemade macaroons, they are both crumbly and slightly chewy.

Vegetable oil spray
¾ cup slivered almonds, dry-roasted and finely chopped
⅔ cup sweetened flaked coconut
⅓ cup all-purpose flour
3 tablespoons unsweetened cocoa powder
Whites of 4 large eggs
½ teaspoon vanilla extract
½ teaspoon imitation coconut flavoring
¼ teaspoon cream of tartar
1 cup sugar

Preheat the oven to 325°F. Lightly spray two baking sheets with vegetable oil spray or line with parchment paper.

In a small bowl, stir together the almonds, coconut, flour, and cocoa.

In a large metal or glass mixing bowl, combine the remaining ingredients except sugar. Beat with an electric mixer on high until foamy. Gradually beat in the sugar. Continue to beat for 2 to 3 minutes, or until the egg whites are glossy and stiff peaks form and remain standing.

Gently fold the almond mixture into the egg white mixture. Drop by rounded teaspoonfuls, 2 inches apart, onto the baking sheets.

Bake one sheet at a time for 12 to 14 minutes, or until the tops of the cookies are dry. Transfer the cookies to a cooling rack; let cool completely.

COOK'S TIP ON PARCHMENT PAPER
It's easy to peel almost anything off parchment paper, and the side of the food touching the parchment will brown nicely. Gourmet shops and supermarkets usually carry this helpful item.

Calories 97	Cholesterol 0 mg
Total Fat 3.5 g	Sodium 20 mg
Saturated 1.0 g	Carbohydrate 16 g
Polyunsaturated 0.5 g	Fiber 1 g
Monounsaturated 1.5 g	Protein 2 g

apple-oat bars

With their combination of crunchiness and smoothness, these bars are winners in a lunch box, on a picnic, or at a cookie exchange.

> **Vegetable oil spray**
> **1 cup uncooked quick-cooking oatmeal**
> **1 cup whole-wheat pastry flour or all-purpose flour**
> **⅔ cup firmly packed dark brown sugar**
> **½ teaspoon ground cinnamon**
> **¼ teaspoon salt**
> **¼ teaspoon baking soda**
> **White of 1 large egg**
> **3 tablespoons acceptable vegetable oil**
> **9-ounce jar or 1 cup apple butter or other fruit butter**
> **3 tablespoons sliced almonds (optional)**

Preheat the oven to 325°F. Lightly spray a 12 × 8 × 2-inch or 11 × 7 × 1½-inch baking pan with vegetable oil spray.

In a medium bowl, stir together the oatmeal, flour, brown sugar, cinnamon, salt, and baking soda.

In a small bowl, lightly beat the egg white with a fork. Add the oil, stirring well. Pour over the oatmeal mixture. Using a fork, stir together thoroughly. Press half the mixture into the prepared pan.

Using a spatula, spread the apple butter over the oatmeal mixture. Sprinkle with the almonds and remaining oat mixture.

Bake until golden brown, about 25 minutes if using a 12 × 8 × 2-inch pan, about 35 minutes if using an 11 × 7 × 1½-inch pan. Let cool in the pan on a cooling rack. Cut into 15 bars.

COOK'S TIP

A 9-ounce bottle of fruit butter isn't quite 1 cup, but it works fine here. If the fruit butter is very thick, whip it with a fork for easier spreading.

without almonds		with almonds	
Calories 132	Cholesterol 0 mg	Calories 140	Cholesterol 0 mg
Total Fat 3.0 g	Sodium 68 mg	Total Fat 4.0 g	Sodium 68 mg
Saturated 0 g	Carbohydrate 25 g	Saturated 0.5 g	Carbohydrate 25 g
Polyunsaturated 1.0 g	Fiber 1 g	Polyunsaturated 1.0 g	Fiber 2 g
Monounsaturated 1.5 g	Protein 2 g	Monounsaturated 2.0 g	Protein 2 g

cheesecake pudding
with tropical fruit

Just because you don't want to heat up your kitchen doesn't mean you have to give up the pleasure of eating creamy, rich-tasting cheesecake.

1 cup nonfat or light sour cream

¼ cup low-fat cream cheese in tub

3 tablespoons sugar

½ teaspoon grated lemon zest

1 tablespoon fresh lemon juice

½ teaspoon vanilla extract

1 medium banana, sliced

8-ounce can pineapple tidbits in their own juice, drained

In a medium mixing bowl, combine the sour cream, cream cheese, sugar, lemon zest, lemon juice, and vanilla. Beat with an electric mixer on low until the mixture is smooth except for the zest.

To assemble, spoon ¼ cup sour cream mixture into each of four 6-ounce ramekins or custard cups. For each serving, arrange the banana slices over the sour cream mixture. Top with the pineapple, making sure the bananas are covered.

Serve immediately, or cover individually with plastic wrap and refrigerate for up to 8 hours.

cheesecake pudding
with kiwifruit and strawberries

Substitute lime zest and juice for lemon zest and juice; 2 medium kiwifruit for banana; and 1 cup sliced fresh strawberries or fresh or frozen blueberries (thawed if frozen) for pineapple.

COOK'S TIP

The juice from the pineapple prevents the bananas from discoloring.

with tropical fruit		with kiwifruit and strawberries	
Calories 193	Cholesterol 8 mg	Calories 181	Cholesterol 8 mg
Total Fat 3.0 g	Sodium 99 mg	Total Fat 3.0 g	Sodium 95 mg
Saturated 1.5 g	Carbohydrate 36 g	Saturated 1.5 g	Carbohydrate 32 g
Polyunsaturated 0 g	Fiber 1 g	Polyunsaturated 0 g	Fiber 2 g
Monounsaturated 1.0 g	Protein 6 g	Monounsaturated 1.0 g	Protein 6 g

individual blueberry bread puddings

serves 6; ½ cup per serving

Rich and creamy, this blueberry-studded bread pudding rises like a soufflé and is as moist and rich tasting as its full-fat kindred. Best of all, it's an elegant mix-in-one-bowl dessert.

Vegetable oil spray

6 thin slices white bread, broken into quarter-size pieces (very low sodium preferred)

1 cup fresh or frozen blueberries (thawed if frozen)

Egg substitute equivalent to 4 eggs

1 cup fat-free milk

⅓ cup sugar

¼ cup all-fruit orange marmalade, divided use

Preheat the oven to 350°F. Lightly spray six 3½- or 4-ounce ramekins or custard cups with vegetable oil spray.

In a medium bowl, stir together the bread, blueberries, egg substitute, milk, sugar, and 2 tablespoons marmalade. Don't overmix; the bread should be mushy, but some identifiable lumps of bread should be visible. Spoon into the ramekins; place on a baking sheet.

Bake for 25 minutes, or until the tops are golden brown and the puddings have risen at least ½ inch above the rims. If you have a quick-read thermometer, the internal temperature should read 155°F.

Meanwhile, in a cup or small bowl, whip the remaining 2 tablespoons marmalade with a fork.

As soon as you take the puddings out of the oven, gently spread 1 teaspoon marmalade over each. Serve immediately. The puddings will start to deflate about 1 minute after removal from the oven.

COOK'S TIP

You can fill the ramekins with the uncooked pudding mixture up to 2 hours before baking. However, the puddings may rise slightly less than usual.

Calories 198	Cholesterol 1 mg
Total Fat 1.5 g	Sodium 241 mg
Saturated 0 g	Carbohydrate 37 g
Polyunsaturated 0 g	Fiber 1 g
Monounsaturated 0.5 g	Protein 8 g

cranberry-orange pudding

If you want a luscious dessert that will fill you up without filling you out, this dish fits the bill. With its rich color and light texture, this unusual pudding could become your new traditional holiday dessert.

> **2 cups fresh or frozen cranberries**
> **2¼ cups water, divided use**
> **½ cup sugar**
> **1 to 1½ teaspoons grated orange zest**
> **¼ cup fresh orange juice**
> **⅓ cup farina (ready-to-cook wheat cereal)**
> **¼ cup fat-free or low-fat plain yogurt**
> **Orange rind curls or thinly grated orange zest (optional)**

In a medium saucepan, combine the cranberries and 1½ cups water. Bring the mixture to a boil over high heat. Reduce the heat; simmer for 8 minutes, or until the cranberries are tender and pop, stirring occasionally.

Strain the mixture into a large mixing bowl, mashing the cranberries. Return the liquid to the saucepan; discard the strained skins. Stir the remaining ¾ cup water, sugar, orange zest, and orange juice into the cranberry liquid. Bring to a boil over high heat. Reduce the heat to medium. Slowly whisk in the farina. Cook for 3 to 4 minutes, or until the mixture has thickened, stirring occasionally.

Pour the mixture into the mixing bowl. Beat with an electric mixer on medium-high for 2 to 3 minutes, or until light and fluffy.

Spoon the pudding into eight champagne glasses, compotes, or individual serving bowls. Top each serving with ½ tablespoon yogurt. Use a toothpick to lightly swirl the yogurt into the pudding. Serve warm or cover with plastic wrap placed directly on the pudding and refrigerate for up to four days. Garnish with orange rind curls or zest.

Calories 95	Cholesterol 0 mg
Total Fat 0 g	Sodium 9 mg
Saturated 0 g	Carbohydrate 23 g
Polyunsaturated 0 g	Fiber 1 g
Monounsaturated 0 g	Protein 1 g

COOK'S TIP

If you don't have fresh or frozen cranberries, you can substitute 2½ cups unsweetened cranberry juice for the cranberries and the 1½ cups water in the first step of this recipe.

COOK'S TIP ON CRANBERRIES

Cranberry season (October through December) is very short, so when you see these berries, it is a good idea to stock up. Buy several packages and put them in the freezer. They will keep for up to 12 months, allowing you to enjoy cranberries all year long.

layered baked apples

The flavors of apricot and cherry blend with hot, bubbly apple juice as these conversation-starting stuffed apples bake. Bread rounds separating the apple layers absorb the juice, so you won't miss one luscious drop.

> Vegetable oil spray
> 4 small, firm tart cooking apples with stems, such as Granny Smith or Braeburn (about 5 ounces each)
> 4 slices light bread
> ¼ cup chopped dried apricots
> ¼ cup dried tart cherries
> 1 tablespoon sugar
> ¼ teaspoon ground cinnamon

Lightly spray four 5- to 6-ounce ceramic or glass custard cups or small ramekins or four muffin cups with vegetable oil spray.

Leaving the stems on for a pretty presentation, slice each apple into 3 horizontal pieces. The top and the bottom pieces should each be about ½ inch thick; the center should be 1½ to 2 inches thick. Keep the slices of each apple together so that the pieces can be reassembled.

Remove the seeds and core from the middle slice of each apple (a melon baller works well). Be sure to keep the outer ring intact. The hole should be about 1 inch in diameter and go all the way through the apple slice. If there are any seeds in the top or bottom sections, remove them as well, making sure not to cut all the way through the apple.

Using a 2-inch-diameter glass, circular cookie cutter, or biscuit cutter, cut 2 circles from each slice of bread. There should be no crust on the circles.

In a small bowl, stir together the remaining ingredients.

Preheat the oven to 375°F.

To assemble, for each serving, place the bottom piece of the apple with the skin side down in a custard cup. Top the apple with a bread circle, then the middle ring of the apple. Press down. Fill the hollowed-out core with one fourth of the apricot and cherry mixture, packing it firmly. Add the second

Calories 154	Cholesterol 0 mg
Total Fat 1.0 g	Sodium 60 mg
Saturated 0 g	Carbohydrate 41 g
Polyunsaturated 0.5 g	Fiber 6 g
Monounsaturated 0 g	Protein 2 g

bread slice and the stem end of the apple. Press down firmly. Lightly spray the top of the apple with vegetable oil spray.

Bake for 30 minutes; if the tops have started to brown, cover the apples with aluminum foil. Bake for 5 to 15 minutes, or until the middle layer of the apple is tender when tested with a fork and the apples have puffed up ½ to 1 inch in height. The tops will have some browned areas. Let the apples cool in the custard cups for 30 minutes; the apples will return to normal size as they cool. Run a knife around the edge of the custard cups to loosen the apples. Gently tip the apples into your hand and place them on plates.

COOK'S TIP

Baking the apples in custard cups allows the apples to maintain their shape as they cool. This lets you serve apple-shaped apples with all five layers showing. For an extra-pretty presentation, sprinkle the serving plates with a little cinnamon or confectioners' sugar before placing the apples on top. If you are short on time, leave the apples whole, but remove the stems, cores, and seeds. Use only two slices of bread; remove and discard the crusts, and break the bread into dime-size pieces. Combine the bread with the filling ingredients and generously stuff each hollowed-out apple, firmly packing the stuffing.

apple dumplings

These plump dumpling delights are filled with light apple pie filling, topped with a sprinkling of sugar, and baked until the crust is golden brown. They are very handy for a lunch box dessert.

> **2 cups all-purpose flour**
> **⅓ cup sugar**
> **½ teaspoon baking powder**
> **⅛ teaspoon salt**
> **¼ cup light stick margarine**
> **½ cup warm water (plus more if needed)**
> **Flour for rolling out dough**
> **Vegetable oil spray**
> **1½ cups light apple pie filling**
> **2 tablespoons fat-free milk**
> **2 tablespoons sugar**

In a medium bowl, stir together the flour, sugar, baking powder, and salt. Using a pastry blender, a fork, or two knives, cut the margarine into the flour until the mixture looks crumbly.

Add the warm water; stir the mixture with a spoon until the dough starts to hold together. Sprinkle a little flour over a flat surface. Shape the dough into a ball with your hands; knead the dough on the flat surface for 1 minute, or until slightly elastic. Add small amounts of flour if the dough is sticky, or add warm water if the dough is dry. Cover the dough with a damp cloth; let rest for 15 minutes at room temperature.

Preheat the oven to 400°F. Lightly spray a baking sheet with vegetable oil spray.

Lightly flour a flat surface. Roll the dough into a 12 × 9-inch rectangle (about ⅛-inch thick). Cut the dough into twelve 3-inch squares.

Spoon 1 tablespoon apple pie filling onto the center of a dough square. Dip a pastry brush into a small amount of water, then moisten the edges of the

Calories 132	Cholesterol 0 mg
Total Fat 2.0 g	Sodium 75 mg
Saturated 0.5 g	Carbohydrate 27 g
Polyunsaturated 0.5 g	Fiber 1 g
Monounsaturated 0.5 g	Protein 2 g

square. Fold the square in half to form a triangle (opposite corners together). Repeat with the remaining filling and dough. Cut two short slits on the top of each dumpling to let the heat escape. Brush the top of each dumpling with milk; sprinkle lightly with sugar.

Bake for 20 to 23 minutes, or until the dumplings are golden brown. Cool for at least 10 minutes before eating (the filling is very hot).

granny smith
caramel apple wedges

serves 2; 1 apple and about 3 tablespoons topping per serving

Drizzle fat-free caramel apple dip over tart green apples, then top them with sprinkles of coconut, dried cranberries, and pumpkin seeds.

2 medium Granny Smith apples, cored and cut into wedges

2 tablespoons fat-free caramel apple dip or fat-free ice cream topping, such as caramel, hot fudge, or butterscotch

8 dried banana chips (about 3 tablespoons)

2 teaspoons dried cranberries

2 teaspoons unsweetened shredded coconut

2 teaspoons unsalted, toasted pumpkin seeds

To assemble, put apple wedges in two small bowls. Drizzle 1 tablespoon dip over each serving. Arrange 4 banana chips on each. Sprinkle with the cranberries, coconut, and pumpkin seeds. Serve immediately.

COOK'S TIP ON FAT-FREE CARAMEL APPLE DIP

Fat-free caramel apple dip is located near the apples in the grocery store produce section.

COOK'S TIP ON TOASTED PUMPKIN SEEDS

Look for unsalted, toasted pumpkin seeds in bulk in the produce, baking, or candy section of your grocery store. During the fall, when pumpkins are available, you can toast your own seeds. Preheat the oven to 375° F. Put 2 cups of pumpkin seeds in a colander and rinse well to remove any pumpkin flesh. Dry the seeds thoroughly with paper towels. Lightly spray a nonstick rimmed baking sheet with vegetable oil spray. Spread the seeds (the hulls are safe to eat) in a single layer, then lightly spray the tops with vegetable oil spray. Bake for 25 to 30 minutes, or until the seeds are lightly golden brown, stirring every 10 minutes. The seeds may pop during cooking. Put the baking sheet on a cooling rack and let cool for 20 to 30 minutes.

Calories 180	Cholesterol 0 mg
Total Fat 3.0 g	Sodium 61 mg
Saturated 1.0 g	Carbohydrate 37 g
Polyunsaturated 1.0 g	Fiber 4 g
Monounsaturated 0.5 g	Protein 2 g

grilled pineapple with port glaze

Warm, heady aromas foreshadow the tastes to come when pineapple sizzles on a grill pan.

> 1 cup tawny or ruby port
> 1 cinnamon stick, about 3 inches long
> 3 whole cloves
> 3 whole black peppercorns or ⅛ teaspoon ground black pepper
> ⅛ teaspoon ground nutmeg
> 1 large pineapple
> Vegetable oil spray

In a small saucepan, stir together the port, cinnamon stick, cloves, pepper-corns, and nutmeg. Bring to a boil over high heat. Reduce the heat to medium-high and continue to boil until the liquid has reduced to ¼ cup, 12 to 15 minutes.

Peel the pineapple lengthwise; slice lengthwise into 18 strips, each about ⅓ inch thick and 1 to 2 inches wide. The strips don't need to be the same width.

Heat an indoor grill pan over high heat. Remove the pan from the heat and lightly spray with vegetable oil spray (being careful not to spray near a gas flame). Grill the pineapple in batches on only one side until dark caramel-colored grill marks appear, about 2 minutes. Or preheat a gas grill on high. Grill about 4 inches from the heat for 2 to 3 minutes on one side. (The grill marks are not likely to be as vivid as when using an indoor grill pan.)

To serve, arrange three slices of pineapple, preferably of various widths, on each plate. Drizzle glaze on and around the pineapple, or arrange all the slices on a platter and drizzle with the sauce. Serve warm or at room temperature.

COOK'S TIP ON SLICING PINEAPPLE

Using a large chef's knife, cut the top and the bottom off the pineapple. Stand the pineapple on end on a cutting board. Slicing from top to bottom, remove 1-inch strips of skin from the pine-apple until the pineapple is clean. Using a sawing motion, cut slices of pineapple about ⅓ inch thick and 1 to 2 inches wide. As you get closer to the core, the strips will become narrower (don't cut into the core). Discard the core. A large pineapple prepared this way should yield 18 or more slices.

Calories 107	Cholesterol 0 mg
Total Fat 0.5 g	Sodium 3 mg
Saturated 0 g	Carbohydrate 22 g
Polyunsaturated 0 g	Fiber 2 g
Monounsaturated 0 g	Protein 1 g

grenadine and melon compote

Pomegranate-flavored grenadine and tart lime juice are the yin-yang tastes clinging to chunks of cool, sweet cantaloupe and honeydew melon. This dish is perfect as a light dessert or the first course at brunch.

4 cups bite-size pieces cantaloupe
4 cups bite-size pieces honeydew melon
¼ cup grenadine
Juice of 2 medium limes
Zest of 2 medium limes
Zest of 1 medium orange

In a large bowl, stir together the cantaloupe, honeydew, grenadine, and lime juice. Sprinkle with the lime and orange zest.

COOK'S TIP

Because melons tend to lose juice as soon as they're cut, this dish shouldn't be made too far in advance. Starting with chilled melons helps minimize the juice loss. You can cut the melons up to 4 hours before serving and refrigerate them in an airtight container. Immediately before serving, drain any excess liquid, stir in the lime juice and grenadine, and sprinkle with the zest.

COOK'S TIP

Leftover compote plus an equal amount of nonfat plain yogurt equals a breakfast smoothie the next day. The compote does not keep well for more than 36 hours.

COOK'S TIP ON SELECTING FRESH MELON

Both honeydew and cantaloupe should be firm and have no obvious bruises or cuts. The bud ends might give a little when pushed. The true test is smell. A sweet, ripe melon smells sweet and ripe.

Calories 88	Cholesterol 0 mg
Total Fat 0.5 g	Sodium 21 mg
Saturated 0 g	Carbohydrate 23 g
Polyunsaturated 0 g	Fiber 1 g
Monounsaturated 0 g	Protein 1 g

crunchy coated
ice cream cones

serves 4; ½ cup ice cream, 1 cone, and 1 tablespoon plus
1 teaspoon granola mixture per serving

You'll feel like a kid again when you eat one of these treats from the freezer.

¼ cup low-fat granola cereal without raisins

1 tablespoon plus 1 teaspoon almond toffee bits

1 tablespoon plus 1 teaspoon semisweet chocolate mini morsels

2 cups fat-free chocolate ice cream or fat-free frozen yogurt

4 sugar wafer ice cream cones (not waffle cones)

Put the granola in a shallow pie pan. Using your fingers or a fork, break up any large pieces. Stir in the toffee bits and chocolate chips.

Scoop ½ cup ice cream onto each of four cones. Working quickly, gently roll the cones over the granola mixture to coat the ice cream completely.

Serve immediately, or prepare the cones for the freezer. Tear off four 12-inch sheets of aluminum foil or plastic wrap. Place each cone upright in the center of one of the pieces. Pull the ends up to the top of the filled cone and gently twist. If using plastic wrap, secure with a twist tie, if desired. Put the cones in the freezer until ready to serve.

Calories 209	Cholesterol 4 mg
Total Fat 3.5 g	Sodium 134 mg
Saturated 1.5 g	Carbohydrate 42 g
Polyunsaturated 0.5 g	Fiber 1 g
Monounsaturated 1.0 g	Protein 5 g

petite baked alaska

In addition to making portion size easy to control, individual servings make everyone feel special. That's certainly true when you're serving this elegant dessert.

1 pint fat-free strawberry frozen yogurt

8 reduced-fat chocolate wafer cookies, crushed (about ¼ cup)

  Vegetable oil spray

½ medium mango or ½ cup bottled mango slices, drained

½ cup fresh raspberries

  Whites of 4 large eggs, at room temperature

⅛ teaspoon cream of tartar

¼ cup sugar

1 teaspoon grated lemon zest

Line four 5-ounce custard cups or ramekins with plastic wrap. Pack ½ cup frozen yogurt into each, pressing firmly to mold the yogurt to the shape of the cup. Sprinkle 1 tablespoon crushed cookies evenly over each. Using a spoon, press the cookies into the yogurt. Cover with plastic wrap; keep in the freezer until ready to use, at least 15 minutes.

Preheat the oven to 450°F. Line a baking sheet with aluminum foil; lightly spray with vegetable oil spray.

Meanwhile, slice the mango if using fresh. Arrange the mango and raspberries on each of four small plates.

In a medium mixing bowl, beat the egg whites with an electric mixer on medium until foamy, about 1 minute. Add the cream of tartar and beat on medium until soft peaks form. Add the sugar, about 1 tablespoon at a time, continuing to beat until stiff peaks form and the sugar has almost dissolved. Add the lemon zest; beat until combined.

Invert the frozen yogurt portions onto the prepared baking sheet. Remove the custard cups and plastic wrap. Working quickly with an icing or regular spatula, spread the meringue topping over each frozen strawberry mound, swirling if desired.

Calories 197	Cholesterol 0 mg
Total Fat 0.5 g	Sodium 126 mg
Saturated 0 g	Carbohydrate 43 g
Polyunsaturated 0 g	Fiber 2 g
Monounsaturated 0 g	Protein 7 g

Bake for 3 to 4 minutes, or until patches of meringue turn golden brown, watching carefully to be sure the meringue doesn't burn. Transfer one baked Alaska onto each plate. Serve immediately.

COOK'S TIP ON BEATING EGG WHITES

To get the most volume, let separated egg whites warm to room temperature before you beat them. (It's easier to separate eggs when they're cold, but the whites won't beat as well.) Equipment also makes a difference: For best results, use copper, stainless steel, or glass bowls, not plastic. Be sure your bowl and utensils are very clean—any grease or even dust can decrease volume.

frozen strawberry softee

Just a hint of cinnamon and orange gives this ice cream a pleasant kick.

- **16-ounce bag frozen unsweetened strawberries, partially thawed**
- **2 cups fat-free or low-fat vanilla ice cream or frozen yogurt, firmly packed**
- **⅓ cup frozen orange juice concentrate**
- **2 tablespoons confectioners' sugar**
- **1 teaspoon vanilla extract**
- **½ teaspoon ground cinnamon**

In a food processor or blender, process all the ingredients until smooth. Put in a 2-quart plastic container or 1-gallon airtight plastic bag and seal tightly. Put in the freezer for 2 hours, or until fairly firm. If the mixture becomes too firm, let it partially thaw on the countertop for 15 to 20 minutes.

Calories 98	Cholesterol 0 mg
Total Fat 0 g	Sodium 34 mg
Saturated 0 g	Carbohydrate 23 g
Polyunsaturated 0 g	Fiber 1 g
Monounsaturated 0 g	Protein 3 g

Appendix a:
THE RELATIONSHIP
BETWEEN HEALTH AND WEIGHT

taking control

You hear all the time about how your diet affects your health. Research confirms that much of how the body functions in both health and disease is related to diet. The good thing about this news is that, unlike with many other things in life, you have control over what you choose to eat.

risk factors for heart disease and stroke

Almost everyone has some risk of heart disease or stroke. The key is to understand your individual situation. Your genes determine some circumstances that you just can't change, but you *can* modify behavior that affects many risk factors.

RISK FACTORS YOU CAN'T CONTROL

Age—As you age, your risk increases.

Sex—Men have a greater risk than women, and they develop heart disease earlier in life. After menopause, however, women's incidence of heart disease increases but never catches up to that of men.

Family history of early heart disease—If a member of your birth family suffered a heart attack or sudden death from heart problems, you're at a higher risk.

Race—Genetics predispose some races to particular health risks. For example, African-Americans have a greater risk of heart disease and stroke than whites.

RISK FACTORS YOU CAN CONTROL OR TREAT

Even if you know that certain risk factors are "in your genes," you can do your best to manage the more controllable factors to lessen your overall risk of heart disease and stroke. Hereditary risk often shows itself in clinical conditions that you can treat. Find out whether high blood pressure, high blood cholesterol, or diabetes runs in your family. Work with your doctor to help prevent or control such conditions. Physical inactivity, diabetes, and exposure to tobacco smoke are the other risk factors that can be controlled or treated.

high blood pressure

Be sure to have your blood pressure checked at least every two years, regardless of whether you need to see your doctor for other reasons. Normal blood pressure levels are below 140/90 mm Hg (millimeters of mercury). If your blood pressure is 140/90 mm Hg or higher on more than two separate visits, you should be treated for high blood pressure.

Often, losing just 10 pounds or so will bring your blood pressure down. Regular exercise and a more healthful diet also will help. For instance, the DASH diet (Dietary Approaches to Stop Hypertension), developed by researchers for the National Heart, Lung, and Blood Institute, is similar to the American Heart Association dietary guidelines (page 301) and has been found to reduce high blood pressure. Both the DASH diet and our guidelines recommend that healthy people limit their daily sodium intake to less than 2,400 milligrams (mg). To follow the AHA guidelines, you need to eat at least five servings of fruits and vegetables and two to four servings of fat-free or low-fat dairy products each day. The DASH diet also places an emphasis on fruits, vegetables, and fat-free dairy products.

If lifestyle changes don't bring your blood pressure levels down to normal, your doctor may prescribe medication.

cigarette smoking

Smokers have twice the risk of heart attack and two to four times the risk of sudden cardiac death of people who don't smoke. Even if you're exposed only to secondhand smoke at work or at home, your risk of death due to heart disease increases significantly. If you quit smoking or eliminate environmental smoke, your risk of heart disease immediately drops.

high blood cholesterol

Ideally, your blood cholesterol level should be below 200 milligrams per deciliter (mg/dl). If it's already too high or you want to keep it from climbing, limit your intake of saturated fat and cholesterol. If you are healthy, the American Heart Association recommends that no more than 10 percent of calories should come from saturated fat and that you should consume less than 300 mg of dietary cholesterol each day. If you have heart disease, you need to limit your saturated fat to no more than 7 percent of calories and your cholesterol intake to less than 200 mg a day.

Many people can lower their blood cholesterol to under 200 mg/dl through diet alone, but some need medication as well. Some of these people are genetically programmed to make too much cholesterol in their bodies. If that is your situation, you are likely to need to take cholesterol-lowering medications as well as follow a low–saturated fat, low-cholesterol diet.

physical inactivity

Exercise—movement of any kind—is good for you. Regular physical activity will help you control or prevent excess weight, high blood pressure, high cholesterol, and diabetes. We urge healthy people to be moderately physically active for a total of at least 30 minutes on most days. Moderate activities, such as walking for pleasure, gardening, housework, and dancing, can have a protective effect if you do 30 minutes or more of them most days of the week. You can spread the activities over the day; they don't have to be in a half-hour segment.

Aerobic exercise, such as brisk walking, running, or cycling, for 30 to 60 minutes three or four times a week will help keep your heart and lungs healthy and help prevent weight gain.

obesity

Overweight (body mass index, or BMI, of 25.0 to 29.9; see Body Mass Index, pages 298–300) and obesity (BMI of 30.0 and above) increase the risk of heart disease, stroke, diabetes, gallbladder disease, arthritis, and some types of cancer. Extra weight and obesity often lead to high blood pressure, high blood cholesterol, sleep apnea, and breathing problems.

In addition to contributing to the risk of heart attack, obesity puts added strain on the heart that can lead to other potentially fatal conditions, such as an enlarged heart, cardiomyopathy (weakness of the heart muscle itself), and irregular heart rhythms. Furthermore, being overweight can make your LDL (low-density lipoprotein, or "bad") cholesterol level rise and your HDL (high-density lipoprotein, or "good") cholesterol level fall.

diabetes

Diabetes, an abnormality in the body's ability to metabolize sugar, is a serious disease in itself, as well as a risk factor for heart disease. In some people with Type 2 diabetes (the most common kind), the pancreas cannot make enough insulin to meet the body's needs. More often the body has difficulty taking insulin into the cells to process sugar. This problem is called insulin resistance, and obesity and physical inactivity lead to it.

Frequently, diabetes can be prevented or controlled by diet, weight management, and exercise. In some cases, however, diabetes requires medication. If you have diabetes, be sure to have regular checkups and work with your doctor or dietitian on a diet appropriate for you. Also work to lower your blood pressure to 130/80 mm Hg. Controlling blood sugar and blood pressure levels is important to help prevent damage to your blood vessels.

the need for weight management

Many, many years ago, the ability to store fat enabled our ancestors to survive times of famine. These days, food is plentiful. If you store too much fat now, your body fat is doing the opposite of what it was designed to do—it's making you sick.

Many experts say we are experiencing an epidemic of obesity. Abdominal fat is so common that we even have pet names for it: rubber tire, beer belly, love handles. Each year about 300,000 Americans die of causes related to obesity. Today, about half the adult population in this country is considered overweight, up from about one fourth two decades ago. It's obviously time to take control by eating a more healthful diet.

OVERWEIGHT AND OBESITY

We all benefit from keeping our calorie intake in balance. If you are concerned that your weight may be affecting your health, use the body mass index to determine your risk.

body mass index

The BMI is a number that is based on weight and height and reflects the amount of overall body fat. To find your BMI:

- Weigh yourself without clothes or shoes.

- Measure your height without shoes.

- Check the chart below. Find your height in the left-hand column and see whether your weight falls into either range listed. If you prefer to calculate your exact BMI, multiply your weight in pounds by 705. Divide by your height in inches; divide again by your height in inches.

Height	Overweight (BMI 25.0–29.9)	Obese (BMI 30.0 and above)
4'10"	119–142 lb	143 lb or more
4'11"	124–147	148
5'0"	128–152	153
5'1"	132–157	158
5'2"	136–163	164
5'3"	141–168	169
5'4"	145–173	174
5'5"	150–179	180
5'6"	155–185	186
5'7"	159–190	191
5'8"	164–196	197
5'9"	169–202	203
5'10"	174–208	209
5'11"	179–214	215
6'0"	184–220	221
6'1"	189–226	227
6'2"	194–232	233
6'3"	200–239	240
6'4"	205–245	246

25.0 to 29.9—Overweight—BMIs in this range indicate a moderate risk of heart and blood vessel disease. A BMI of 25 translates to about 10 percent over ideal body weight.

30 or more—Obesity—This means a high risk of heart and blood vessel disease, with 30 or more extra pounds of fat.

40 or more—Extreme obesity.

Below 25—A BMI from 18.5 to 24.9 is considered healthy. BMIs less than 18.5 are considered underweight.

- If you have a BMI of 30 or above, discuss your weight loss plan with your doctor.

waist measurement

Bodybuilders with large muscles may have a high BMI but very little body fat, so they're at lower risk than their BMI indicates. So are people, usually women, who carry their excess fat in their pelvic area or their hips. For people in either of these groups, a waist measurement (taken just above the navel) may be a better risk indicator than the BMI. Women with a waistline of 35 inches or more have a high risk of heart and blood vessel disease. Men with a waistline of 40 inches or more have a high risk.

next steps

If you are at a healthful weight, you need only to stay there. By eating a healthful diet and getting regular exercise, you will guard against weight gain.

If you are overweight or obese, you probably already want to lose weight. You may not realize, however, that losing just 10 or 20 pounds can make a big difference in your blood pressure and cholesterol levels (see "Losing Weight in Good Health," page 309).

Obesity is a chronic disease, like high blood pressure or diabetes. You can control it with diet and physical activity. This book will show you how to put all the pieces together.

OBESITY IN OUR CHILDREN

About 5 million children in the United States are overweight. Like adults in this country, American children are eating more, especially snacks, and exercising less. About half these children will continue to have a weight problem after they grow up. To help your children, lead by example. Eat a healthful diet and show that you believe that exercise is important.

Taking weight off can be hard. The best "cure" is prevention—don't put it on in the first place. It is vitally important to keep children from developing a lifelong weight problem. Teach your children to eat a nutritious diet and follow good exercise habits. It may be the most important thing you do for their health now, and it will help keep them healthier for the rest of their lives.

you are what you eat

Whether you are following a low-calorie eating plan to lose weight or just want to watch your calories and maintain your present weight, you need to know how to choose healthful foods. That's where the easy-to-follow

American Heart Association dietary guidelines and the Healthy Heart Food Pyramid can help you succeed.

the american heart association dietary guidelines

By following a few easy suggestions, healthy people over two years old can help prevent heart disease, stroke, obesity, and the many other problems that obesity can cause.

SEVEN STEPS TO GOOD NUTRITION

1. Eat at least six servings of grain products and starchy vegetables daily.

2. Eat at least five servings of fruits and vegetables daily. Include at least one serving of citrus fruit or a vegetable high in vitamin C and one serving of a dark green, leafy vegetable or deep yellow vegetable.

3. Eat no more than 6 ounces (cooked weight) of lean meat, seafood, or skinless poultry per day. Have at least two servings of fish per week.

4. Include two or more servings of fat-free and low-fat dairy products if you are an adult and three to four servings if you are a child or an adolescent.

5. Choose a diet low in saturated fat, trans fat, and cholesterol and moderate in salt (sodium) and sugar. Eat no more than 10 percent of your calories as saturated fat. Limit yourself to less than 300 mg of cholesterol and less than 2,400 mg of sodium daily.

6. If you drink alcohol, limit yourself to one drink per day if you are a woman and two drinks per day if you are a man.

7. Balance food intake with physical activity to achieve and maintain a healthful weight.

These guidelines are based on the ideas of moderation and balance, not "good foods" and "bad foods." That means you can have a small amount of anything on occasion. When you bend the rules, make up for it by cutting down on fat and calories later that day or even later that week. You can afford small splurges once in a while if you follow the guidelines most of the time.

the healthy heart food pyramid

The Healthy Heart Food Pyramid gives you a picture of the principles set forth in our guidelines. It shows you at a glance the various food groups that make up a nutritious diet and the proportions of each that you should eat. For information on how to choose foods from these groups to integrate into your eating plan, see the section on shopping in "Low-Calorie Cooking for Life" (page 316).

THE BASE OF THE PYRAMID: BREADS, CEREALS, PASTA, AND STARCHY VEGETABLES

Whole-grain or enriched breads, grains, and pasta provide plenty of nutrients and relatively few calories. Whole grains are good sources of soluble fiber, which can help lower your blood cholesterol.

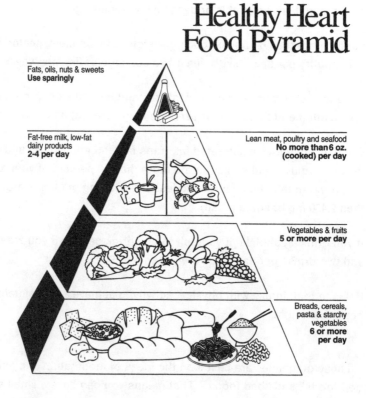

Healthy Heart Food Pyramid

Fats, oils, nuts & sweets
Use sparingly

Fat-free milk, low-fat dairy products
2-4 per day

Lean meat, poultry and seafood
No more than 6 oz. (cooked) per day

Vegetables & fruits
5 or more per day

Breads, cereals, pasta & starchy vegetables
6 or more per day

Starchy vegetables and legumes are also part of the base of the pyramid. White potatoes, sweet potatoes, and beans are nutrition bargains. Just be careful about adding fat. Beans—not green beans, which count as a vegetable—are a great source of fiber.

Substitute beans or grains for meat at least twice a week. You will probably save on calories and fat, and you will definitely cut down on dietary cholesterol.

---

one serving size =

1 slice of regular bread or 2 slices of light bread

½ of a 2-ounce bagel

1 2- to 3-ounce muffin (the size of a large egg)

½ cup of cooked rice, pasta, or hot cereal

1 cup of flaked cereal

1 3-ounce potato

½ cup of cooked beans (not green beans)

THE NEXT STEP: VEGETABLES AND FRUITS

Eating a variety of vegetables and fruits has been found to be significant in maintaining a healthful weight. The foods in this category are loaded with vitamins, fiber, and other nutrients, and most are low in calories, saturated fat, and sodium. (See "Fruits and Vegetables," page 317, for information about the exceptions.)

---

one serving size =

1 medium piece or ½ cup of fruit

¾ cup of fruit juice or vegetable juice

1 cup of a raw leafy vegetable

½ cup of any other vegetable, cooked or raw (chopped)

CLIMBING THE PYRAMID:
MEATS, POULTRY, SEAFOOD,
AND DAIRY PRODUCTS

meats, poultry, and seafood

You need some protein every day. Because animal-based foods contain saturated fat and cholesterol along with protein, however, you'll want to limit yourself to a total of 6 ounces (cooked weight) of meat, poultry, and seafood per day. Trying the entrée recipes in this cookbook will make that easier. Each serving contains a maximum of 3 ounces of cooked meat, poultry, or seafood. Emphasizing grains, fruits, and vegetables in your meal planning also helps.

Meat is a good source of protein. Just be careful to select lean varieties and trim all the visible fat. Skinless poultry, another good source, has less saturated fat than red meats. Seafood contains less saturated fat than meat or poultry. In your two servings of fish a week, you may want to include salmon or other fish that are high in omega-3 fat, a special kind of unsaturated fat that may have health benefits for your heart. The American Heart Association does not recommend fish oil supplements unless prescribed by your doctor.

Shrimp, lobster, crab, crayfish, and most other shellfish are very low in calories and saturated fat but high in cholesterol. You can eat shellfish occasionally and keep within the recommended limit of 300 mg of cholesterol per day.

---

one serving size =

3 ounces of cooked meat, poultry, or seafood (4 ounces raw)

---

dairy products

Dairy products are good sources of calcium and protein, but whole milk contains both fat and cholesterol. Choose fat-free and low-fat dairy foods, and eat less of them than of the foods in the lower parts of the pyramid.

THE TOP OF THE PYRAMID: FATS, OILS, NUTS, AND SWEETS

Topping the pyramid are the foods you should eat in small amounts. They usually contain lots of fat and/or sugar and are high in calories.

If you want to cut calories, start at the top! Cutting down on fat is one of the best ways. If you're trying to lose weight, eat less than 30 percent of your calories as fat, averaged over a week.

Protecting your heart and blood vessels is another important reason to limit the amount and kinds of fat in your diet. That's because certain fats (saturated fat, trans fat, and cholesterol) raise the level of LDL cholesterol, or "bad cholesterol," in your blood. LDL cholesterol and other substances can build up in the inner walls of your arteries as plaque. Called atherosclerosis, such buildup in the blood vessel wall can lead to heart disease, heart attack, and stroke.

saturated fat, trans fat, and cholesterol

Saturated fat comes from both animal- and plant-based foods. Animal-based foods high in saturated fat include butter and other whole-milk dairy products, organ meats, lard, and fat from beef, pork, and chicken. Plant-based foods containing saturated fat include coconut, coconut oil, palm kernel oil, palm oil, and cocoa butter. A high intake of saturated fat may increase your risk of developing insulin resistance, which may in turn increase your risk of diabetes.

Trans fats are created when vegetable oil is hydrogenated (hydrogen is added) to make it solid. The most common sources of trans fats are margarine and commercially baked products such as cookies, crackers, and breads.

Cholesterol in foods comes only from animal products. It's in all meats, poultry, seafood, and animal fats, such as butter and lard. The richest sources are egg yolks and organ meats. If you are healthy, you can have up to 300 mg of cholesterol per day. If you have heart disease or high cholesterol, that number drops to 200 mg.

polyunsaturated and monounsaturated fats

With this information in mind, you can see that if you're going to cook with fat, it's wise to choose the polyunsaturated and monounsaturated varieties. They don't raise the level of LDL cholesterol.

The most important thing when planning your meals is to look at your *saturated fat intake.* No more than 10 percent of your total calories per week should come from saturated fat if you are healthy. We recommend that most people with heart disease or high cholesterol eat no more than 7 percent of calories as saturated fat. Your doctor may tailor this recommendation to your individual needs.

---

one day's total =

5 to 8 teaspoons of monounsaturated and polyunsaturated fats (5 teaspoons if you're restricting calories). Count margarine, oils, salad dressing, and fat in prepared foods.

OTHER CONSIDERATIONS

sodium

One teaspoon of salt contains about 2,400 mg of sodium, our recommended daily maximum of sodium for healthy people. The high sodium levels in some common processed foods will quickly add up to that maximum. These foods include canned soups, canned tomatoes and tomato products, pickles, bread, and cheese. One way to watch your sodium intake is to choose no-salt-added or low- or reduced-sodium products when they are available. Another way is to look on food labels for "hidden" sources of sodium, such as monosodium glutamate (MSG), sodium bicarbonate, sodium nitrite, sodium propionate, and sodium citrate, and avoid them when you can. You need a small amount of sodium in your diet, but you get enough from the natural content in food.

sugar

Sugar is not linked to heart or blood vessel disease. However, sugar provides extra calories with no other nutrition. Cutting down on these empty calories can help you maintain a healthful balance between caloric intake and dietary needs. When you want something sweet, fresh fruit is a nutritious choice. Or try one of the dessert recipes in this cookbook (pages 268–294). Many of them provide the benefits of whole grains, dairy products, or fruit without excessive sugar.

alcohol

The subject of alcohol is complicated. Some research shows that people who drink in moderation have some protection against heart disease. Other research shows that excessive drinking is associated with high blood pressure and stroke. In addition, alcohol is a major source of calories and can contribute to obesity. The many other problems associated with excessive drinking are well known.

We do not recommend that anyone start drinking as protection against heart disease. The risks heavily outweigh any small benefit to health.

too much of a good thing

In the 1980s, restaurants began serving food in huge portions so customers would feel they were getting more than their money's worth. Some people think this is when the obesity epidemic began in the United States. Gradually we have become used to eating food in large quantities. It's certainly hard to resist the lure of a bargain, but **it's not a bargain if it ends up on your body as fat!**

Learn how to visualize a reasonable serving and try to stay within that limit both at restaurants and at home. For example, a box of spaghetti lists two ounces (dried weight) as a serving. That translates into one cup of cooked spaghetti. At a typical restaurant, you may be served three or four cups as an entrée. If you're limiting calories, we recommend a serving of one cup for a main dish or one-half cup for a side dish. Take the rest home, or share your entrée with a friend.

Using measuring cups and spoons and a food scale will help you learn how much food makes one serving, as will the boxed information in this appendix. When you have mastered serving sizes, you can stop measuring for every meal. It's a good idea to recheck your portions about once a month, however. Estimated servings do tend to creep up in size!

For quick reference, the palm of an average-size woman is about the size of a 3-ounce serving of meat, poultry, or seafood. The size of the fist represents about one cup. For a measure of a teaspoon, use the tip of your thumb; for a tablespoon, the tip of your thumb to the first joint.

For portion control, try using smaller plates at home. A meal that covers a salad plate seems like more food than one that occupies only two thirds of a dinner plate.

Appendix b:
LOSING WEIGHT
IN GOOD HEALTH

You've decided that you want to lose weight. You know that weight loss is quite likely to make you feel better, can help lower blood pressure and blood cholesterol, and, long range, will reduce or at least help you control your risk for heart disease, stroke, diabetes, and arthritis. But do you know how to lose weight and keep it off safely and most effectively? The discussion on the following pages will give you the details, but the bottom line is simple: If you consume fewer calories and increase your physical activity on a regular basis, you will lose weight. To maintain your ideal weight, eat only the calories your body needs. The same principles hold true whether you follow the American Heart Association dietary guidelines for healthy people (page 301), create your own plan, or join a weight-loss program.

The chart below shows the range of calories the average person needs to consume on a daily basis to maintain or lose weight.

	DAILY CALORIES NEEDED TO MAINTAIN WEIGHT	DAILY CALORIES NEEDED TO LOSE WEIGHT
Men	1,800 to 2,500	1,500 to 1,800
Women	1,500 to 2,000	1,200 to 1,500

the importance of safe weight loss

The best way to lose weight is gradually—one to two pounds a week. At this rate, you are more likely to be able to keep the weight off.

weight-loss programs

If you decide to join a weight-loss program, look for the right one. Find a program that advocates gradual weight loss; a nutritious, well-balanced eating plan; and plenty of physical activity. Avoid any program that provides fewer than 1,200 calories a day for a woman or 1,500 calories a day for a man unless you are under medical supervision. Carefully examine any promises—if they sound too good to be true, they probably are. You didn't gain weight overnight, and you shouldn't lose it that quickly either.

If you are too busy to go to meetings or prefer privacy, you may want to use a weight-loss website with 24-hour services and anonymity. Some free websites furnish very good information, including meal plans designed by professional dietitians. Sites that charge a fee offer more-personalized services. Use the same guidelines to choose a website that you'd use for a traditional weight-loss program.

pitfalls of fad diets

The American Heart Association's food pyramid (page 302) illustrates what kinds of food you need and how much of them to eat for a nutritionally balanced diet. The pyramid is compatible with reputable weight-loss programs. Eating a balanced diet is especially important when you reduce your caloric intake. You'll want every calorie to contribute to good nutrition.

One of the most popular diets now is the high-protein, low-carbohydrate diet, which may contain more than 50 percent of calories as fat. Our experts say that eating unlimited amounts of meat and high-fat dairy products loaded with saturated fat will increase your risk of heart disease. You may lose weight for a time, but you run the risk of raising your blood cholesterol level to new heights even weeks after you've stopped the diet.

Fad diets often advocate eating designated amounts of one or certain foods. Among those continuing to make the rounds are the cabbage soup diet, the grapefruit diet, and the hot-dog diet. Simply put, such diets are not nutritionally sound. Be skeptical of diets that:

❖ Promise a large or quick weight loss. Remember that losing more than two pounds a week can be harmful.

❖ Champion "miracle" foods. (No food "burns" calories.)

❖ Insist on set menus or food combinations.

❖ Forbid certain foods.

❖ Disagree with what most nutrition authorities say.

❖ Sound too good to be true.

water loss

If you are losing five or more pounds a week, much of the weight lost is water. As soon as you revert to your usual diet, the water comes right back, and with it the same pounds you lost before.

a simple equation:
diet + exercise = health

Fat, particularly saturated fat, can have a great impact on your health by raising your blood cholesterol level. Calories are important, too, because they directly affect your body weight. You can take in calories without consuming fat, but you can't eat fat without taking in calories.

Fat (saturated and unsaturated) is the most concentrated source of calories in your diet. Therefore, if everything else remains unchanged and you cut down on fat, you'll automatically cut down on calories. Fat has 9 calories per gram, more than twice the calories of an equal weight of protein or carbohydrate (each has about 4 calories per gram).

It's easy to get so caught up in the hoopla over the variety of fat-free foods now available that you forget that fat free doesn't mean calorie free. Manufacturers of fat-free and low-fat products frequently replace fats with sugars and sodium. Check nutrition labels carefully for the number of calories.

counting calories and
making calories count

As we've said, when you are counting calories, you need to make sure that every calorie counts. Each one should pull its weight by providing some of the nutrients you need—vitamins, minerals, antioxidants, fiber, flavonoids, and other phytochemicals (plant chemicals) that haven't even been identified yet. But no one food group can give you all the nourishment you need. This is why eating a variety of foods is so important.

It's a no-brainer that a 100-calorie pear is a more healthful choice than a 100-calorie soft drink. The pear provides fiber, vitamins A and C, and B vitamins, including folic acid, potassium, and other minerals. The soft drink basically offers sugar with a little phosphorus. But what about whether to have beef, a good source of iron and zinc, or salmon, a good source of omega-3 fats, a special kind of unsaturated fat that helps reduce your risk of heart disease? If you've eaten beef every night for a week but no salmon for a month, you know the better choice for tonight is the salmon with the different nutrients it has to offer.

The decisions can get much more difficult, as the box below shows. Fortunately, help is at hand. Many cookbooks, such as this one, list the calorie counts for recipes. Foods packaged in the United States have labels that tell the calorie counts, along with other nutrition facts. Additionally, many books that list calorie counts are widely available. With such resources, you can make delicious decisions about spending your calorie allotment wisely.

---

can you choose the food that's lower in calories?

Most people think they know just what they're getting when they eat certain foods, but they are often surprised by the hard facts. Here are a few examples of calorie comparisons:

12 ounces club soda (0) OR tonic water (130)

2 tablespoons ranch dressing (160) OR vinaigrette (61)

1 tablespoon regular stick margarine (100) OR regular sour cream (26)

½ cup refried beans made with lard (130) OR refried beans without fat (70)

1 3½-inch bagel (195) OR 1 English muffin (134)

1 ounce Cheddar (114) OR 1 ounce soft goat cheese (76)

½ cup tuna packed in water (99) OR ½ cup fat-free cottage cheese (80)

1 kiwifruit (46) OR 3 apricots (51) OR 1 banana (105)

Eating a variety of foods doesn't mean eating a cinnamon roll for breakfast, a doughnut for an afternoon snack, and a piece of pie at dinner. It doesn't mean eating one item from each food group if it's the same item repeatedly. If you eat broiled chicken, a baked potato, and a salad of iceberg lettuce and tomato every day, you are missing out on the nutrients other foods would provide. You'll also become bored and more likely to turn to high-calorie foods, looking for something to tantalize your taste buds.

When choosing among the food groups, keep in mind another kind of variety—texture—to satisfy your sensory needs.

the importance of being active

Eating well and being physically active are key to a healthful lifestyle. To lose weight, you need to increase your physical activity and decrease your calories. Exercise also helps keep excess weight off.

To get an idea of how many calories you need every day to maintain weight, multiply the number of pounds you weigh now by 15 calories. This represents the average number of calories used in one day if you're moderately active. If you get very little exercise, multiply your weight by 13 instead of 15. Less-active people burn fewer calories.

Using this information, you can plan your calorie intake for maintenance or weight loss. For example, you may need 1,800 calories a day to maintain your weight. If you want to lose weight, give yourself a small deficit every day. Eat 1,500 calories a day and exercise more often. By eating 200 to 300 calories fewer and burning 200 to 300 more in exercise each day, you should lose about a pound a week, a weight loss that will be steady, sure, and safe.

Being physically active also helps manage most of the other risk factors for heart and blood vessel disease.

start slowly

If you haven't been exercising, it's best to start slowly. Check with your doctor to determine how much activity is okay for you.

Walking is one of the best forms of physical activity. You already know how, you can do it almost anywhere, and you don't need any special equipment except comfortable walking shoes.

Start walking for 10 minutes a day four or five days a week. Each week add 5 minutes a day to your walking time until you're up to a total of 30 minutes a day on most days. This is enough activity to help you lose weight. Of course, the more you walk, and the faster the pace, the more calories you burn.

have fun

Make your exercise enjoyable. Pick an interesting place to walk, and take different routes to get there. Try dancing, swimming, water aerobics, tennis, or golf if you prefer. Just engage in some physical activity almost every day if possible.

Other kinds of activity burn calories too: housework, yard work, taking groceries to and from the car, walking the dog. Walk down the block to see your neighbor instead of telephoning or e-mailing, and take the stairs instead of the elevator every time you can. Once you change your approach from finding what's easiest and least active to choosing an active alternative, you will burn up more calories and get the most benefit from your low-calorie diet.

Variety is every bit as important in choosing physical activities as in choosing foods. You may want to walk several days a week, ride your bicycle sometimes, and garden on the weekend. And remember, the activity doesn't have to be done all at once. The amount of time is cumulative throughout the day.

lifelong habits for low-cal living

Let enjoying a low-calorie eating plan become habit forming. Once you integrate several basic changes into your daily routine, you will be living the low-cal life without feeling deprived in the least.

Here are just a few suggestions.

✦ Drink lots of fluids. Instead of snacking, enjoy a large glass of cool, refreshing water, a cup of hot tea or low-sodium broth, or a small glass of fruit or vegetable juice. The body is often more thirsty than hungry.

✦ Know what counts. Don't worry too much about measuring your green beans or lettuce, but do measure your breakfast cereal and your Carrot Cake (page 271).

✦ Sit down to eat. Better yet, take time to eat a sit-down meal with your family or friends. You may not be able to do this every day, but mealtime is a good time to find out what is going on. You may talk more and eat less!

✦ Serve yourself small portions.

✦ Eat slowly. You'll have time to be aware that you feel satisfied and therefore may be less likely to overeat.

✦ Don't take second helpings.

try a little help
from your friends

Losing weight is much easier with support from your family and friends. Ask for their help, and be specific about the kind of help you want. Maybe it's positive words to boost your motivation. Hearing "I'm so proud of you for resisting that piece of cake" will make you want to keep trying. Maybe it's exercising with you. Let a walking buddy or group keep you going—even when you want to quit. Involving other people will make you feel more committed—and being aware of healthful eating habits and "getting physical" will benefit them as well.

Losing weight means making a commitment to change your routine. Trimming calories from your plate, choosing to move, and soliciting a little help from your friends can make all the difference in your weight and your health.

Appendix c:
LOW-CALORIE COOKING FOR LIFE

shopping

You'll find so many low-calorie, nonfat, and low-fat products, not to mention a bounty of fresh produce, in the supermarket these days that shopping with healthful eating as your goal will be easier than ever.

Here are a few tips to help you get started.

* Using the American Heart Association's dietary guidelines (page 301), the Healthy Heart Food Pyramid (pages 302–306), and/or your weight-loss program guide, make a weekly meal plan. Use the meal plan to make a grocery list, but feel free to make adjustments if you find appealing, healthful foods that aren't on your list.

* Shop for the whole week. The fewer trips you make, the less impulse buying you'll do.

* Don't shop on an empty stomach. Your resolve will be low, and you'll be likely to put all kinds of things in the cart.

* Ignore the store's specials if the foods are high in calories, saturated fat, or cholesterol and therefore don't fit in with your meal plan.

* Read the nutrition labels on prepared foods to make sure they're low in calories, saturated fat, and cholesterol. (See "Food Labels," page 320.)

* If it's more convenient, you can compare nutrition labels on the Internet just as you would at the grocery store.

wise buys

You have become familiar with the Healthy Heart Food Pyramid food groups, listed on the following pages, and with how many servings to eat from each group (see page 302 for a refresher). You've also heard us emphasize the benefits of variety in your food choices. Now you're ready to find out the shopping specifics so you can put all that knowledge to work.

BREADS, CEREALS, PASTA, AND STARCHY VEGETABLES

There's much more to this group than white bread, spaghetti, and mashed potatoes. Experiment with different grains, such as brown rice, bulgur, and quinoa (for examples, see recipes on pages 138, 212, and 242). Cook grains in different forms, including orzo and polenta (see recipes on pages 82 and 116). Try different kinds of bread, such as whole or cracked wheat, rye, and pumpernickel, that have more fiber than white bread.

Substituting beans (not green), peas, lentils, or tofu for meat at least twice a week can save you money as well as calories.

Check labels for calorie, saturated fat, cholesterol, and sodium counts. Also look for good sources of fiber, such as oatmeal and oat bran. All else being equal, a higher fiber content is better for you.

Shop carefully for commercially baked breads and rolls; they may be high in calories and saturated fat, so read the labels. (See pages 319–321.) It's much better to bake your own when you can. Try the recipes in this book (pages 1–294), or adjust your own favorites by using the "Ingredient Substitutions" list on pages 326–327.

FRUITS AND VEGETABLES

Fruits and vegetables can be a dieter's dream come true. You will feel satisfied without consuming many calories or adding saturated fat. The most popular fruits and nonstarchy vegetables in the United States are iceberg lettuce (the least nutritious variety), tomatoes, bananas, orange juice, and apples. Don't get stuck on these five! So many fruits and vegetables are available now, many of them year-round, that you can try something different every week. It's easy to eat five or six servings of fruits and vegetables each day. You can start with two fruits at breakfast by drinking a half cup of orange juice and eating half a banana on your cereal. Plan a vegetable snack into your daily routine, and you are halfway to your goal. Have at least one dark green leafy vegetable or one deep yellow or orange vegetable every day.

Although most fruits and vegetables are low in calories and fat, be aware of the exceptions. Avocados and olives are high in calories and fat, although the fat is largely monounsaturated. Coconut is high in saturated fat. (See page 319 for more information on different kinds of fat.)

Always read the labels on frozen and canned vegetables. Many of them contain added fat, such as from sauces. Some canned vegetables are high in sodium. Look for no-salt-added canned vegetables, or rinse before using. And don't add lots of margarine, cheese, or sour cream to your vegetables, or you'll negate their healthful benefits.

Fresh fruits or those canned in water are lower in calories than the same fruits canned in juice or syrup. Choose frozen fruits without added sugar.

MEATS, POULTRY, SEAFOOD, DAIRY PRODUCTS, AND EGGS

meats, poultry, and seafood

Meats, poultry, and seafood lose about 25 percent of their weight during cooking. For each 3-ounce cooked serving, buy 4 ounces, excluding visible fat and bone, of the raw food.

Choose only lean cuts of beef, such as round steak, sirloin tip, tenderloin, and flank steak. Look for lean cuts of pork, such as center-cut ham, tenderloin, and loin chops. Buy only lean ground beef and pork (no more than 10 percent fat). All cuts of veal except cutlets are lean. The leg is the leanest cut of lamb. Limit your intake of liver and other organ meats, which are very high in cholesterol.

Trim all visible fat from your meat choices.

Poultry cooked without skin is an excellent protein choice. However, when using whole chickens and turkeys, cook them with the skin on to keep the meat from drying out. Remove the skin before eating the poultry. When buying ground poultry, select only that ground without the skin.

Avoid self-basting turkeys because commercial basting fats are highly saturated. Even if the turkey is basted in broth, the broth is usually high in sodium. It's better to baste with an unsalted broth or cook the turkey in an oven-cooking bag, which produces a more healthful "self-basted" turkey.

For your two or more servings of fish a week, good choices are fish containing high levels of omega-3 fat, which raises your level of beneficial cholesterol. Some fish high in omega-3 are Atlantic and coho salmon, albacore tuna, mackerel, carp, lake whitefish, sweet smelt, and lake and brook trout. If you choose canned tuna or salmon, buy these products packed in water, not in oil, or vacuum-packed in foil pouches.

dairy products

Drinking fat-free milk is certainly a good way to get your dairy servings, but many other dairy products also are available. Some of them are fat-free evaporated milk, fat-free dry milk, cheese made from fat-free or part-skim milk, nonfat or low-fat yogurt, and fat-free or low-fat frozen yogurt, fat-free or low-fat ice cream, sorbets, and sherbets. If you now use cream, switch to fat-free milk or to a polyunsaturated nondairy creamer or whitener.

> **Caution:** Two percent milk is **not** low fat. The milk labeled
> 1 percent or ½ percent is low fat. Skim milk is fat free. Whole
> milk has 4 percent fat.

eggs

In general, it's a good idea to use egg whites or egg substitute rather than whole eggs. One large egg yolk contains about 213 mg of cholesterol, about two thirds of your entire allowance for the day. Egg whites and egg substitute contain no cholesterol and are an excellent source of protein. Also, they contain no fat and are lower in calories than whole eggs. In most recipes, two egg whites will substitute nicely for a whole egg.

Be sure to eat only cooked eggs and egg whites; raw eggs can carry salmonella, which causes food poisoning.

FATS, OILS, NUTS, AND SWEETS

fats and oils

When reading the labels on packaged goods, pay particular attention to the kinds of fat and oil listed.

Select polyunsaturated and monounsaturated fats and oils for as much as possible of your daily fat allowance. You'll find polyunsaturated fats in vegetable oils, such as safflower, sunflower, soybean, and corn, and in some fish and fish oils. The most common sources of monounsaturated fat in cooking oils are olive oil and canola oil. Look for them in commercial products, such as margarines and salad dressings, as well. It's also easy to make your own low-calorie dressings using our recipes on pages 68–69.

Choose products that are low in saturated fat, often present in commercial baked goods. Butter, lard, and tallow from animals and coconut, palm, and palm kernel oils from plants are common examples of saturated fat.

Trans fat, another type to avoid, is found in products with hydrogenated or partially hydrogenated oil or fat. Highly processed foods, such as margarine, shortening, and crackers and other snack foods, are likely to contain a lot of trans fat. Choose liquid or tub margarines or stick margarines that have a liquid oil listed as the first ingredient and have no more than 2 grams of saturated fat per tablespoon. (The more liquid the form of the margarine, the less trans fat it contains.) By shopping for products with a low saturated fat content, you'll also get a low trans fat content. (For more information, see "Saturated Fat, Trans Fat, and Cholesterol," pages 305–306.)

nuts and seeds

Nuts and seeds are good sources of protein, but they are higher in calories than you may realize. (A quarter-cup of nuts or seeds averages 194 calories.) They are also high in fat. Most of the fat is unsaturated, but some nuts, such as Brazil and macadamia, are quite high in saturated fat. Buy nuts and seeds in their natural unsalted state, and dry-roast them for added flavor. Have a few for a snack, or sprinkle some in other foods to add both taste and crunch.

BEVERAGES

If you're trying to lose weight, avoid sugared beverages, such as carbonated or fruit drinks, and alcoholic drinks, such as beer, wine, and liquor. Apart from adding calories to your diet, alcohol can also raise blood pressure.

DESSERTS

Look for nutritious desserts, like the ones in this cookbook, that are lower in fat and calories than the typical desserts. Build occasional sweet treats into your eating plan. If you crave chocolate, once in a while it's okay to savor one piece of really good chocolate after a meal when your hunger is already satisfied. Or make Chocolate Angel Food Cake, page 270. If you love high-fat desserts, share one serving with friends.

food labels

You can take advantage of much useful information by reading and comparing food labels, required by the U.S. Food and Drug Administration (FDA) on food packaged in the United States. The label tells the number of calories and the amount of total fat, saturated fat, cholesterol, sodium, carbohydrates, fiber, sugars, and protein per serving. The label also tells you what percentages of the U.S. Recommended Daily Allowances (RDA) for vitamins A and C, calcium, and iron are in each serving. For example, if you eat a serving of a food that contains 100 percent of the RDA for iron, you don't need any additional iron that day.

The FDA also has established criteria for making certain claims on food labels. For instance, a product labeled "low-calorie" is allowed to contain no more than 40 calories per serving. "Reduced-calorie" means the product has at least one fourth fewer calories than the full-calorie version of the same food.

AMERICAN HEART ASSOCIATION FOOD CERTIFICATION

To help consumers make better food choices, the American Heart Association introduced its Food Certification Program in 1995. This program is designed to help consumers quickly and easily select grocery-store foods that can be part of a balanced, heart-healthy eating plan. The heart-check mark on a food package means that the product meets the Association's food criteria for saturated fat and cholesterol for healthy people over two years of age.

American Heart Association

Meets American Heart Association food criteria for saturated fat and cholesterol for healthy people over age 2.

cooking

Cooking when you have plenty of time can be relaxing and fun. In reality, however, today's hectic schedules can make everyday meal preparation a challenge. It's easy to rely on high-fat, high-calorie fast food, but with a little preparation, you can take control right in your own kitchen. Here are some handy hints:

❖ Commit: Make health a top priority.

❖ Make time for three meals a day. If you find that you often eat fast food in the car, learn to keep supplies on hand so you can take along a low-calorie meal-on-the-go. You can easily prepare a brown-bag meal, such as a sandwich on whole-wheat bread and some grapes, in the same time you'd sit in the fast-food drive-through.

◆ Have snacks ready to grab in a hurry: rinsed fruit, cut-up raw vegetables, healthful muffins, and fat-free yogurt.

methods

For a lifetime of healthful eating, you will want to not only serve recipes from this and other healthful cookbooks but also create some of your own recipes or adapt your favorites. Choose from the cooking methods listed below. All lend themselves to reducing calories, saturated fat, and cholesterol. Avoid cooking techniques, such as frying, that add a lot of fat or allow food to cook in its own fat.

BAKING

Bake poultry, seafood, and meat in covered cookware with a little liquid. The moisture that the liquid adds makes this method particularly good for seafood or chicken breasts, which tend to be a little dry. (See Chicken Kiev, page 103.) Using parchment paper or aluminum foil, create packets of poultry, seafood, or meat with vegetables. Baking in packets, or *en papillote,* keeps the moisture in and blends the flavors—and with no pans to wash.

BRAISING OR STEWING

Braising is an excellent way to cook meat, poultry, or vegetables. Use enough liquid to keep the dish from drying out or sticking and to make broth if you like. Cook over a low setting on the stove or at 300°F to 325°F in the oven. If you're braising or stewing meat or poultry, such as for pot roast, cook it a day ahead and refrigerate it overnight. The fat will congeal, and you can remove it easily before reheating the dish. (See Royal Pot Roast with Gravy, pages 166–167.)

GRILLING OR BROILING

Grilling meat or poultry or broiling it on a rack allows the fat to drip away. Grilling and broiling are also easy ways to cook seafood, fruits, and vegetables. For extra flavor, marinate foods in wine or fruit juice with herbs and spices before cooking. (See Grilled Sirloin with Chimichurri Sauce, page 163.)

MICROWAVE COOKING

This fast, easy cooking method requires no added fat. Because the heat of microwave cooking is moist, food doesn't usually stick to the pan.

POACHING

To poach chicken or seafood, immerse it in a pan of simmering water or fat-free, low-salt broth on the stovetop. Salmon is especially good prepared this way. (See Citrus-Poached Fish Fillets, page 77.)

ROASTING

Roast meat or poultry, usually uncovered, on a rack in the oven so the meat doesn't sit in fat drippings. For basting, use low-sodium, fat-free liquids, such as no-salt-added tomato juice, fruit juice, table wine, or fat-free, low-sodium broth. (See One-Dish Roast Chicken Dinner, page 100.)

STEAMING

Cooking vegetables in a steamer basket over simmering water preserves their natural flavor, color, and nutritional value. (See Tarragon Balsamic Green Beans, page 224.) Add herbs to the steaming water to give the vegetables even more flavor. A Chinese bamboo steamer, which looks like a stack of round baskets, will cook a whole meal at the same time. Put the basket with the food needing the most time on the bottom, and add each basket at the proper time so all the foods will steam at once.

STIR-FRYING

Stir-frying in a wok or large skillet over high temperature uses the constant movement of the food to keep it from sticking and burning. Stir-fry vegetables, meat, poultry, or seafood in a small amount of oil. When a stir-fry recipe calls for soy sauce, use the kind with the lowest sodium or dilute regular soy sauce with an equal amount of water. (See Turkey Lo Mein, pages 142–143.)

equipment

The right kitchen tools can help you reduce fat and calories in your cooking. Here are a few suggestions about equipment we find especially helpful for this.

❖ Nonstick pots and pans, including a large ovenproof skillet with a tight-fitting lid.

❖ A roasting pan with a rack.

* A ridged stovetop grill pan.

* A steamer—a regular steamer, a collapsible metal steamer, or a set of Chinese bamboo steamers. A spaghetti cooker can double as a steamer.

* A fat separator to remove fat from meat drippings or broth.

adapting your own recipes healthfully

When you're cooking your favorite dishes, use the following tips and the information in "Ingredient Substitutions," pages 325–327, to cut down on calories, saturated fat, and sodium.

* Trim all visible fat before cooking meat.

* After browning lean ground beef or pork, put it into a strainer or colander. Rinse it under hot running water, and let the water and fat drain. Wipe the skillet with a paper towel. Return the browned meat to the skillet, add seasonings, and proceed with the recipe. This rinsing process reduces the fat by about 50 percent.

* Marinate leaner cuts of meat to add flavor and make them more tender. Experiment with herbs, spices, wines, flavored vinegars, and fruit juices. Red wine is good with beef, or try lemon juice with chicken. Don't use "cooking wines." They are high in sodium and have poor flavor.

* Skin chicken and remove all visible fat below the skin before cooking. Raw skin will be easier to remove if you grasp it with paper towels. You may leave the skin on when roasting whole chickens, but remove it before eating the chicken. (Always scrub the cutting surface and utensils well with hot sudsy water after preparing poultry for cooking.)

* Substitute microwaved turkey bacon for the fried pork variety.

* Use more vegetables and less poultry, seafood, or meat in soups, stews, and casseroles. Shredded or finely chopped vegetables are great for stretching ground poultry or meat.

* When preparing omelets, use only one egg yolk per portion. Add a few extra egg whites to make more generous servings, or use egg substitute.

* Make fat-free gravy by shaking 1 teaspoon of cornstarch and 1 cup of room-temperature fat-free, low-sodium broth in a jar with a tight-fitting lid.

Heat the rest of the broth in a saucepan and add the blended liquid. Simmer until thickened.

◆ Thicken sauces by reducing them; that is, boil the liquid away until the sauce is about half the original volume. Another good way to thicken sauces and make them creamy at the same time is to add nonfat or low-fat sour cream or fat-free evaporated milk.

◆ Cut down on fat in creamy salad dressing by mixing in some nonfat or low-fat sour cream or yogurt or fat-free milk.

◆ Make your own chicken broth and beef broth without added salt, especially if you can't find canned fat-free, low-sodium broth. Refrigerate your broth overnight, then skim the hardened fat off the top. To have small amounts of broth handy, freeze the defatted broth in an ice-cube tray and bag the cubes. A quicker but less flavorful alternative is to make broth using low-sodium bouillon granules.

◆ Flavor rice or pasta by cooking it in fat-free, low-sodium broth. Leave out the salt, and add wine, juice, herbs, or spices.

◆ Instead of salt, use fresh herbs generously for added flavor. The following is only a partial list of complementary pairings. Enjoy experimenting with other combinations as well.

  ◆ Basil—tomatoes, green salads, poultry
  ◆ Dill—cucumbers, green beans, squash, seafood
  ◆ Parsley—soups, stews, green peas, sauces, salad dressings
  ◆ Cilantro—salsas, southwestern dishes, Asian dishes
  ◆ Oregano—pizza, spaghetti sauce, tomatoes
  ◆ Chives—cottage cheese, potatoes, seafood
  ◆ Rosemary—potatoes, cabbage, grilled meats, poultry
  ◆ Mint—lamb, tabbouleh, and other Middle Eastern dishes

ingredient substitutions

You don't need to throw away old family recipes just because you want to eat healthfully. By making a few simple ingredient substitutions, you can fit almost any recipe into your eating plan. The chart on the following pages shows some common examples.

IF YOUR OWN RECIPE CALLS FOR	USE
All-purpose flour	2 teaspoons of cornstarch for every 1 tablespoon of flour (saves 30 calories).
Broth or bouillon	Low-sodium bouillon granules or cubes, reconstituted according to package directions; homemade or commercially prepared fat-free, low-sodium broth.
Butter, melted butter, or shortening	Acceptable margarine or acceptable oil. When possible, use fat-free or light tub, light stick, or fat-free spray margarine. However, if the type of fat is critical to the recipe, especially in baked goods, you may need to use a stick margarine, such as corn oil stick margarine, that lists liquid vegetable oil as its first ingredient (see page ix).
Butter or oil for sautéing	Fat-free, low-sodium broth; vegetable oil spray; wine; fruit or vegetable juice.
Cream	Polyunsaturated nondairy coffee creamer; undiluted fat-free evaporated milk.
Eggs	Cholesterol-free egg substitutes; 2 egg whites for 1 whole egg.
Evaporated milk	Fat-free evaporated milk.
Flavored salts, such as onion salt, garlic salt, and celery salt	Onion powder, garlic powder, celery seeds or flakes. Use about one fourth of the amount of flavored salt indicated in the recipe.
Ice cream	Fat-free, low-fat, or light ice cream; nonfat or low-fat frozen yogurt; sorbet; sherbet.
Oil in baking	Unsweetened applesauce.
Salt	No-salt-added seasoning blends.
Tomato juice	No-salt-added tomato juice; 6-ounce can of no-salt-added tomato paste diluted with 3 cans of water.
Tomato sauce	6-ounce can of no-salt-added tomato paste diluted with 1 can of water.

Unsweetened baking chocolate	3 tablespoons cocoa powder plus 1 tablespoon polyunsaturated oil or unsaturated, unsalted margarine for every 1-ounce square of chocolate.
Vegetable oil for sautéing or to prepare pan	Vegetable oil spray; fat-free or light tub, light stick, or fat-free spray margarine; acceptable margarine. However, if the type of fat is critical to the recipe, especially in baked goods, you may need to use a stick margarine, such as corn oil stick margarine, that lists liquid vegetable oil as its first ingredient (see page ix).
Whipping cream	Fat-free evaporated milk (thoroughly chilled before whipping).
Whole milk	Fat-free milk.

Appendix d:
EQUIVALENTS

Here are approximate equivalents for some items often called for in this book. Keep in mind that some foods, especially produce, vary widely between regions and by season. This list is merely a guideline to simplify your shopping.

INGREDIENT	MEASUREMENT
Basil leaves, fresh	⅔ ounce = ½ cup
Bell pepper, any color	1 medium = 1 cup chopped or sliced
Carrot	1 medium = ⅓ to ½ cup chopped or sliced, ½ cup shredded
Celery	1 medium rib = ½ cup chopped or sliced
Cheese, hard, such as Parmesan	4 ounces = 1 cup grated 3½ ounces = 1 cup shredded
Cheese, semihard, such as Cheddar, mozzarella, or Swiss	4 ounces = 1 cup grated
Cheese, soft, such as blue, feta, or goat	1 ounce, crumbled = ¼ cup
Cucumber	1 medium = 1 cup sliced
Lemon juice	1 medium = 3 tablespoons
Lemon zest	1 medium = 2 to 3 teaspoons
Lime juice	1 medium = 1½ to 2 tablespoons
Lime zest	1 medium = 1 teaspoon
Mushrooms (domestic)	1 pound = 5 cups sliced or 6 cups chopped
Onions, green	8 to 9 medium = 1 cup sliced (green and white parts)
Onions, white or yellow	1 large = 1 cup chopped 1 medium = ⅔ cup chopped 1 small = ⅓ cup chopped
Orange juice	1 medium = ⅓ to ½ cup
Orange zest	1 medium = 1½ to 2 tablespoons
Strawberries, fresh	1 pint = 2 cups sliced or chopped
Tomatoes	2 large, 3 medium, or 4 small = 1½ to 2 cups, chopped

Appendix e:
AMERICAN HEART ASSOCIATION
NATIONAL CENTER AND AFFILIATES

For more information about our programs and services, call 1-800-AHA-USA1 (1-800-242-8721) or contact us online at www.americanheart.org. For information about the American Stroke Association, a division of the American Heart Association, call 1-888-4STROKE (1-888-478-7653).

NATIONAL CENTER
American Heart Association
7272 Greenville Avenue
Dallas, TX 75231-4596
214-373-6300

AFFILIATES
Florida/Puerto Rico Affiliate
St. Petersburg, FL

Greater Midwest Affiliate
Illinois, Indiana, Michigan, Minnesota, North Dakota, South Dakota, Wisconsin
Chicago, IL

Heartland Affiliate
Arkansas, Iowa, Kansas, Missouri, Nebraska, Oklahoma
Topeka, KS

Heritage Affiliate
Connecticut, Long Island, New Jersey, New York City
New York, NY

Mid-Atlantic Affiliate
District of Coumbia, Maryland, North Carolina, South Carolina, Virginia
Glen Allen, VA

Northeast Affiliate
Maine, Massachusetts, New Hampshire, New York State (except New York
City and Long Island), Rhode Island, Vermont
Framingham, MA

Ohio Valley Affiliate
Kentucky, Ohio, West Virginia
Columbus, OH

Pacific/Mountain Affiliate
Alaska, Arizona, Colorado, Hawaii, Idaho, Montana, New Mexico, Oregon,
Washington, Wyoming
Seattle, WA

Pennsylvania/Delaware Affiliate
Delaware, Pennsylvania
Wormleysburg, PA

Southeast Affiliate
Alabama, Georgia, Louisiana, Mississippi, Tennessee
Marietta, GA

Texas Affiliate
Austin, TX

Western States Affiliate
California, Nevada, Utah
Los Angeles, CA

index